*The*

# NATIONAL PARKS

*and other Wild Places of*

# CANADA

# The
# NATIONAL PARKS
## and other Wild Places of
# CANADA

Blake Maybank • Peter Mertz

NEW HOLLAND

First published in 2001 by New Holland Publishers (UK) Ltd
London • Cape Town • Sydney • Auckland

2 4 6 8 10 9 7 5 3 1

Garfield House, 86 Edgware Road, London W2 2EA, United Kingdom

80 McKenzie Street, Cape Town 8001, South Africa

Level 1/Unit 4, 14 Aquatic Drive, Frenchs Forest, NSW 2086, Australia

218 Lake Road, Northcote, Auckland, New Zealand

ISBN 1 85974 696 9

Project Manager:Jo Hemmings
Series Editor: Mike Unwin
Copy Editor: Richard Hammond
Designer: Behram Kapadia
Cover Design: Alan Marshall
Cartography: William Smuts
Index: Blueline Editorial Services
Production: Joan Woodroffe

Reproduction by Pica Digital Pte Ltd, Singapore
Printed and bound in Singapore by Star Standard Industries Pte Ltd

**Publishers' Note**

Throughout this book species are, where possible, referred to by their common as opposed to scientific names for ease of reference by the general reader. Many of the titles listed in the further reading section on page 174 provide full scientific names for species found in Canada. The maps contained in the book are intended as 'locators' only; detailed, large-scale maps should be consulted when planning a trip. It is important to note that access, accommodation and other details vary as new transport methods and facilities develop. Permits are required for all Canadian parks, and it essential that visitors consult the appropriate park authorities before any visit. Remember that trail routes can vary, and weather conditions can alter dramatically within minutes. Although the publishers, author and consultants have made every effort to ensure that the information contained in this book was correct at the time of going to press, they accept no responsibility for any loss, injury or inconvenience sustained by any person using the book.

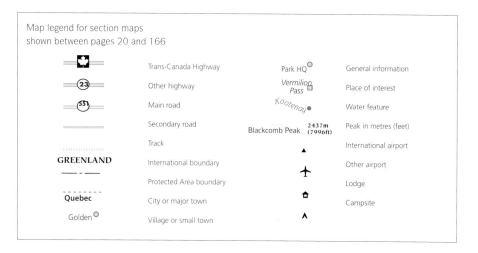

Map legend for section maps
shown between pages 20 and 166

| | | | |
|---|---|---|---|
| Trans-Canada Highway | Park HQ | General information |
| Other highway | Vermilion Pass | Place of interest |
| Main road | Kootenay | Water feature |
| Secondary road | Blackcomb Peak 2437m (7996ft) | Peak in metres (feet) |
| Track | ▲ | International airport |
| **GREENLAND** International boundary | ✈ | Other airport |
| Protected Area boundary | | |
| **Quebec** City or major town | ⌂ | Lodge |
| Golden Village or small town | ⋀ | Campsite |

Illustrations appearing in the preliminary pages are as follows:
Half title: Female Lynx; Title pages: Male Elk, Jasper National Park; Pages 4–5:
Autumn leaves, La Mauricie National Park; Pages 6–7: Castle Mountain in winter, Banff National Park; Pages 8–9: Jacques Cartier River Valley at Le Perdreau.

### AUTHOR'S DEDICATION
*For Martine, my most fortuitous discovery of my Parks Canada career.*

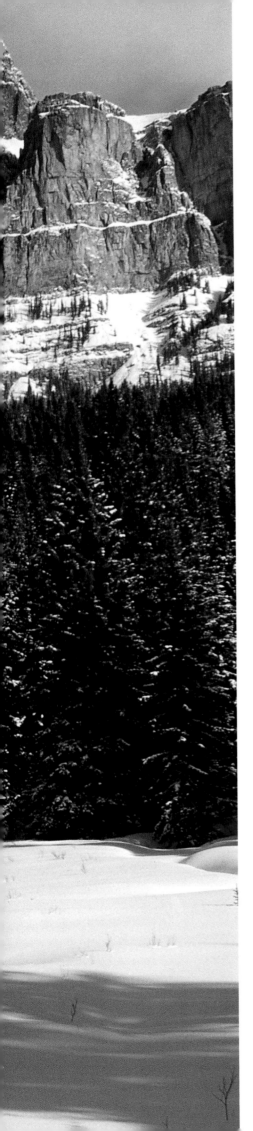

# CONTENTS

Map Legend  4
Foreword  9
Introduction  10
Map of Canada  16

### BRITISH COLUMBIA  18
Pacific Rim National Park Reserve  20
Yoho National Park  26
Mount Revelstoke National Park // Glacier
National Park  29
Kootenay National Park  32
Gwaii Haanas National Park Reserve  35
Garibaldi Provincial Park  38

### PRAIRIE PROVINCES (ALBERTA,
### SASKATCHEWAN, MANITOBA)  42
Prince Albert National Park  44
Banff National Park  50
Wood Buffalo National Park  56
Jasper National Park  60
Cypress Hills Interprovincial Park  64
Grasslands National Park  67
Waterton Lakes National Park  70
Riding Mountain National Park  73
Dinosaur Provincial Park  76
Elk Island National Park  79

### ONTARIO  82
Point Pelee National Park  84
Pukaskwa National Park  87
Georgian Bay Islands National Park  90
Algonquin Provincial Park  93
Bruce Peninsula National Park / Fathom

Five National Marine Park  96
St Lawrence Islands National Park  99

### QUÉBEC  102
La Mauricie National Park  104
Forillon National Park // Bonaventure Island
Provincial Park  108
Saguenay – St. Lawrence
Marine Park  112
Mingan Archipelago National Park
Reserve  115

### ATLANTIC CANADA  118
Gros Morne National Park  120
Cape Breton Highlands
National Park  126
Fundy National Park  130
Kejimkujik National Park  134
Kouchibouguac National Park  137
Prince Edward Island National Park  140
Terra Nova National Park  143

### NORTH OF 60° (YUKON TERRITORY,
### NORTHWEST TERRITORIES, NUNAVUT)  146
Kluane National Park Reserve  148
Auyuittuq National Park  154
Nahanni National Park  158
Wapusk National Park  161
Ivvavik National Park // Vuntut National
Park  164
Aulavik National Park//Tuktut Nogait
National Park//Quttinirpaaq
National Park  167

Summary of Conservation Areas  170
Useful Addresses/Further Reading  172
Index  174
Acknowledgements  176

# FOREWORD

Canada is justly celebrated as a land of abundant natural beauty. Its many national and provincial parks encompass wide-open spaces and pristine wilderness, and protect a spectacular flora and fauna that draw visitors from around the world.

These natural riches, however, should not be taken for granted. Despite Canada's vast size and seemingly endless tracts of unspoiled country, the natural environment remains threatened by development. As in many nations, Canada's wonderful green image does not always reflect reality. At the time of writing, the national parks system is only two-thirds complete. Of the 39 national park natural regions across the country that require at least representative areas to be protected, 15 still have little or no protection. Furthermore, the status of Canada's existing parks has come under renewed scrutiny. In 2000, the Federal Panel on the Ecological Integrity of Canada's National Parks made substantial recommendations and issued a clear warning about the ecological damage done to the nation's parks:

In much of Canada, protected areas have become ecological islands, disconnected from other areas of remaining natural habitat. Increasingly, urban development, agriculture, industrial forestry, or other land uses surround national parks and other conservation areas, affecting the viability of park ecosystems.

This book brings you the beauty and grandeur of Canada's spectacular wilderness. Blake Maybank's authoritative and accessible text takes you into a world of natural wonders, which are beautifully captured by Peter Mertz's evocative photographs. But Canada's special places need to be protected by more than just the hard covers of a book. Canada needs the political will and concern of people everywhere to reverse the trends currently eroding its parks and wilderness. Canadians must learn that they have only this generation to salvage something of that legacy.

I hope that you enjoy this book, and will in turn be encouraged to visit Canada's national and provincial parks. Your support will be a step further in securing their future for generations to come.

Elizabeth May
Executive Director, Sierra Club of Canada

# INTRODUCTION

*'We need an enrichment other than material prosperity and to gain it we have only to look around at what our country has to offer...*
*We have something here that no other country has.'*
GREY OWL (WA-SHA-QUON-ASIN)

Grey Owl spoke to the world concerning Canada's Wilderness in the 1930s, and his words still ring true today. One hundred and fifteen years after the first Canadian national park was created, the world's expanding population has put relentless pressure on the planet, and wild, untouched places are increasingly rare and threatened. Excluding Antarctica, 20 per cent of the world's remaining wilderness is in Canada. Indeed, Canada retains an image of a large untouched wilderness, and if the reality is tarnished by modern development, there is still much land worthy of, and requiring, protection. The creation and maintenance of national parks are one tool to achieve this aim, and yet less than 2.5 per cent of this vast country is currently protected within a national park.

The population of Canada is 30 million, and is growing. However, 95 per cent of these people live within 500 kilometres (300 miles) of the country's southern border with the United States. Large, wilderness national parks are far removed from the major cities. The parks, however, despite being removed from the daily affairs of most Canadians, nourish the Canadian soul, and beguile the world.

Many of Canada's national parks have received international recognition. Since 1972, UNESCO has declared 11 World Heritage Sites in Canada, as well as two more that straddle the border with the United States. These 13 sites include 9 of Canada's national parks: Nahanni; Wood Buffalo; Gros Morne; the Canadian Rocky Mountain Parks (Banff, Jasper, Yoho, Kootenay); Waterton; and Kluane.

## History

While land in Canada is also protected through Canadian Wildlife Service Wildlife Refuges, National Historic Parks, Provincial and Municipal Parks, conservation groups, and private holdings, national parks have pride of place, and arguably provide the most thorough legislated protection of the wilderness in Canada. This book deals primarily with the national parks, but includes several provincial parks to complement them. Hundreds of provincial parks exist, and while most are primarily recreation-based, they also usually protect a habitat. This book includes all Canada's national parks, and also four selected provincial parks; two were chosen for habitats that are unrepresented in national parks (Cypress Hills Interprovincial Park and Dinosaur Provincial Park), and two for offering a wilderness experience close to major urban areas (Garibaldi Provincial Park near Vancouver, and Algonquin Provincial Park near Toronto).

Although the first Europeans to visit Canada were the Norse, it was the English and the French who ultimately competed for the country's wealth, and provided the impetus for the country's exploration and European settlement. Of course, the country was already occupied (see

*Left: Lush meadows carpet the lower slopes of Black Tusk Mountain in Garibaldi Provincial Park, British Columbia.*
*Above: The Orca, or Killer Whale, is a welcome sight in the waters of Canada's Pacific Coast.*

Aboriginal Peoples, below). Today Canada is an officially bilingual country (French and English) of thirty million people, with most of the country's eight million Francophones living in the provinces of Québec and New Brunswick.

Economic concerns were the motivating force behind the establishment of Canada's first national parks. In 1885 the Trans-Continental Railway was considered crucial to the development of the country, and it was thought that the creation of parks would entice visits from well-heeled visitors, who would in turn use the new rail system. In the year the railway was completed, a small reserve was created around the hot sulphur springs in Banff, where thermal waters lured the unwell and other travellers. Eventually the federal government reserved the land for itself and created Rocky Mountain Park, later renamed Banff National Park. The popularity of this park quickly led to the creation of others, each a focus for tourism.

In 1911 the government created the Dominion Parks Branch (today Parks Canada) to administer parks under the new Dominion Forest Reserves and Parks Act. The first Commissioner of Parks was James B. Harkin, an enlightened man who combined a passion for wilderness with a pragmatic economic outlook. His lobbying led to the National Parks Act of 1930, which restricted much industrial development inside national parks. He also increased the number of parks from five to eighteen, and established many parks in new regions. He convinced politicians of the benefits of tourism, and encouraged the development of facilities and access routes to enable visitors to explore the parks.

Below: *Canada's parks embrace a variety of habitats, most of them grand in their scale. The wild Gulf of St. Lawrence dominates the landscapes of Saguenay National Marine Park* (below left), *while in Saskatchewan rolling prairies characterise Grasslands National Park* (below right).

In the ensuing years, some parks were exploited for commercial interests, and several were eliminated or reduced in size. The growing environmental movement helped create a new National Parks Policy in 1964, which committed governments to long-term management of the parks. A plan was created, based upon the division of Canada into 39 natural regions, with the intention of creating a park within each region of sufficient size to protect a representative sample of the habitat. This goal has not yet been realised as the economic downturn of the 1980s caused huge cuts in the operating budgets of Parks Canada. Some Natural Regions may never be protected within a park.

There are 40 national parks in Canada, some fully established, and some awaiting the outcome of treaty negotiations with First Nations groups. Today, Canada's national parks, despite still being under-resourced, with fewer staff burdened by increasing pressures and responsibilities, continue to offer an exquisite introduction into the true nature of the second largest country in the world.

## Biogeographical Development

Canada has an intricate and complex biogeography. The underlying landforms were shaped by the westward movement of the North American tectonic plate that uplifted the Rocky Mountains of British Columbia, Alberta, and the Yukon. These young mountains are still growing. The west coast of Canada, lying near the plate subduction zone, is still an active earthquake region. The rocky upland areas of eastern Canada, in Québec, Newfoundland, New Brunswick, Prince Edward Island and Nova Scotia, are the ancient remnants of the Appalachian Mountains, formed long ago when the North American plate had an eastern motion.

The rest of Canada is dominated by four main regions. The Arctic region of the high north is a land of permafrost,

ice, mountains, and a very short summer. The great Canadian Shield comprises the oldest surficial rocks on the planet, some more than four billion years old: a rolling landscape of rock, coniferous forest, and countless lakes linked by thousands of winding rivers. The Interior Plains is an immense flat area whose bedrock base was overlain by material scraped from the Canadian Shield and the mountains by the glaciers that, at least five times in the past two million years, have covered most of the country in ice several kilometres thick. The glaciers also are responsible for carving out the other dominant Canadian landscape, the Great Lakes and the St. Lawrence River that drains them.

## Wildlife

During the glacial periods, most of Canada was barren of wildlife. The last glacial retreat was but 12,000 years ago, and since then wildlife has recolonised the country, both from the south, and from the few unglaciated areas. No part of Canada is tropical or sub-tropical and, typical of countries closer to the poles, there is not a large amount of biodiversity. Canada has fewer than 200 species of mammal, and only 550 bird species of annual occurrence, most of which are migrants. Canada is the largest country in the world to have no endemic bird species, and there are but a handful of endemic insects and plants, although more of the former are now being found.

## Environment Considerations

Canada faces the same economic pressures on its natural resources as the rest of the world. Its responsibility for environmental stewardship is arguably greater than that of most countries, as Canada controls a significant proportion of the world's remaining wilderness and fresh water. The country can be proud of its system of national parks, but many of its ecosystems remain unprotected (espe-cially marine areas), and there are few effective controls on the exploitation of its natural resources. The country's citizens waste water, use large amounts of fossil fuels in transportation systems, and control the climate in their homes. The country is only now emerging from a long period of poor economic health, a situation that places additional pressure on the desire to develop resources rather than protect environments. Consequently, governments at all levels in Canada have been slow to act upon environmental issues. In Canada, as elsewhere, advocacy groups exist to lobby for environmental change. Some of the larger national environmental organisations include the Canadian Parks and Wilderness Society, the Canadian Nature Federation, Sierra Club Canada, Canadian Nature Conservancy, World Wildlife – Canada, and Greenpeace.

## Aboriginal Peoples

Europeans were not the first to arrive on Canada's shores. Even before the end of the last glacial period, 12,000 years ago, people had migrated to North America from Asia, travelling across the Bering Sea on a land bridge that then existed. They spread out across both North and South America, settling almost everywhere, quickly developing an astonishing diversity of culture, language, theology, and lifestyle. Many aboriginal peoples fared badly as a result of European contact. And while the Europeans' (British and French) interactions with the aboriginal peoples in Canada were arguably less bloody than elsewhere on the continent,

Below: *The dense coniferous forests of Jasper National Park* (below, left) *are typical of much of Canada's boreal region. North of 60° however, trees are scarce, and the Arctic landscape of parks such as Auyuittuq* (below right) *is characterised by permafrost and great sheets of glacial ice.*

disease, displacement, and destruction of resources caused an enormous upheaval in these peoples' way of life.

There are more than 630 different aboriginal communities in Canada today. These include the Inuit and the Inuvialuit of the far North, as well as the many 'First Nations' peoples further South. Many of the First Nations peoples live in reserves, and some are currently pursuing legal action over the status of land to which they hold an ancestral inheritance. In some national parks, traditional First Nations subsistence lifestyle practices (hunting and trapping) are permitted to continue. New parks under development in the North involve First Nations peoples in every stage of the development process, as well as in the protection and administration of the parks.

## Visitor Activities

The current National Parks Act and Policy places maintenance of ecological integrity as the foremost responsibility of Parks Canada. A secondary responsibility is to permit visitors to visit and learn about the national parks, as long as the parks' resources are not thereby threatened. Furthermore, where practical, parks allow for certain types of outdoor recreation. Some of the present visitor activities arise from decisions made much earlier this century, and so several parks possess golf courses, tennis courts, downhill ski resorts, bowling greens, etc. No new developments of this nature are currently permitted. The general intention is to allow only low-impact visitor activities, such as hiking,

*Below: The wildlife of Canada's parks ranges from the elusive wolverine (below, left) to the impressive Humpback Whale (below, right), that can be seen off both the Pacific and Atlantic coasts.*

canoeing, cross-country skiing, sight-seeing, swimming, picnicking, and camping. Mountain biking and horse riding are permitted on a few designated trails, and the use of off-road vehicles is generally not allowed, although a few snowmobile trails do exist. Sport fishing is permitted, although strictly regulated, and is currently under review.

Once past the entrance gates, most 'frontcountry' activities may be freely carried out, but most parks have supplementary permit requirements for travel into the 'backcountry', or for certain specialised activities such as mountain climbing or spelunking, to ensure the participants are adequately provisioned and prepared, and that park resources are protected.

Access to national parks south of 60° North is straightforward, as roads lead to, and usually through, all the 'southern' parks. North of 60° only Kluane National Park is accessible by road.

## Fees and Accessibility

Most parks charge fees for their facilities and services, including entry, camping, fishing, special programmes, and others. There is no nationwide pass available as yet and fees vary between parks, and change from year to year. Contact specific parks to learn current fee schedules, or consult the Parks Canada web site (see Useful Addresses, p.172).

Parks Canada, as part of a federal government initiative, undertook to make its facilities and programs accessible to people with hearing, mental, mobility, speech, and visual impairments, so that they too can visit, enjoy, and understand Canada's national parks and historic sites. Specific improvements vary from park to park, but often include: accessible Visitor Centres and other public buildings;

accessible washrooms; lowered information counters; barrier-free trails; proper lighting levels; close-captioning of audio-visual presentations; large-print brochures; audio cassettes of park information; TDDs (Telephone Devices for the Deaf); and all-terrain wheelchairs. Contact the park for specific information regarding what is available.

## Some Practical Considerations

Since most of the parks are true wilderness parks, there are potential natural hazards that all visitors should understand. Some hazards are park specific, and are dealt with in the corresponding park chapter in this book, but a few are relevant to most of Canada's parks and are mentioned below.

**Bears** occur in most of Canada's national parks. All three species (Black, Grizzly and Polar) should be treated seriously. Bears generally choose to avoid humans. However, attacks do occur, usually when bears become habituated to humans; when bears are surprised; or when they are forced to defend themselves, their young or their food. 'You Are in Bear Country' is as close to a Parks Canada mantra as you will find. Parks Canada provides visitors with literature regarding the risks posed by bears, with which you must familiarize yourself before you enter a park.

No **other wildlife** poses the same threat as do bears. However, you should never feed or approach any wildlife. Elk and Moose have been known to charge during the autumn rut, and smaller animals such as raccoon, skunk, or fox sometimes carry rabies. There are two species of poisonous rattlesnake in Canada; though neither is aggressive, they should be treated with respect. In the rare event of a bite, seek immediate medical assistance.

**Biting insects** are a feature of summers in any northern climate. Mosquitoes are widespread, while Black Flies are restricted to boreal forests (though there is a lot of boreal forest in Canada). Other biting insects include Horse Flies, Deer Flies, Sand Flies, and No-See-Ums (midges). None are normally vectors of any disease. To repel biting insects either wear bug-proof clothing, or use a repellent with DEET as an active ingredient. Insects are attracted to darker colours, and to fragrances, so wear light-coloured clothing, use scent-free soaps and deodorants, and avoid perfume.

**Hypothermia** is a risk from late autumn through early spring in all national parks, and year-round at higher elevations in the mountains and in the Arctic. Hypothermia is caused by exposure to cold, compounded by wetness, wind, and exhaustion. Most cases develop in fairly mild air temperatures between -1° C (30° F) and 10°C (50° F). As the body cools, the victim shivers, as blood is redirected away from outer parts of the body to the vital organs. This leads to uncontrolled shivering, slurred speech, loss of co-ordination, stupor, collapse, and eventually death.

Before you enter one of Canada's parks, learn about hypothermia. Wear warm clothing and good rain gear (wool clothing keeps warm when wet); do not eat snow; protect high heat-loss areas: head, neck, underarms, groin; wear a hat; keep dry; and avoid cold winds. Change wet clothing as soon as possible and avoid overheating the body. Eat foods with a high energy content and ensure that you make camp before fatigue sets in.

Below: *Many of Canada's parks are dominated by forests of trees such as aspen (below, middle), while the widespread bogs harbour wildflowers such as Canada Burnet (below, right) and the insectivorous Sundew (below, left).*

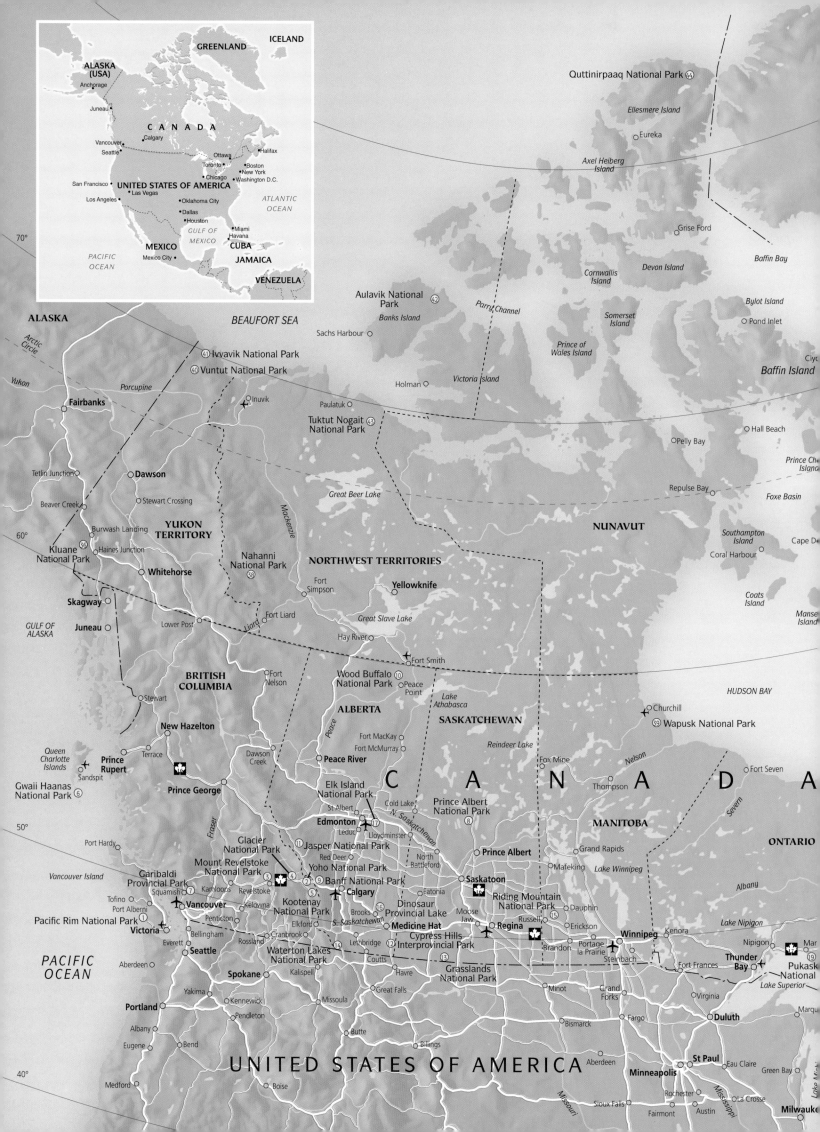

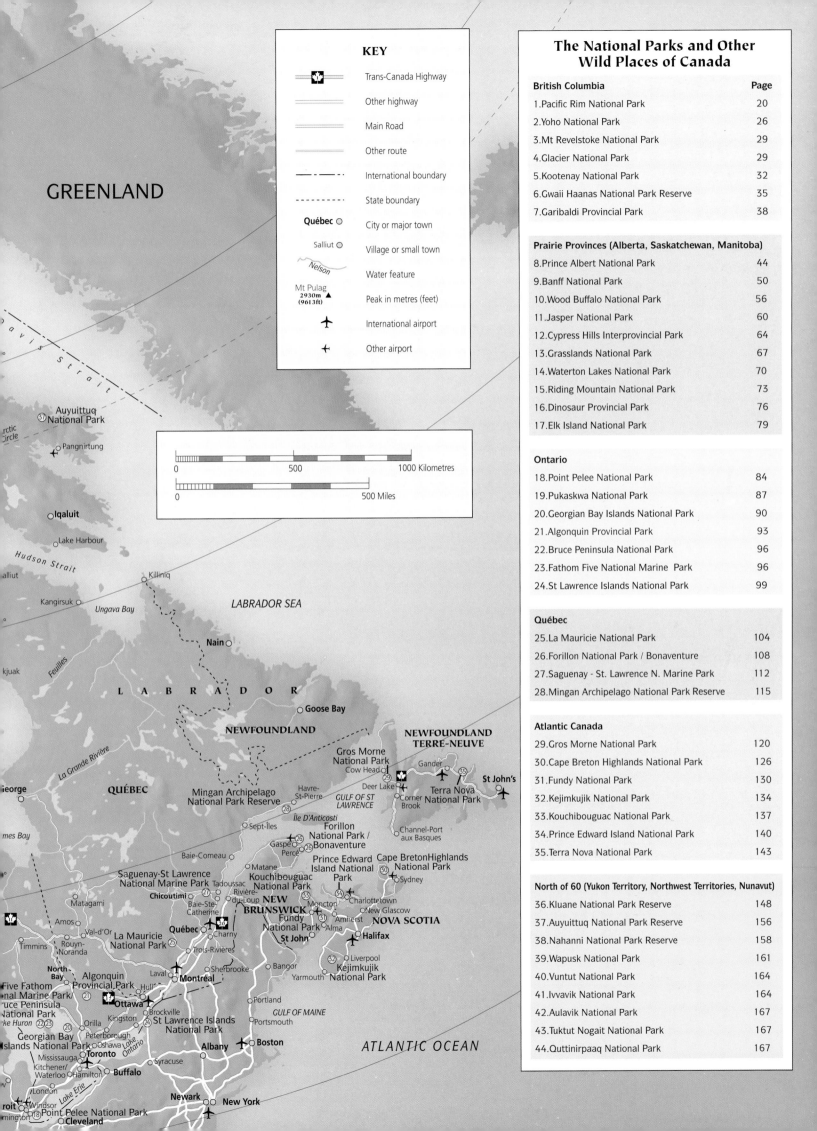

GREENLAND

## KEY

| | |
|---|---|
| ⬛ | Trans-Canada Highway |
| | Other highway |
| | Main Road |
| | Other route |
| –·–·– | International boundary |
| – – – | State boundary |
| Québec ◯ | City or major town |
| Salliut ◯ | Village or small town |
| *Nelson* | Water feature |
| Mt Pulag ▲ 2930m (9613ft) | Peak in metres (feet) |
| ✈ | International airport |
| ✈ | Other airport |

Scale:
0 — 500 — 1000 Kilometres
0 — 500 Miles

## The National Parks and Other Wild Places of Canada

| British Columbia | Page |
|---|---|
| 1. Pacific Rim National Park | 20 |
| 2. Yoho National Park | 26 |
| 3. Mt Revelstoke National Park | 29 |
| 4. Glacier National Park | 29 |
| 5. Kootenay National Park | 32 |
| 6. Gwaii Haanas National Park Reserve | 35 |
| 7. Garibaldi Provincial Park | 38 |

**Prairie Provinces (Alberta, Saskatchewan, Manitoba)**
| | |
|---|---|
| 8. Prince Albert National Park | 44 |
| 9. Banff National Park | 50 |
| 10. Wood Buffalo National Park | 56 |
| 11. Jasper National Park | 60 |
| 12. Cypress Hills Interprovincial Park | 64 |
| 13. Grasslands National Park | 67 |
| 14. Waterton Lakes National Park | 70 |
| 15. Riding Mountain National Park | 73 |
| 16. Dinosaur Provincial Park | 76 |
| 17. Elk Island National Park | 79 |

**Ontario**
| | |
|---|---|
| 18. Point Pelee National Park | 84 |
| 19. Pukaskwa National Park | 87 |
| 20. Georgian Bay Islands National Park | 90 |
| 21. Algonquin Provincial Park | 93 |
| 22. Bruce Peninsula National Park | 96 |
| 23. Fathom Five National Marine Park | 96 |
| 24. St Lawrence Islands National Park | 99 |

**Québec**
| | |
|---|---|
| 25. La Mauricie National Park | 104 |
| 26. Forillon National Park / Bonaventure | 108 |
| 27. Saguenay - St. Lawrence N. Marine Park | 112 |
| 28. Mingan Archipelago National Park Reserve | 115 |

**Atlantic Canada**
| | |
|---|---|
| 29. Gros Morne National Park | 120 |
| 30. Cape Breton Highlands National Park | 126 |
| 31. Fundy National Park | 130 |
| 32. Kejimkujik National Park | 134 |
| 33. Kouchibouguac National Park | 137 |
| 34. Prince Edward Island National Park | 140 |
| 35. Terra Nova National Park | 143 |

**North of 60 (Yukon Territory, Northwest Territories, Nunavut)**
| | |
|---|---|
| 36. Kluane National Park Reserve | 148 |
| 37. Auyuittuq National Park Reserve | 156 |
| 38. Nahanni National Park Reserve | 158 |
| 39. Wapusk National Park | 161 |
| 40. Vuntut National Park | 164 |
| 41. Ivvavik National Park | 164 |
| 42. Aulavik National Park | 167 |
| 43. Tuktut Nogait National Park | 167 |
| 44. Quttinirpaaq National Park | 167 |

# BRITISH COLUMBIA

Brit| ritish Columbia (B.C.) is the third largest province in Canada, and the only one bordering the Pacific Ocean. To quote from *British Columbia: A Natural History*, by Richard & Sydney Cannings, 'British Columbia is a marvellous place for anyone who is curious about nature. It has more species of living things than any other Canadian province.' People are drawn to B.C.'s mountains, rainforests, and Pacific Ocean.

There are four mountain national parks (Glacier, Yoho, Kootenay, and Mt. Revelstoke), and many Provincial Parks (Garibaldi is featured herein). The mountains offer scenery, physical challenges, and nature – fragile alpine wildflower meadows, and alluring wildlife including Mountain Goats, Grizzly Bears, Hoary Marmots, Pikas, and numerous birds, such as White-tailed Ptarmigan and Golden Eagles. British Columbia's rainforests are internationally famous, not least for the threat posed by the lumber industry. Rainforest is protected within Pacific Rim National Park Reserve and Gwaii Haanas National Park Reserve, as well as Cathedral Grove and several provincial parks. The massive hemlocks and other coniferous trees of the rainforest are home to many plants and animals, including Marbled Murrelets, seabirds which nest high in the trees. For the ocean, Pacific Rim National Park is a favourite destination, with whale watching a focus, with both Gray Whales and Orcas on offer.

The author's favourite B.C. destination is the Okanagan Valley, a dry southern interior valley, a land of sagebrush, vineyards, and riverine habitat, surrounded by forested mountains. The province is at the forefront of many environmental campaigns, particularly with respect to destructive logging practices, and the threats to the few remaining untouched old-growth forests. Come and see for yourself why the province deserves our respect and protection.

# PACIFIC RIM NATIONAL PARK RESERVE

## Canada's Ocean Park

'We watched the ocean and the sky together . . .'
PERCY BYSSHE SHELLEY, LETTER TO MARIA GISBOURNE

Pacific Rim National Park is managed and marketed in three 'units' of outstanding natural beauty. The entire strip of the park (286 square kilometres, 110 square miles) extends 150 kilometres (93 miles) north to south. The agreement to establish the park in principle was signed in 1970, although the final disposition of the park lands, and their management, awaits the settlement of a land claim dispute with the local First Nations group, the Nuu-chah-nulth, who have lived in the area for thousands of years.

Despite the majesty of the towering rainforest, the ocean and the weather dominate life in Pacific Rim National Park. Though Pacific Rim is not the only Canadian Park bordering an ocean, nowhere else is the ocean such a dominant aspect of the local environment. Visitors are thrilled by walking among giant old-growth Western Hemlock and Sitka Spruce, but their foremost memories will be of the relentless surf pounding the long sandy beaches, and the seemingly equally relentless rain that may fill the sky for days at a time. The ocean and the sky together evoke powerful and lifelong emotions for all who venture here.

### Long Beach

The northern Long Beach is by far the most heavily visited unit of Pacific Rim, as it is easily accessible by paved road. The prominent feature of this unit is Long Beach, 11 kilometres (7 miles) long, though the entire unit offers an excellent opportunity to explore the different environments of the park: ocean; intertidal; beach; and forest. The 2 kilometre (1 1/4 mile) Rainforest Trail is a superb introduction to the impressive coastal rainforests of Vancouver Island; some of the Red Cedars are more than 800 years old, while the Western Hemlocks are a sprightly 300 years. Ferns, mosses, and lichens abound, including Licorice Fern and Feather Moss. Mammals and birds are hard to see, but the bird song is pervasive,

*Opposite, above: Botanical Beach can be reached by adventurous hikers on the West Coast Trail.*

*Opposite, bottom left: Pods of Killer Whales are occasionally seen in the coastal waters and bays of the national park.*

*Opposite, bottom right: The Sea Otter has been reintroduced to the region, and now occurs close to the park.*

*Above, right: Whale-watching tours are a popular attraction for visitors to Vancouver Island.*

Previous pages:
Page 18: *Pacific Rim National Park protects great tracts of towering old-growth coastal rainforest.* Page 19: *The Western Wood Lily thrives in the forests of British Columbia.*

**Location:** On central west coast of Vancouver Island, British Columbia. Park has three sections: Long Beach Unit; Broken Group Islands Unit; West Coast Trail Unit.

**Climate:** Marine, changeable with heavy rainfall (300 cm/120 in annually). Mean average temperatures: summer 14°C/57°F; winter 6°C/43°F. Frequent fog in summer. Most rainfall in autumn and winter.

**When to Go:** Open year-round. High season in the Long Beach Unit is July–August. Some park services closed during low season, November–March.

**Access:** Long Beach Unit: by road from Port Alberni (91 km/57 miles) on Hwy 4 (285km/178 miles from Victoria). Broken Group Islands Unit: by boat from either Ucluelet or Bamfield. West Coast Trail Unit: by foot, from trail heads at Bamfield or Port Renfrew (100 km/60 miles from Victoria).

**Facilities:** Park (Long Beach Unit): Visitor Centre, trails, picnic sites, on-site exhibits, campgrounds, viewpoints, golf course. Broken Group Islands Unit: primitive campsites. West Coast Trail Unit: primitive campsites. Local communities: commercial accommodations (reservations advised July/August); medical clinic; dentist; pharmacy; police; bank; gas station; groceries; restaurants.

**Watching Nature:** Marine mammals: sea lions, seals, Gray Whales (best mid-March to mid-April). Seabirds, shorebirds, and forest birds. Exploring rainforest.

**Visitor Activities:** hiking, birding, canoeing, kayaking, camping, golfing, scuba diving, fishing, swimming, surfing, beach combing.

**Special Notes:** (1) Respect notices regarding local shellfish contamination. (2) More than 300 earthquake tremors annually, though most are too small to be felt.

Above: *Sunlight only occasionally penetrates the dense forest of giant Western Hemlock and Sitka Spruce.*

Right: *Fungi flourish in the damp conditions of the forest floor.*

particularly the Winter Wren and Varied Thrush. With luck you might glimpse the striking Pileated Woodpecker, the largest woodpecker in Canada, or see the reclusive Blue Grouse, or the diminutive Brown Creeper. Mammals disappear easily in such thick forests; you might encounter Mule Deer, raccoon, River Otter, or Red Squirrel, but you are most unlikely to see Black Bear, wolf, or cougar. Sharp observation may reveal a Pacific Tree Frog among the low-level vegetation of the rainforest.

A walk along the beach is the best way to explore the seashore, but take special care on the beach at high tide, especially if it is windy, as waves can be unexpectedly strong and far-reaching. At low tide rocky headland pools become exposed, and all offer surprises; look for Finger Limpets, Acorn Barnacles, Purple Shore Crabs, Tidepool Sculpins, and Ochre Starfish. In migration shorebirds feed among the rocks, especially Ruddy and Black Turnstones, Surfbirds, and occasionally Rock Sandpipers.

There are good opportunities for intertidal exploration in Florence Bay, at the south end of Long Beach.

## Broken Group Islands

The Broken Group Islands consist of more than 100 islands in Barkley Sound; the island group is 60 square kilometres (24 square miles), and is named after its appearance, suggesting one large island broken into many smaller ones. This part of Vancouver Island's coastline is known as 'Graveyard of the Pacific', as storms, rain, fog, and strong tidal currents have wrecked many ships. Because the islands are undeveloped, and offshore, it is necessary to explore them by boat, and given the dangerous waters, trip preparation is very important. Visitors who wish to explore and camp in the park must be experienced in navigation, reading weather, and wilderness survival. There are a number of primitive campsites; contact the park for information regarding access, and boating regulations.

## The West Coast Trail

For certain adventurous, and necessarily fit, individuals, the ultimate Pacific Rim experience is hiking the famous West Coast Trail, a 75-kilometre (46-mile) trek along an historic telegraph route originally constructed to aid the rescue of shipwreck victims. This is a difficult backcountry challenge through dense, wet forest, along sandy and rocky beaches, and across numerous streams and rivers.

All hikes of the trail, and the use of backcountry campsites, must be prearranged with park authorities. Access is controlled, and strict limits are set on the number of hikers annually, through a reservation system. Contact the park for information: (250) 726-7721.

## Wildlife

The park is home to a fine array of wildlife, but the impenetrable rainforest and the rolling ocean, make viewing difficult. On both land and ocean birds are the most obvious animals, with more than 250 species, but

Left: *The Western Sandpiper is one of many shorebirds that follow the Pacific flyway through the park in spring and autumn.*

*Above: The Steller's Jay is a noisy and conspicuous bird, easily identified by its crest and dark blue plumage.*

only about one-fifth are breeders, with the rest migrants, many using the Pacific Flyway between Alaska and points south. Loons, grebes, and sea ducks spend the winter at sea, while shorebirds are mostly seen in spring and autumn. Many of the most visible breeders use the coastline, including Brandt's and Pelagic Cormorants, Black Oystercatchers, and Tufted Puffins.

## Logging Threats

Pacific Rim National Park protects the Pacific Coast Mountain natural region. This region is under intense pressure from logging companies who seek to exploit the large, mature trees of the rainforest. The park only protects a narrow strip of this critical habitat, and most large terrestrial mammals require large territories, and so regularly move out of the park, where they are unprotected. The logging of Canada's west coast rainforests is now a high profile international environmental issue.

The Long Beach and West Coast Trail Units do not contain complete watersheds, and are thus not ecologically secure. They are at risk from human activities that abut the park boundaries, especially logging. The Broken Group Islands are intact and more secure. Offshore shipping can present a risk of oil spills; the last major spill occurred in 1989, and its impacts are still being assessed.

*Right: The park's backcountry offers challenging hikes into a wilderness of rainforest, rivers and undeveloped beaches.*

*Below: From Schooner Bay, Tofino, visitors may explore the coastline under sail.*

# YOHO
# NATIONAL PARK

## Waterfalls, Glaciers and Fossil Beds

*'...and snowy summits old in story.'*
ALFRED, LORD TENNYSON, THE REVENGE

Established in 1886, Yoho National Park has since has had its boundaries increased to its present size of 1,313 square kilometres (507 square miles). It is situated to the east of Golden, British Columbia, and although by world standards a large park, it is the smallest of four contiguous mountain national parks (the others are Kootenay, Banff, and Jasper), which together constitute a UNESCO World Heritage Site. 'Yoho' means 'awe' and is the name the Cree First Nations people gave to this area, signifying the respect these early visitors had for this impressive area of natural beauty.

The Continental Divide runs through the park, and east-west travel across the high mountains is through the Kicking Horse Pass, a wide valley that passes through the park. The side valleys leading into the Kicking Horse Pass are steep and narrow, with numerous waterfalls. The large Wapta and Waputik ice-sheets cover the northern part of the park; waters from these

glaciers trickle down either side of the divide, flowing west into the Pacific Ocean, and east into Hudson Bay.

### Off the Beaten Track

Yoho National Park lies on the busy Trans-Canada highway and so visitors have to drive away from the heavy traffic on the highway into the park's interior to discover the many attractions. One of the most spectacular sights in the park is the Takakkaw Falls. A 13-km (8-mile) road winds up the Yoho Valley leading to the falls (Takakkaw means "magnificent" in Cree), one of the highest waterfalls in Canada, at 254 m (847 ft). At the road's end, there are also several trailheads providing access deeper into the park, and there are walking trails to Laughing Falls and Twin Falls. The name 'Wapta' ('running water') now attached to a glacier, waterfall, lake, and mountain in this region, was originally applied by the Cree to the Kicking Horse River. The Wapta Falls are viewed at the end of an easy 2.4-km (1.5-mile) trail, but reaching the glacier, which lies beyond the established trails, requires a major backcountry mountain excursion.

There are also many fine campsites and trails at the Lake O'Hara area that provide a spectacular alpine experience. Hikers are welcome, but there is a limit to the number of people using the commercial bus service to visit this fragile area, and bicycles are not permitted on the main road to the lake.

*Opposite above: Lake O'Hara offers a base from which to explore Yoho's spectacular alpine landscape.*

*Opposite below: Extraordinary geological formations line the eroded cliffs above Hoodoo Creek.*

*Above right: The Red-breasted Nuthatch is resident in valley coniferous forests.*

**Location:** Borders the west side of Banff National Park, on the Trans-Canada Highway. Field townsite (in the park) is 55 km (34 miles) east of Golden, British Columbia, and 27 km (17 miles) west of Lake Louise, Alberta.

**Climate:** Highly changeable, with many local mountain influences. Summer is from mid-June to mid-September, with average highs of 20°C (68°F) and lows of 5°C (41°F). Above 1,500 metres (5,000 ft), freezing temperatures and snow are not uncommon in the summer.

**When to Go:** Open year-round, but most services only available May to October; most of the park is inaccessible in winter.

**Access:** By road, on the Trans-Canada Highway. Nearest International airport at Calgary, 210 km (131 miles) east.

**Facilities:** Park: trails, viewpoints, picnicking, campgrounds, on-site exhibits, Visitor Centre. Town of Field: post office, restaurants, general store, Greyhound bus flag stop, lodges, guest houses.

**Watching Nature:** White Mountain Rhododendron and Moss Campion are among many wildflowers in alpine meadows. Clark's Nutcrackers and Common Ravens are conspicuous birds throughout the park, and visitors frequently sight elk, Mountain Goat, and Mule Deer.

**Visitor Activities:** camping, hiking (360 km/225 miles of trails), mountaineering, canoeing, kayaking, mountain biking, horseback riding.

**Special Notes:** (1) Western Canada Annual Parks Pass is accepted. (2) It is illegal to collect fossils anywhere in any national park.

## The Burgess Shales

In the interior of the park, north-west of the town of Field, is the world famous fossil site, The Burgess Shales. The site now lies within a restricted area, and was discovered in 1909 by Charles D. Walcott, the Secretary of the Smithsonian Institute in Washington, U.S.A. while riding near the Emerald Lake. It is considered one of the most important fossil sites in the world and was recognised by UNESCO as a World Heritage Site in 1981. Hundreds of thousands of soft-bodied fossils have been recovered from the site, and been dated to more than half a billion years ago, greatly refining our understanding of evolution. More than 120 fossil species have been described, including Opabinia, with its five eyes and an elephant-like trunk tipped with a claw, Pikaia, a wormlike primitive chordate, the oldest-known ancestor of modern vertebrates, and Marrella, or 'lace crab', the most common fossil in the beds. Visitors may pay for a guided tour of the site, for which reservations are required. The Burgess Shales are displayed at the Field and Lake Louise Visitor Centres, and at Emerald Lake. At this latter site there is a telescope to view the Shale, and an outdoor exhibit illustrating many of the fossil discoveries. In addition, there is an hour's interpretive trail that circles the beautiful Emerald Lake.

## Shrinking Boundaries

Both the backcountry and the more accessible areas closer to the highway are beginning to suffer from over use. Also, intensive logging of forest adjacent to the Yoho National Park boundary has put pressure on the plants and animals within the relatively small park area. The size of the park has also been reduced recently as some of the forest that is now being logged is delisted land that was formerly within the park's boundaries.

Above: *The impressive Takakkaw Falls are the highest in the Rockies.*

Right: *The tranquil waters of Emerald Lake provide an idyllic setting for boaters (no motorised craft are allowed).*

# MOUNT REVELSTOKE AND GLACIER NATIONAL PARKS

## The Summit and the Pass

*'There was a time in this fair land when the railroads did not run,*
*When the wild majestic mountains stood alone against the sun.'*

GORDON LIGHTFOOT, CANADIAN RAILROAD TRILOGY

Mount Revelstoke and Glacier National Parks lie within the Columbia Mountains ecosystem, between the cities of Golden and Revelstoke. Mount Revelstoke National Park was established in 1914 and is one of Canada's smallest mountain parks, only 260 square kilometres (100 square miles). The park was established due to local pressure on the federal government to build a road to the summit of Mount Revelstoke, already the focus of a popular trail. Glacier National Park is much larger, 1,349 square kilometres (520 square miles), more than half of which is above the treeline, and 10 per cent of which is covered in glaciers. It was established in 1886, at the same time as Yoho National Park, to entice visitors to take the railroad through the mountains and view the spectacular scenery. Glacier and Revelstoke both contain steep mountains, deep, confined valleys, and numerous glaciers, waterfalls, and avalanche paths.

*Above right: Mount Revelstoke's Skunk Cabbage Nature Trail explores the marshy terrain of the low valleys.*

Mountain climbing is very popular at Mount Revelstoke, and Glacier protects one of Canada's most extensive cave systems, the Nakimu Caves, where there are excellent opportunities for caving in the numerous underground caverns, grottos, and corridors.

### The Summit

The road to the summit of Mount Revelstoke, the Meadows-in-the-Sky Parkway (26 km/16 miles long) is the only one in any of Canada's national parks where visitors may drive their own vehicles above the treeline to subalpine meadows just below the summit. Although Mt. Revelstoke is relatively diminutive, visitors have a fascinating insight into how vegetation can change with altitude, starting in the low valleys with lush old-growth forests of cedar and pine (some cedars on the Giant Cedars nature trail are 1,000 years old), and rising through subalpine forest, to alpine meadows and tundra. The altitude change is also reflected in the birdlife. Remarkably, there are four species of chickadees (Black-capped, Mountain, Boreal and Chestnut-backed), as well as MacGillivray's Warbler, Blue Grouse,

---

**Location**: Both parks lie on the Trans-Canada highway, between the towns of Golden and Revelstoke, British Columbia.

**Climate**: High annual rainfall, heavy snowfall, and relatively moderate winter temperatures. Highly unpredictable weather. Glacier average temperatures are slightly lower than Mount Revelstoke. Glacier receives more rain in summer and more snow in winter.

**When to Go**: Open year-round, but most facilities open only May through October.

**Access**: Via Trans-Canada Highway. Mt. Revelstoke: City of Revelstoke is 410 km (256 miles) west of Calgary, 575 km (360 miles) east of Vancouver. Glacier: Visitor centre at Rogers Pass Summit is 342 km (214 miles) from Calgary and 643 km (402 miles) from Vancouver. Nearest communities: Golden, 80 km (50 miles) east, and Revelstoke 72 km (45 miles) west; both are serviced by small, chartered aircraft.

**Facilities**: Both parks: picnicking, camping, trails, viewpoints. Revelstoke: scenic drive (summer only) to summit of Mt. Revelstoke (a shuttle bus takes visitors the last 2 km (1¼ miles) to the summit. Parkway is open from mid-July to mid-October). Glacier: two campgrounds (80 sites). Gas and convenience store at summit of Rogers Pass. Commercial lodge at eastern park boundary.

**Watching Nature**: Beaver, elk, White-tailed Deer, muskrat. Alpine animals, such as Grizzly Bear and Hoary Marmot, are less often seen.

**Visitor Activities**: Hiking, picnicking, camping, cross-country skiing, ski touring, snowshoeing. Excellent mountain climbing and caving.

**Special Notes**: (1) Western Canada Annual Parks Pass is accepted. (2) Beware of avalanches.

*[Map labels: ALASKA, CANADA, Vancouver, To Mica Creek, 23, Columbia River, COLUMBIA MOUNTAINS, Eva Lake, Clachnacudainn Icefield, To Glacier NP, Mt Revelstoke ??m (3412ft), To Kamloops, Mount Revelstoke National Park, Revelstoke, Illecillewaet River, 0 5 km, 0 3 miles, N]*

Above: *Devil's Club grows in the damp forest understorey.*

Below right: *The Giant Cedar Nature Trail passes amongst trees over 1,000 years old.*

Below: *The Black-capped Chickadee is one of four species found across the region's broad altitudinal range.*

Black and Vaux's Swifts, Three-toed Woodpecker, Olive-sided Flycatcher, Northern Hawk-Owl, and near the summit, Golden Eagle, White-tailed Ptarmigan, American Pipit, and Gray-crowned Rosy-Finch.

## The Mountain Pass

The Rogers Pass summit is named after Major A.B. Rogers who, in 1882, while surveying for the transcontinental railroad, first realised that this pass could provide the long sought-after rail route through the Selkirk Mountains. The first scheduled pasenger rail service began in 1886, but the steep mountain slopes and heavy snowfall combined to cause many avalanches, and it was difficult and dangerous work to keep the railroad open through the pass. After one avalanche in 1910, in which 62 people died, it was decided that a tunnel should be built through the mountains, and in 1962 the Trans-Canada Highway was routed through the new Connaught Tunnel, ensuring much safer travel. In winter, however, the highway is frequently closed to permit the triggering of avalanches by artillery, a preventive measure to avoid massive falls of snow.

## Climbing and Caving

There are excellent opportunities for mountain climbing at Mount Revelstoke. There are fine climbs on

rock, snow, and ice at all standards of difficulty, with a great deal, in particular, for the intermediate mountaineer. At Glacier, the extensive Nakimu Caves provide excellent opportunities for caving in underground caverns, grottos, and corridors that extend for 5.9 kilometres (3¾ miles). Access is restricted.

## Room to Roam

Both parks protect important elements of the Columbia Mountains natural ecosytem, but neither is large enough to protect completely those species that have large ranges, such as Grizzly Bear and Mountain Caribou, which do wander outside the park. Also, the loss of old-growth forest through logging outside both parks threatens those species that depend on it.

Left: *Avalanche Mountain is an imposing sight after heavy winter snowfalls.*

Below: *Yellow Glacier Lilies bring a splash of spring colour to Rogers Pass.*

# KOOTENAY NATIONAL PARK

## Marble Canyons, Paint Pots, and Hot Springs

*'I have desired to go where springs not fail.'*

GERARD MANLEY HOPKINS

Kootenay National Park covers an area of 1,406 square kilometres (543 square miles), stretching 16 km (10 miles) either side of the Banff-Windermere Highway that runs over the Vermilion Pass and along the Kootenay Valley. The park was established in 1920 and is the youngest of four contiguous mountain national parks that comprise a UNESCO World Heritage Site (the other parks are Yoho, Banff, and Jasper). The K'tunaxa (later anglicised to Kootenai) means either 'people from beyond the hills' or 'people of the water', which is how the people that lived in this mountainous area were perceived by the Blackfoot First Nations people of the Western Plains. Within the park there is plenty to see, including limestone-walled canyons fed by cascading waterfalls, and the sacred town of Radium Hot Springs, a gathering place for the Kootenai and now a favourite destination for park visitors wishing to relax in its therapeutic waters.

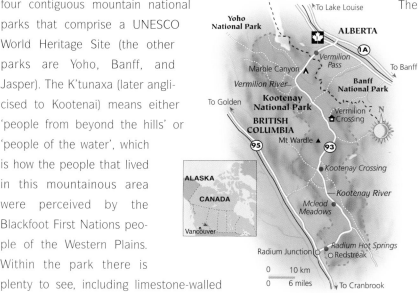

## An Accessible Mountain Park

The Banff-Windermere Highway (93) winds north to south along the length of the park, over the Vermilion Pass and along the Vermilion River Valley and the Kootenay River, a total distance of 94 km (59 miles). There are numerous roadside attractions, beginning with the summit of the Vermilion Pass, and the adjacent Fireweed Trail. Heading south, and descending in elevation along a 0.8-km (1/2-mile) trail, is the Marble Canyon, a limestone-walled canyon headed by a vigorous waterfall. A little further on are the Paint Pots – iron-rich mineral springs that bubble through small pools staining the earth dark red. An on-site exhibit, at the end of a 1.5-km (1-mile) trail, explains the Paint Pots science and its history. There is a panoramic vista at the Kootenay Valley viewpoint, where the valley can be seen set against the Mitchell and Vermilion Mountain Ranges. Near the small settlement of Radium Hot Springs, the Clear Lake Trail is an easy stroll along a boardwalk around a pretty, clear, spring-fed lake.

*Opposite above: Boom Lake reflects the panoramic vista of the Kootenay Valley.*

*Opposite, bottom left: Mule Deer are amongst several ungulate species that may be seen feeding in the valleys close to the road.*

*Opposite, bottom right: Rocky Mountain Goats generally frequent steeper terrain.*

*Above, right: The Paint Pots, small mineral springs stained red by dissolved iron.*

**Location:** Borders Banff National Park to the north-east, Assiniboine Provincial Park to the east, and Yoho National Park to the north-west.

**Climate:** Highly changeable. Summer is from mid-June to mid-September, with average highs of 20°C (68°F) and lows of 5°C (41°F). Above 1,500 metres (5,000 feet), there may be freezing temperatures and snow in summer.

**When to go:** Open year-round, but many facilities only open mid-May–September. Peak season July–August, and advance reservations for commercial accommodation recommended.

**Access:** By road; on Hwy 93 off Trans-Canada Hwy. Distance from Radium townsite to: Banff 132 km/83 miles; Lake Louise 131km/82 miles; Calgary 260 km/163 miles.

**Facilities:** Trails, on-site exhibits, visitor centres, nature shop, viewpoints, campgrounds. Radium Hot Springs complex is open year-round, but hours of opening and admission fees vary seasonally. Swimsuits and towels for rent.

**Watching Nature:** Kootenay and Vermilion valleys provide good roadside wildlife viewing; also Rocky Mountain Goats, elk, Bighorn Sheep (Radium Hot Springs area), White-tailed and Mule Deer. Less common are moose, coyote, and Black Bear. Excellent birding in June and July.

**Visitor Activities:** Hiking, back-packing, nature photography, canoeing, kayaking, mountain climbing, swimming, rafting, mountain biking, horse riding, cross-country skiing, snowshoeing, winter camping.

**Special Notes:** Western Canada Annual Parks Pass is accepted.

## Radium Hot Springs

The most visited attraction in Kootenay National Park is the small village of Radium Hot Springs. The hot springs themselves are just to the North, and do indeed contain trace amounts of Radium, but in amounts far too insignificant to pose any risk. The springs have long been sacred to the Kootenai First Nation, and remain extremely popular with park visitors today, seeking to relax, and soak away the stresses of the modern world. There is a hot soaking pool (40°C, 104°F), and a cooler swimming pool.

## Pressures from People

Kootenay National Park protects part of the western component of the Rocky Mountains natural region. There are numerous threats to the ecological stability of this long, narrow, and heavily-visited park, including poaching, overuse of backcountry areas (the park receives more than 1.5 million visitors a year), collisions between wildlife and vehicles, intensive logging at the park borders, and the (usually accidental) introduction of non-native plant species.

# GWAII HAANAS NATIONAL PARK RESERVE HAIDA HERITAGE SITE

## Islands of Wonder and Beauty

*'Tales, marvellous tales of isles where good men rest.'*

JAMES FLECKER

Gwaii Haanas National Park Reserve is a group of 138 islands at the southern end of the Queen Charlotte Islands that stretch for more than 90 kilometres (56 miles). Although the islands bear a name chosen by Europeans (Queen Charlotte was the Queen of George III, King of Great Britain), these 138 islands are known by the Haida, the first and enduring residents of these marvellous isles, as Gwaii Haanas, 'islands of wonder of beauty.' In the 1980s environmentalists fought to protect the islands, and in 1988 their actions, broadcast to the world, resulted in the signing of an agreement to protect the Gwaii Haanas, along with 3,400 square kilometres (1,360 square miles) of the surrounding ocean. The islands remain undeveloped and unexploited, and offer a wilderness experience unlike any other in Canada.

*Above, right: The magnificent cedar totem poles on Sgaan Gwaii were erected by the Haida – the islands' indigenous inhabitants – and are now a World Heritage Site.*

### The Canadian Galapagos

The Queen Charlotte Islands are relatively isolated from the rest of British Columbia, and there is some evidence that part of them escaped glaciation during the last ice age. Consequently, the flora and fauna have evolved a distinctive flavour; some species common on the mainland are absent here, while others have evolved subspecific differences. There are seven distinct mammals, including the world's largest race of Black Bear and Pine Marten, as well as a distinctive Short-tailed Weasel. Birds have evolved differences too, such as Saw-whet Owl, Steller's Jay, and Hairy Woodpecker. The archipelago contains deep fjords, above which the San Christoval mountains rise to 1,123 metres (3,743 feet). The lower elevations contain one of the finest old-growth rainforests on the Pacific coast. Nearly a million seabirds nest in Gwaii Haanas, many in burrows, such as Rhinoceros Auklets, Ancient Murrelets, Tufted and Horned Puffins, and Leach's Stormy Petrels. The adjacent sea is rich in life, with Gray Whales migrating north in spring, and frequent sightings of Killer, Humpback, Sei, Fin, and Minke Whales. There is also a large colony of Steller's Sea Lions.

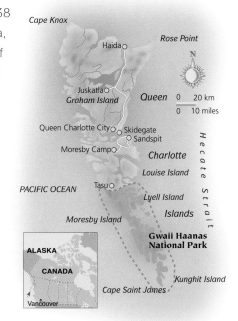

**Location**: Southern part of Haida Gwaii (Queen Charlotte Islands), a remote archipelago off the British Columbia coast, 640 km (400 miles) north of Vancouver, British Columbia.

**Climate**: Cool, relatively dry and sunny from mid-May to mid-September; rainy season beginning mid-August. West side much wetter than east, receiving 800 cm (315 in) annual rainfall. August mean average temperature 14.5°C (59°F). Sea fog common July–October. Frequent, strong, unpredictable winds. Weather extremely changeable; storms can appear suddenly.

**When to go**: Open all year, but most visit in summer.

**Access**: By air: daily commercial flights from Vancouver to Sandspit. Regular service between Prince Rupert and points on the Islands. Charter float planes and helicopters at Sandspit, Queen Charlotte, and Masset. A 20-minute ferry ride between Graham and Moresby Islands. By boat: BC Ferries provides service between the Queen Charlotte Islands and Prince Rupert.

**Facilities**: No facilities in the park. Island towns (Queen Charlotte, Masset, Sandspit): commercial accommodation; museum, medical facilities; pharmacy; police; bank; gas station; groceries; restaurants.

**Watching Nature**: Sea mammals, seabirds. Boat charters are the easiest way to see wildlife.

**Visitor Activities**: Boating, canoeing, kayaking, nature photography.

Right: *Principe Channel is one of the many waterways that, for centuries, have allowed passage between the islands – weather permitting.*

## The Haida

The Haida have lived on the islands for hundreds of generations, sustained by the environment's richness. A nomadic lifestyle was unnecessary, and leisure time allowed the growth of an elaborate society with unique customs, traditions, and art. They erected magnificent totem poles of cedar to proclaim their families' history, and built superb wooden canoes to navigate the treacherous waters. In 1981, the island of Sgaan Gwaii, with its impressive totem and funerary poles, was declared a World Heritage Site. Despite the Haida's mastery of land and sea they had to endure the arrival of European diseases, such as smallpox and tuberculosis, which decimated their numbers. Yet the Haida have survived, and their descendants have carried their culture into the new millennium.

## Travel in Gwaii Haanas

Travelling to and within Gwaii Haanas should not be undertaken lightly, and the safest approach is to employ the services of approved local guides. Travelling solo is discouraged; those who venture independently into Gwaii Haanas will be heading into remote areas, far removed from assistance should something go wrong. Planning, knowledge, and experience are essential. If in doubt regarding your ability, travel with a licensed tour operator. Independent travellers to Gwaii Haanas must make an advance reservation or obtain a stand-by space. In addition to reservations there are six stand-by spaces available daily on a first come-first served basis,

Below: *Marine mammals thrive in the rich waters of the islands. Gray Whales (below) migrate north though the region in spring, while Steller's Sea Lions (Opposite, bottom) are permanent residents.*

at 8:00 a.m. at the Queen Charlotte Visitor Information Centre. If you are going stand-by allow extra days in your itinerary, as you may have to wait. Everyone travelling in Gwaii Haanas must register each trip they take.

A 90-minute orientation session is mandatory for all visitors before entering Gwaii Haanas, Skedans and T'anuu. Please allow enough time in your schedule to attend. The session covers public safety, camping practices, hazards, natural and cultural heritage, and the Haida Gwaii Watchmen Program. Haida Gwaii Watchmen serve as site guardians throughout the area at K'una (Skedans), T'anuu (Tanu), Hlk'yaah (Windy Bay), Gandl'kin (Hotspring Island) and Sgaan Gwaii (Anthony Island), and their base camps have been established at sites of cultural and natural significance. In addition to protecting the sites' cultural features, Haida Gwaii Watchmen teach first-hand the Haida culture, and provide basic information services and emergency assistance to visitors.

## A Delicate Balance

Gwaii Haanas National Park Reserve protects three natural areas: the Pacific Coast Mountains, Hecate Strait, and Queen Charlotte Islands Shelf. Despite protection, and carefully controlled access, there are still threats from introduced mammals (such as raccoons, beaver, and deer) on some islands, which disrupt the indigenous ecosystem. Over-fishing offshore, and the impact of campers also pose a threat to this delicate environment. The park remains a reserve pending land claim disputes with the Haida Nation. The area is co-managed by Parks Canada as a National Park Reserve, and by the Council of the Haida Nation as a Haida Heritage Site. Thus all stakeholders presently share all aspects of planning, management and operations, pending the resolution of their dispute over land ownership through the British Columbia Treaty Negotiations Process.

# GARIBALDI PROVINCIAL PARK

## Whistler's Wilderness Neighbour

*'The Trail is the stage on which all the drama, the burlesque, the*
*tragedy, and the comedy of the wilderness is played.'*

GREY OWL (WA-SHA-QUON-ASIN)

**Location:** In the Coastal Mountains of SW British Columbia.

**Climate:** Short warm summers, and long snowy winters. Snow may stay on the ground in alpine areas from November until late July; there are permanent ice-packs on higher peaks. Weather is variable, and may change quickly. High annual precipitation: the Diamond Head area receives 1950 cm (780 in) of snowfall in winter.

**When to go:** Most visits are from late July through early September, when snow packs have receded. Alpine skiers visit in winter, often by heli-skiing, but through only approved operators with autho-rised clearance.

**Access:** Access to the western half of the park from Highway 99, north from Vancouver. The south-ernmost access point, near Squamish, is 75 km (47 miles) north of Vancouver. The north-ern-most parking lot is on the east side of Highway 99, 13 km (8 miles) north of Whistler. The iso-lated eastern half of the park is accessible by forestry roads lead-ing south from Mount Currie, east of Pemberton.

**Facilities:** Park: trails; backcountry campsites; picnic sites. Nearby communities of Squamish, Whistler and Pemberton: all typical services including food, fuel, shopping, commercial accommodations, and medical services.

**Watching Nature:** Alpine wild-flowers, particularly in August. Squamish River attracts winter concentrations of Bald Eagles.

**Visitor Activities:** Hiking, fishing, cross-country skiing, alpine ski-ing, mountain biking (designated trails only), nature photography.

**Special Notes:** Know your limits and abilities, especially if travel-ling independently.

Garibaldi Provincial Park was established in 1920 and is one of the earliest provincial parks in Canada. It lies to the north of Vancouver – the largest city in British Columbia and the third-largest urban area in Canada – and the whole park covers an area of 1,950 square kilometres (750 square miles). While Garibaldi Provincial Park is close to the international jet-set town of Whistler, it maintains a sense of physical remoteness because access to the park's interior can be made only on foot. As a result, the park's alpine wilderness remain rela-tively unimpaired and there are some stunning opportunities for activity-based holidays among high mountain peaks, glaciers, alpine meadows, and pristine lakes.

### Trekking Poles and Ski Poles

The most popular and easily accessible areas of the park are along Highway 99, the Sea to Sky Highway, along the west side of the park. Diamond Head is located in the south-west portion of the park that includes Mount Garibaldi, and is the starting point for many hiking, mountain biking and cross-country skiing trails that lead to designated wilderness camping areas. Garibaldi Lake is situated in the heart of the park, and is accessible by trails from a parking area at Rubble Creek. Along the way there are many other prominent features, including the Black Tusk, Panorama Ridge, Helm Glacier, the Sphinx, and Castle Towers. A popular trip amongst visitors is to hike to Garibaldi Lake, camp overnight, and then climb to the peak of Black Tusk, at 2,315 m (7,595 ft) the following morning.

Further north many trails lead to Singing Pass where there are some excellent panoramic views. The mountains and glaciers surrounding Wedgemount Lake are popular with climbers, and this is one of the most rigorous hikes in the park. In winter, many local skiers undertake challenging ski touring along trails with such prosaic names as the Spearhead Traverse or the Musical Bumps.

### The Brackendale Eagle Reserve

Each autumn thousands of Bald Eagles from across southern British Columbia congregate along the Squamish River just outside Garibaldi Provincial Park, where they seek spawning salmon. The Squamish River

*Opposite: Shannon Falls may be seen from the Sea to Sky Highway, along the west side of the park.*

*Above right: The Green False Hellebore is one of many wild flower species that flourish in the park, seen at their best during August.*

Above: *At 2,315 metres (7,595 feet) Black Tusk Cone is one of Garibaldi's most distinctive features.*

and its tributaries, the Cheakamus and the Mamquam, contain numerous gravel beds favoured by spawning salmon, and each autumn 350,000 Chum Salmon arrive to breed, lay eggs, and die. The rivers do not freeze due to the moderating influence of the nearby Strait of Georgia, and provide a rich feeding ground for the Bald Eagles that roost on the large cottonwood trees lining the rivers. Recent censuses have tallied more than 3,500 eagles at a time and, as a result of local pressure on the provincial government to protect the area from development, the 550-hectare (1,354-acre) Brackendale Eagle Reserve has now been established.

## Future Concerns

The provincial government of British Columbia has had a more aggressive policy of creating provincial parks than any other provincial government in Canada, and although the British Columbia park legislation does not confer the same degree of protection as National Parks, it does go some way to spare the designated areas the more overt forms of human exploitation. However, intensive use of Garibaldi Provincial Park's backcountry resources may lead to environmental degradation unless access is controlled. Also, global warming is reducing the size and thickness of the park's glaciers, with unknown impacts on

vegetation and wildlife. Over-fishing of salmon in the Pacific Ocean is also reducing the spawning run in the Squamish River, which will have an enormous potential impact on the autumn eagle congregation.

Top, right: *Garibaldi Lake, in the heart of the park, is a popular base for hikers, who often camp overnight here.*

Right, middle and bottom: *Bald Eagles* (middle) *congregate in thousands along the Squamish River each autumn. They feed upon the salmon* (bottom) *that arrive to spawn and die on the gravel beds.*

# PRAIRIE PROVINCES

Canadians speak of Alberta, Saskatchewan, and Manitoba collectively as the Prairie Provinces, an inaccurate appellation, but understandable as most people live in the Grassland Ecological Region, just north of the U.S. border. Only the region's southern third is actually prairie; the Boreal Ecological Region comprises half the landmass, the remainder being the Rocky Mountains to the west and the SubArctic Ecological Region in the northeast. The Grasslands are the most heavily modified, with agriculture having disturbed or displaced the original landscape; consequently, precious little grassland remains, but some is now protected in parks.

This region of Canada contains the most-visited and oldest national park (Banff), the largest (Wood Buffalo), and the author's favourite (Prince Albert). The region also has the most diversity, including grasslands (Grasslands NP), mountains (Waterton Lakes NP), foothills (Cypress Hills Interprovincial Park), badlands (Dinosaur Provincial Park), Aspen Parkland (Elk Island NP), boreal forest (Riding Mountain NP), and SubArctic Tundra (Wapusk NP). There are historic sites, each featuring stories inextricably linked with the nature of the land, including Head-Smashed-In Buffalo Jump (Alberta), Fort Walsh (Saskatchewan), and Lower Fort Garry (Manitoba).

There is plant and animal diversity to match that of habitat. Special wildlife includes the Whooping Cranes of Wood Buffalo, the Black-tailed Prairie Dogs of Grasslands, the Beluga Whales at Churchill, the fossils at Dinosaur Provincial Park, the Polar Bears at Wapusk, and the wolves in Riding Mountain and Prince Albert. All three provinces maintain a system of provincial parks, including: Whiteshell and Bird's Hill in Manitoba; Wildcat Hill, Moose Mountain, and Clearwater River in Saskatchewan; and Kannanaskis (Peter Lougheed), Writing-on-Stone and Notikewin in Alberta.

# PRINCE ALBERT NATIONAL PARK

## Canada's Quintessential Landscape

'Ajawaan; a small, deep lake that, like a splash of quicksilver, lies gleaming in its setting of the wooded hills that stretch in long, heaving undulations into the North, to the Arctic Sea.'

GREY OWL (WA-SHA-QUON-ASIN)

Prince Albert National Park personifies the authentic Canadian wilderness. Established in 1927, the park covers 3,875 square kilometres (1,496 square miles) of wilderness and is the largest park within the Taiga region (the other parks are Wood Buffalo, Riding Mountain, Pukaskwa, La Mauricie, Nahanni, Georgian Bay Islands, and Algonquin Provincial Park). Although the park is easily accessible by road from the nearby cities of Saskatoon and Prince Albert, the park itself is wild,

Opposite above: *Waskesiu Lake, towards the east of the park, is fringed with forests of Trembling Aspen and White Spruce.*

Opposite, below left: *Canada Geese breed near water. The northern forms of this species are smaller than those further south.*

Opposite, below right: *Boreal Forest, including Black Spruce bogs, dominates much of the park landscape.*

Above, right: *The conspicuous Bunchberry may be found growing beside the Mud Creek Trail.*

Previous pages:
Page 42: *Open prairie, with waving grasses and wildflowers, once covered the southern part of the region, but now exists only in isolated fragments.* Page 43: *American White Pelicans breed in various localities throughout the region.*

and to go past the frontcountry – to experience the true Taiga wilderness – can be done only by hiking or paddling. The park's landscape is a seemingly endless expanse of forests, lakes, and rivers of the Precambrian Shield and Boreal Plains that reflect the true measure of the country; it is a landscape that has guided transportation and exploration, encouraged resource extraction, and shaped the history and present cultural mythology of the nation.

### The Accessible Taiga

'Far enough away to gain seclusion, yet within reach of those whose genuine interest prompts them to make the trip.' Grey Owl

An ideal way to explore the park is to follow one or several of the sixteen trails that explore the variety of habitats within the park and cover a combined length of 160 km (100 miles).

Treebeard Trail wanders through an old-growth forest of White Spruce and Balsam Fir, some of the largest trees in the park. Beard-like lichen hangs from evergreen branches, and club mosses such as Ground Cedar and Running Pine carpet the forest floor. Pileated and Black-backed Woodpeckers are present, and with luck you might catch a glimpse of a Great Gray Owl. The Boundary Bog Trail passes through a mixedwoods forest culminating in a boardwalk stroll over a bog, a key feature of the Taiga landscape. The Sphagnum

**Location:** 60 km (38 miles) north of the city of Prince Albert, Saskatchewan. By road: 228 km (142 miles) from Saskatoon, 809 km (506 miles) from Winnipeg, and 843 km (527 miles) from Calgary.

**Climate:** Long, cold winters, pleasant springs and autumns, and warm summers. Annual precipitation is 40 cm (16 in), one third as snow.

**When to Go:** Open year-round, but most park facilities only available May–September. Peak season July–August, when advance bookings for commercial accommodations recommended.

**Access:** Airport in Saskatoon. Car rental agencies in Saskatoon and Prince Albert.

**Facilities:** Park: Visitor Centre (nature bookstore); interpretive outdoor theatre; campgrounds; picnic grounds; on-site exhibits; trails. Waskesiu townsite: museum; gas station; restaurants; commercial accommodations (motels, cabins). All medical facilities in city of Prince Albert.

**Watching Nature:** Excellent mammal watching, especially along the scenic drive to The Narrows; look for Black Bear, Mule and White-tailed Deer, moose, elk, Red Fox, and beaver. Excellent birding throughout the park, including White Pelicans feeding on most lakes in summer, including their colony on Lavallee Lake (restricted access), the second largest colony in North America.

**Visitor Activities:** Hiking, backpacking, cycling, tennis, lawn bowling, golf (18 holes), paddlewheel cruises, swimming, canoeing, and cross-country skiing.

**Special Notes:** Do not approach wildlife, even in urban areas.

Above: *From a boardwalk on the Boundary Bog Trail, the unusual fauna and flora of this habitat can be closely observed.*

Right: *The Height-of-Land Tower offers a bird's-eye view of the forest, and straddles a divide; from here water flows north to the Churchill River, and south to the Saskatchewan River.*

Moss of the bog harbours various carnivorous plants, including Pitcher Plant, Bladderwort, and two Sundews. The shoreline of diminutive Yotin Lake is a good spot to watch for nesting Common Loons and Willets, and to search for Dragonflies. The Mud Creek Trail follows the shoreline of Waskesiu Lake and Mud Creek, alternating between forests of Trembling Aspen and White Spruce. Both beaver and River Otter can regularly be seen, the former especially at dawn or dusk, and this is an excellent trail for wildflowers (Twinflower, Bunchberry, Sweet-scented Bedstraw), and breeding birds (Connecticut Warbler, Bald Eagle, Belted Kingfisher).

## Diversity Within Uniformity

A glance at the park's landscape gives a misleading impression of green uniformity, but closer inspection reveals the incredible diversity of life that exists in the variety of habitats. While Prince Albert National Park is truly in the Taiga, it is towards the southern edge, and there are elements of other habitats within its boundaries, most notably an outlier of fescue grassland in the southwest of the park. Elk, once prairie specialists, are widespread in the park, and there are a few free-roaming

Plains Bison. Moose, White-tailed and Mule Deer, are widespread, while a few small herds of Woodland Caribou linger in the north of the park. The park supports healthy populations of Timber Wolves and Black Bears, as well as smaller carnivores, including coyote, lynx, bobcat, fisher, martin, and otter. The variety of habitats provides for numerous wildflowers, such as Striped Coralroot, Yellow Locoweed, Prickly Pear Cactus, Sphagnum Moss, Pitcher Plant, and Calypso Orchid. The diversity within the park also attracts many birds, including eight species of owls and more than 20 kinds of wood warbler, including Connecticut, Canada, and Blackburnian. The second largest colony of American White Pelicans in North America can be seen at Lavallee Lake, an area in the northwest quadrant of the park that is off-limits to visitors.

## Grey Owl (Wa-sha-quon-asin)

The history of Prince Albert National Park is inextricably bound with the life of the author Grey Owl (Wa-Sha-Quon-Asin in Ojibway, or 'He Who Walks By Night'). This naturalist-writer, a former trapper turned conservationist, and purportedly a Native Indian, was hired by the National Parks Branch in 1931 to re-establish

Above, left: *The Water Arum prefers moister habitats in the park.*

Above: *The Common Bladderwort is a carnivorous species that flourishes in the thick Sphagnum Moss of the bogs.*

Left: *Lucky hikers on the Treebeard Trail might catch a glimpse of a Great Gray Owl amongst the giant spruce and fir trees.*

Opposite: *The park supports a healthy population of predators, including Black Bears.*

Below: *The elusive lynx preys on smaller mammals up to the size of young deer.*

beaver colonies in National Parks, and to promote the ideas of conservation through writing and speeches. Most of his work was in Prince Albert National Park, which he made his home. Immediately following his death from pneumonia in 1938, newspapers worldwide trumpeted the widely-known, but suppressed, news that Grey Owl was actually an Englishman, Archibald Stansfeld Belaney, who had worn the persona of Indian trapper and raconteur as convincingly as he had worn his buckskins. He was a bigamist, a drunkard, a poseur, and, some say, a complete fraud, but his passion for the preservation of the Canadian Wilderness was genuine, as were the positive changes he effected. The cabin in which he worked still stands in the park, on the shores of the lovely Ajawaan Lake, and although it is a long hike to the cabin, the trek is made by many who wish to touch this historic shrine to Grey Owl's passionate teachings.

## The Threat of Isolation

Prince Albert National Park protects a section of the Southern Boreal Plains where there are three different life zones: boreal forest, aspen parkland, and fescue grassland. Intensifying forestry and agricultural development outside the park borders are making the park – and the life zones it protects – increasingly isolated, and are threatening to turn the park into a Taiga island. These developments are having an impact on the spread of plants and on the free movement of animals, such as elk and caribou, which are affected by hunting pressures and the ecological barriers presented by logging clear-cuts. Over-fishing by sportsmen has depleted the populations of some fish species in several of the larger lakes in the park, and a long history of fire suppression has resulted in an unhealthy number of over-mature trees and a forest mosaic that is ecologically out of balance.

# BANFF NATIONAL PARK

## First and Foremost

*'We need an enrichment other than material prosperity and to gain it we have only to look around at what our country has to offer... We have something here that no other country has.'*

GREY OWL (WA-SHA-QUON-ASIN)

Banff National Park, formerly Rocky Mountain Park, was established in 1885, and was the first National Park to be established in Canada and only the third in the world after Yellowstone National Park in the United States and Royal National Park in Australia.

The historic heart of Banff is the Cave and Basin Hot Springs on Sulphur Mountain, the site of acrimonious competing commercial ownership claims in the late 19th century. In 1885, the government reserved 26 square kilometres (10 square miles) around the springs. Two years later, the area was expanded and named Rocky Mountain Park, and the Lake Louise area was added in 1902. The park's name was changed to Banff in 1930, and after several further boundary adjustments the park now covers 6,641 square kilometres (2,656 square miles).

Opposite, above: *Hoodoo Lookout affords panoramic views of Bow River Valley.*

Opposite, below left: *Female Bighorn Sheep differ from the males in their smaller horns and slighter build.*

Opposite below right: *Mule Deer live in small family groups; only the males have antlers.*

Above, right: *Three separate waterfalls tumble down Johnston Canyon to the Bow River below.*

Banff is one of four contiguous mountain parks that have been designated as a UNESCO World Heritage Site (the other parks are Yoho, Kootenay, and Jasper). While Jasper is the largest of these, Banff is the most visited, with more than four and a half million people arriving each year.

### By Road or By Trail

There are a number of short road trips that lead around the town of Banff, including the Vermilion Lake Drive and the road to the man-made Lake Minnewanka ('Minnewanka' is the First Nations name for 'water spirits'). Longer excursions include the Bow Valley Parkway drive to Lake Louise (infinitely preferable to the Trans-Canada Highway), which branches off the Banff-Windermere Highway that passes through Kootenay National Park. A little further north of Lake Louise, the Trans-Canada Highway heads west through Yoho National Park, while the Icefields Parkway continues north to Jasper National Park, over the Bow Summit and Sunset Pass, and alongside the impressive Columbia Icefields. Many consider the Icefields Parkway the most scenic drive in the world.

The landscapes can be well appreciated by road, but explorations on foot reveal intricacies and subtleties easily missed from the comfort of the car. There are dozens of frontcountry and backcountry trails to explore.

**Location**: In Alberta, in the Canadian Rocky Mountains east of the Continental Divide. It is 128 km (80 miles) west of Calgary, and 850 km (530 miles) east of Vancouver.

**Climate**: Highly changeable, and many local mountain influences. Average high temperatures for Banff townsite are July: 22°C (72°F), January: -15°C (4 °F). Year-round the temperature decreases 1° for every 200 m (670 ft) rise. In alpine areas snow can occur in any month. In montane (valley) areas summers are wetter than winters, and summer precipitation is rain. Prepare for a variety of weather at any season.

**When to Go**: Open year-round; a few services only available seasonally. May and October are the least visited months. During summer, and peak skiing season, book accommodations well in advance. Adverse weather can force temporary closures of highways, especially in winter.

**Access**: Road: by vehicle or bus from east or west along the Trans-Canada Highway. Nearest international airport in Calgary.

**Facilities**: Park: Visitor Centres; on-site exhibits; campgrounds; scenic drives, picnic grounds; trails; outdoor theatres, hot springs. Banff and Lake Louise townsites; commercial accommodations (motels, cabins, B&B, hostel); hospital; gas station.

**Watching Nature**: Extensive opportunities, with seasonal highlights. Inquire with the park.

**Visitor Activities**: Hiking; scenic drives; mountaineering; horseback riding; cross-country skiing; downhill skiing near Banff townsite; hot mineral springs; boating, canoeing, golfing, kayaking.

Right: Heavy snowfalls
create a magical winter
landscape around Lake
Louise.

Below: *Skiing, both downhill and cross-country, is
Banff's greatest winter
attraction.*

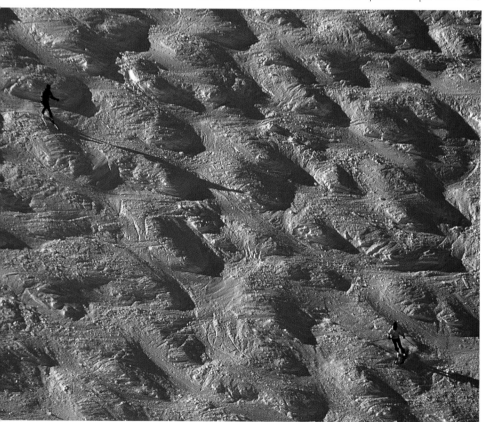

Johnstone Canyon is a popular trail that has an asphalt surface to withstand the many steps of visitors wishing to view the two waterfalls that tumble down the canyon to the Bow River. Black Swifts, Cordilleran Flycatchers, and American Dippers nest here, and there are frequent sightings of Harlequin Ducks in the rapids of the Bow River. The Fenland trail offers a quiet escape from the more popular park attractions, and beaver are regularly seen. Mistaya Canyon is a ten-minute walk off the Icefields parkway, where the Mistaya River has created some beautiful rock formations, including a natural arch. The alpine environment takes a bit more work to reach, but is accessible either on the Parker Ridge trail (a 2.4-km/1.5-mile round trip) or the Sunshine Meadows (a 5-km/3-mile walk from the Sunshine ski area parking lot). Alpine wildflowers are a summer attraction at these two sites, and there are mammals and birds, including Pika (in rockpiles above 1,800 m/6,000 feet), Hoary Marmots (above 2,500 m/6,800 feet), White-tailed Ptarmigan, Gray-crowned Rosy-Finches, and American Pipits. Below the alpine areas, the two most popular areas for birding include the Bow Valley Parkway, and the Vermilion Lakes, which is the most important site in the park for migrant birds.

## Water and Rocks

As well as the magnificent peaks shaped by water, snow, ice, and avalanche, Banff has other sites that reveal a long history of interaction between rock and water. The Castleguard Cave system is the largest Karst cave system in Canada and one of the finest in the world. A total of 16.2 kilometres (10 miles) of caving has been mapped. The cave system contains numerous remarkable and pristine cave features and supports several cave-dependent animals, including several species of bats. The Cave and Basin hot springs, along the base of Sulphur Mountain, are a National Historic Site as they are the birthplace of Canada's National Parks, and have been restored to their turn-of-the-century appearance. Further along the Bow River near Tunnel Mountain Drive, Hoodoos (pillars of sedimentary rock that have been formed by the differential erosion of soft and hard sedimentary rock) can be seen poking out of the landscape.

## Lake Louise

Lake Louise is one of the most stunning natural sights in the world. It flows into the Bow River, and faces the mountains of the continental divide to the west, which form the border with British Columbia. It is best viewed, and least crowded, at dawn and dusk. The local Stoney First Nations people knew Lake Louise as 'Lake of the Little Fishes', though the first European visitor renamed it Emerald Lake in 1882, and it was renamed two years later after Louise, the daughter of Queen Victoria. The town is roughly 40 kilometres (25 miles) northwest of Banff, further upstream along the Bow River, which flows through both communities. Moraine Lake (15 minutes from Lake Louise by road) is arguably as beautiful as Lake Louise, though it is much less visited. A commercial gondola is available from June to September, which offers excellent views of Lake Louise, Victoria Glacier, and the surrounding mountains.

## The Perils of Popularity

The ability of the park's authorities to protect this important part of the Rocky Mountains is under threat from the pressure sustained by the increasing number of visitors to the area. Currently, further park developments have been halted, and attempts are being made to rectify some of the damage that has already been done. There is, however, conflict between those wishing to preserve the park's wilderness and those wishing to expand the tourism infrastructure within the park boundaries. Poaching and external park developments also pose difficulties, but the greatest risk is to the park's montane habitat, which has borne the brunt of park infrastructure development.

Above: *Hoary Marmots are amongst several mammal species that the visitor may encounter.*

Below: *The Second Vermilion Lake is accessible on a short drive from Banff townsite.*

Overleaf: *Moraine Lake in the Valley of the Ten Peaks typifies the grandeur of Banff's landscapes.*

# WOOD BUFFALO NATIONAL PARK

## A Vast Expanse

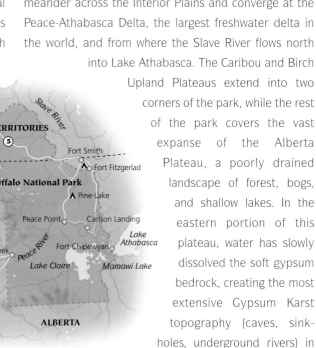

*'He thought he saw a Buffalo upon the chimney-piece . . .'*

LEWIS CARROLL, ALICE IN WONDERLAND

Wood Buffalo National Park was established in 1922 and is Canada's largest national park. The total area covered by the park is 44,802 square kilometres (17,299 square miles), which is an area greater than that covered by countries such as Switzerland, The Netherlands, and Taiwan. In 1983 the park was designated as a UNESCO World Heritage Site, recognising the park authority's attempt to protect the world's largest free-roaming bison herd as well as the biologically rich Peace-Athabasca Delta, and an extensive area of unique salt plains, the only remaining nesting ground of the Whooping Crane. This highly endangered bird winters on the Gulf Coast of Texas, returning to the park in small numbers every spring.

Opposite above: *Little Buffalo River Falls is one of the many interesting geological features of the heavily eroded landscape protected by this huge park.*

Opposite below: *In summer, a rich variety of plant life can be found in the park, including Calypso Orchid (left), Saline Shooting-Star (centre), and Cut-leaved Anenome (right).*

Above right: *The umistakable bold markings of the Tiger Swallowtail enable easy identification of this butterfly.*

Large rivers (the Peace, Athabasca, and Beaver) meander across the Interior Plains and converge at the Peace-Athabasca Delta, the largest freshwater delta in the world, and from where the Slave River flows north into Lake Athabasca. The Caribou and Birch Upland Plateaus extend into two corners of the park, while the rest of the park covers the vast expanse of the Alberta Plateau, a poorly drained landscape of forest, bogs, and shallow lakes. In the eastern portion of this plateau, water has slowly dissolved the soft gypsum bedrock, creating the most extensive Gypsum Karst topography (caves, sinkholes, underground rivers) in North America. Just southwest of Fort Smith, at the base of a low escarpment, mineral-laden water emerges from springs, and the salty precipitate has affected the flora and fauna of a wide area, known as the Salt Plains.

## Special Species

The reason that Wood Buffalo National Park was initially established was to protect the largest remaining free-roaming and self-regulating herd of bison in the world. Though 'bison' is the scientific name, 'buffalo' is the widespread common term that is used for the animals, even though they are unrelated to the true buffalo found in Africa and Asia. Two races exist in the

**Location:** Straddles the Northwest Territories/Alberta border. Road distances to Fort Smith from Yellowknife: 748 km/468 miles; from Hay River: 174 km/109 miles; from Edmonton: 1,310 km/818 miles.

**Climate:** Summers are short, warm, and dry, with long hours of daylight. Autumns are cool and windy. Winters are long and cold. High and low mean temperatures: July 23/10°C (72/50°F); January -22/-32°C (-8/-26°F). Frequent winter temperatures below -40°C/F. Annual precipitation 215 mm (8 in), 70% as snow.

**When to Go:** Open year-round, though most visit park from June–September. Most park facilities closed October–May.

**Access:** All-weather gravel road (Hwy 5) from Hay River, on the McKenzie Highway. By air from Edmonton or Yellowknife.

**Facilities:** Park: trails, picnic sites, campgrounds, Visitor Centre (Fort Smith), trails, on-site exhibits. Fort Smith: Hotels, campground, and B&B's, restaurants, stores, gas stations, vehicle rental, canoe and water craft rental, airport. Information centre.

**Watching Nature:** Bison, moose, and Sandhill Cranes. Productive viewing sites: Salt Plains Viewpoint, Grosbeak Lake, Sweetgrass (Peace-Athabasca Delta, by boat from Fort Chipewyan). Winter viewing of Northern Lights.

**Visitor Activities:** Hiking, backpacking, nature photography, canoeing, fishing, and cross-country skiing.

**Special Notes:** (1) Do not approach bison. (2) Park roads are all-weather gravel and may become slippery when wet. (3) Contact park for backcountry and water travel hazards.

Right: *The Sandhill Crane also breeds in the park, and is more likely to be seen by visitors than its relative, the endangered Whooping Crane.*

resupply helicopter flight stumbled upon two adult and one young Whooping Crane, a species whose entire world population at that time numbered approximately 20 birds. Up until that time the birds were known to winter in Aransas, Texas, but their breeding grounds were unknown. In subsequent years all the nesting sites have been mapped, and a continuing intensive international conservation effort has succeeded in raising the wild population to over 180. Cranes normally successfully raise only one of two chicks, and so over the years – to continue to increase the numbers of this special species – surplus eggs have been removed and the chicks raised in captivity for either breeding or subsequent release. The Whooping Crane nesting area, in the remote north-central part of the park, is off limits to all visitors.

Wood Buffalo National Park is also home to the northernmost populations of a number of species of animals, including White Pelican, and the Red-sided Garter Snake, whose most northerly known hibernaculum (an underground winter hibernating site) is located at the Salt River Day-use Area. The snakes, toward the end of April, emerge from the ground to mate prior to migrating to their summer feeding grounds.

Below: *The Wood Buffalo, more properly known as a bison, is unrelated to the true buffalos of Africa and Asia.*

park, the Plains Bison and the Wood Bison, which though appearing distinctly different, are genetically almost identical.

Wood Buffalo is also responsible for the protection of Whooping Crane. In 1954 the crew of a forest-fire

## A Cultural Crossroads

First Nations people have inhabited the Wood Buffalo region for more than eight thousand years. The European fur traders, who arrived in the early 1700s, named the different tribes they met the Beaver, Slavey, and Chipewyan. The Beaver and Slavey moved west with the fur trade, and today's park communities are mostly made up of Cree, Chipewyan, Métis, and non-First Nations people. Subsistence hunting, fishing and commercial trapping still occur in Wood Buffalo National Park, and traditional activities are considered an important part of the park's cultural mosaic.

## The Peace-Athabasca Delta

Since the retreat of the glaciers 12,000 years ago, the deltas of the Peace and Athabasca Rivers converged, and have been expanding ever since, forming the largest freshwater delta in the world (over 5,000 square km/1,900 square miles), creating channels, shallow lakes, sedge meadows, and hundreds of sloughs and treed levees. The area is extraordinarily productive for breeding birds, particularly waterfowl, and millions use the area to refuel their migration. There is also an abundance of mammals, including high concentrations of muskrat, beaver, bison, wolves, and moose. Historically, spring floods enriched the area with an annual deposit of rich silt eroded upstream, but since the construction of a dam on the Peace River in the 1960s, the river volume has dropped by more than 40 per cent, and spring flooding is now a rarity. Several solutions are currently being pursued to maintain a healthy delta.

## Protecting the Park

Wood Buffalo National Park protects an outstanding example of the Northern Boreal Plains region. Commercial logging in the south of the park, a vestige of the 1950s when the government was trying to promote economic development of the north, was halted in 1992. However, the water cycles in the Peace-Athabaska Delta continue to be disrupted. Ensuring the health of the bison herds, and continuing to maintain suitable nesting habitat for the Whooping Crane represent major conservation challenges. The present practice of allowing many forest fires to burn naturally is occasionally controversial, as is the unrealised plan to build a dam on the Slave River, outside the park boundaries.

Above: *American White Pelicans may be seen along the Slave River, the northernmost colony for this species.*

Below: *The Mountain Avens bears distinctive seedheads.*

# JASPER NATIONAL PARK

## The Icefields and the Divide

*'Where the rivers change direction, across the Great Divide.'*

KATE WOLF

Jasper National Park covers 10,878 square kilometres (4,200 square miles) and is the northernmost and largest of Canada's four contiguous Rocky Mountain National Parks. Together the four parks (Jasper, Yoho, Kootenay and Banff) comprise a UNESCO World Heritage Site. Jasper is a land of divides: the Main Range of the Rocky Mountains split waters flowing into the Pacific and the Arctic; Jasper's southern boundary separates it from its three sister Rocky Mountain parks; and its size and remoteness from urban areas dissociate it from the commercial glitter of Banff.

Visitors are drawn to Jasper's relative remoteness, captivating scenery, and abundant wildlife, particularly large mammals. Despite its distance from major urban centres, nearly two million people visit the park each year, and more pass through on its highways. Attractions include the Columbia Icefield, Maligne Canyon and Lake, Sunwapta Falls, Miette Hot Springs, and especially the Icefields Parkway, one of the world's most scenic drives, which links Jasper with Lake Louise via the Sunwapta Pass.

### The Columbia Icefields and Divided Waters

The Columbia Icefields dominate Jasper's scenery and are a highlight for those who drive the Icefields Parkway. Many visitors are satisfied with a trip to the Visitor Centre, and a stroll along the interpretive trail to the foot of the glacier, while others take commercial coach tours on vehicles especially designed for travel on the glacier. From the toe of the Columbia Glacier, the Athabasca River flows north and east through the park for nearly 150 kilometres (94 miles), a short step on its long trip to the Arctic Ocean. The portion of the river within Jasper National Park has been designated a Canadian Heritage River. Waters melting from the unseen western side of the Columbia Icefields flow into the Pacific Ocean, while the Southesk and Brazeau rivers in the southeasterly corner of the park join the North Saskatchewan River, and eventually reach Hudson Bay.

*Opposite, above: Bighorn Sheep find good grazing around the shores of Celestine Lake.*

*Opposite, bottom left: The Grizzly Bear is the larger and more elusive of the two bear species found in the park.*

*Opposite, bottom right: The male elk, or Wapiti, possesses an impressive pair of antlers.*

*Above right: The Red-tailed Hawk is the most common member of its family in North America.*

**Location:** By road: 370 km (192 miles) west of Edmonton, 404 km (256 miles) north-west of Calgary, 805 km (500 miles) north-east of Vancouver, and 226 km (141 miles) north of Lake Louise.

**Climate:** Unpredictable and highly variable, due to mountain effects. Average high and low temperatures in Jasper townsite: July 22.5°C (72°F); January -7°C (14°F). Columbia Icefield: July 15°C (58°F); January: -10°C (14°F). Snow is possible at high elevations even in summer.

**When to Go:** Open year-round. Peak season July–August, when advance bookings for commercial accommodations recommended. Visitor Centre open seven days a week all year-round. Icefields Visitor Centre open seven days a week May 1–October 15.

**Access:** International airports in Edmonton, Calgary, Vancouver. Scheduled bus and train service from Vancouver and Edmonton. Car rental agencies in Jasper.

**Facilities:** Park: Visitor Centres; on-site exhibits; campgrounds; picnic grounds; trails; outdoor theatre. Jasper townsite: commercial accommodations (B&B, motels, cabins,, and hostel).

**Watching Nature:** Mammals, including elk, Bighorn Sheep, Mountain Goat, and caribou. Birdwatching and alpine plants.

**Visitor Activities:** Hiking; scenic drives; mountaineering; horseback riding; cross-country skiing; downhill skiing near Jasper townsite; hot mineral springs.

**Special Notes:** (1) Western Canada Annual Parks Pass is accepted. (2) Do not approach elk, even in urban areas.

Above: *Clark's Nutcracker feeds on pine seeds, and is locally common in high forests at the timberline.*

## Three Life Zones

There are three important life zones in the park, each defined by climatic changes that occur with changes in elevation. The Montane Forest Zone is the lowest, and contains the wide river valleys and adjacent Douglas-Fir forests. This is the zone all visitors experience, as most park and community services lie within it, including Jasper townsite. This zone possesses the greatest number and diversity of plants and animals, as it is the warmest, with the longest growing season. Here you'll find Trembling Aspen, Wild Rose, Black-billed Magpie, Ruffed Grouse, elk, and White-tailed Deer. The Subalpine Forest Zone rises higher to the tree line, and is home to Subalpine Fir, Engleman Spruce, White Rhododendron, Clark's Nutcracker, Spruce Grouse, Moose, and Woodland Caribou. The Alpine Tundra Zone lies above the treeline wherever there is not permanent ice, and typical species include White Mountain Avens, Alpine Marsh Marigold, Common Raven, White-tailed Ptarmigan, Bighorn Sheep, and Mountain Goat. Samples of all the zones are accessible via the park's extensive series of trails, of which there are more than 1,000 kilometres (600 miles) in total.

## Charismatic Mega-Fauna

Most visitors to Jasper seek out the numerous larger mammal species that inhabit the park. Fifty-three species of mammals are found in the park, though attention is drawn to those species that are more easily visible. Among the smaller mammals that are frequently encountered are Columbian Ground Squirrels, Hoary Marmots (alpine zone), Pikas, and beaver. The park is blessed with seven ungulates, all popular with visitors: elk; caribou; moose; White-tailed Deer; Mule

Below: *The turbulent waters of the Maligne River offer an exciting challenge for river rafters.*

Deer; Bighorn Sheep; and Mountain Goat. Most sightings occur beside or near the roads, especially in spring when the animals come to lick road salt off the highway. If you encounter animals near a road, do not stop your car and disrupt traffic; stop off only in designated areas.

Most of the carnivores that inhabit the park are rarely seen, although Coyotes often patrol road edges for animals struck by cars. Mountain Lions and wolves are resident, but are elusive. Black Bears and Grizzly Bears are less shy, but are best seen from a distance. Read the park literature regarding bear safety, and take heed of all warning signs. Park staff go to great lengths to ensure that bears and people rarely mix. So far the pol-

icy seems to be working, as the park supports a healthy population of more than 100 Grizzly Bears, and is a vital refuge for this endangered species.

## A Brief History

First Nations people have been in the area for more than 8,000 years. Smallpox, brought to North America by Europeans, was carried to the mountains by tribes from further east, and the Jasper area was mostly unpopulated when the first European trappers arrived. Jasper Forest Reserve was created in 1907 to protect watersheds in anticipation of the arrival of two transcontinental railways through the Athabasca Valley. Tourism development and resource extraction (wood, coal, lime-

stone) occurred until the establishment of the National Parks Act in 1930. The railway era of the early part of the 1900s spurred the establishment of what today is Jasper National Park.

## Land Development

Jasper National Park preserves a fine portion of the Front and Main Ranges of the Rocky Mountains. Park resources are threatened by logging and mining activity on adjacent land, and by poachers. Within the park, animals are frequent victims of collisions with vehicles, and the animals' preferred wintering area in the Lower Athabasca Valley is reduced with each new human development.

Above: *The rugged Queen Elizabeth Range in the Maligne Valley looms over Jasper's forests.*

# CYPRESS HILLS INTERPROVINCIAL PARK

## The Thunder Breeding Hills

*'Spring on the Prairies, it comes like a surprise...'*
CONNIE KALDOR, SPRING ON THE PRAIRIES

Cypress Hills Interprovincial Park covers an area of 250 square kilometres (96 square miles) and is divided into two portions that are administered by the provinces of Alberta and Saskatchewan. The First Nations people who lived in the Cypress Hills area for thousands of years thought the weather was created here and so gave the region the name 'Thunder Breeding Hills'. The name used today comes from the early Métis hunters who mistook the area's pines for Cypress and named the area 'Les Montagnes des Cypres'.

Driving to the hills southwest from Maple Creek, at an elevation of 1,055 metres (3,517 feet), there is a gradual, almost imperceptible, rise in elevation to the Cypress Hills Plateau, at 1,500 metres (5,000 feet). The flat prairies and peaceful ennui of the grasslands are replaced by coniferous forest, where the air is cooler and wetter, and there is the pervasive smell of pine. The Cypress Hills Plateau is higher than anywhere further east in Canada south of the Arctic, and high enough that several of the highest areas in the park escaped glaciation. Many of the plants and animals that thrive on this prairie upland island are typical of the foothills of the Rocky Mountains far away to the west of the country. Lodgepole Pine is the dominant tree in the park. There, are moose and elk, and many bird species reach their eastern limits in the park, including MacGillivray's Warbler, Townsend's Solitaire and Trumpeter Swan.

Opposite: *Trembling Aspen bring colour to the prairies.*

Above, right: *Fort Walsh was a base for the Northwest Mounted Police during early settlement in the region.*

### Les Montagnes Des Cypres

The First Nations people who hunted in and around the hills were the Assiniboine, Blackfoot, Sioux, and Cree. With European contact came horses, guns, alcohol, disease, and a devastating upheaval of their way of life. As the population of buffalo declined in the 1870s, many illegal independent trading posts were built, where unscrupulous men exchanged whisky for furs. In 1873, a group of wolf hunters rode from Fort Benton, Montana, in search of Cree Indians who they believed had stolen some horses. They stayed to rest and drink at two adjacent trading posts in the Cypress Hills, built by Moses Soloman and Abe Farwell. A group of Assiniboine was encamped nearby, and when a horse wandered off, the men accused the Indians of theft. More than 20 Assiniboine were massacred and their

**Location**: Saskatchewan portion's West Block is 52 km (33 miles) south-west of Maple Creek, and Centre Block is 27 km (17 miles) south of Maple Creek. The Alberta portion is 70 km (44 miles) south-east of Medicine Hat, Alberta.

**Climate:** Fairly dry year-round, hot in summer, cold in winter. Frequently windy. Thunderstorms occur in summer.

**When to Go:** Open year-round, but most park services and facilities only open from June–September.

**Access:** Saskatchewan: by road, Maple Creek is just south of the TransCanada Hwy on Hwy 21. Access Centre Block on Hwy 21, West Block on Hwy 271. Nearest major airport is in Regina, Saskatchewan, 383 km (240 miles) east of Maple Creek. Alberta: by road, south on Hwy 41 from Medicine Hat, Alberta (on Trans-Canada Hwy). Closest major airport is in Calgary, Alberta, 293 km (183 miles) north-west.

**Facilities:** Campgrounds, trails, on-site exhibits. Saskatchewan only: Visitor Centre, commercial accommodations. Full services (including stores, gas station, restaurant, vehicle rental) in Medicine Hat, Alberta, and Maple Creek, Saskatchewan.

**Watching Nature:** Excellent birding, diverse wildflowers, interesting geological features.

**Visitor Activities:** Hiking, swimming, horseback riding, boating, fishing, ice-fishing, cross-country skiing, nature photography, auto-tours.

camp burned. This tragedy spurred the arrival of the Northwest Mounted Police to administer law in the then Northwest Territories. Their first base of operations was Fort Walsh, in the West Block of the Saskatchewan Cypress Hills, and now a popular National Historic Site. The original trading posts have also been reconstructed.

## West Block Auto-Tour

An Auto-Tour has been developed between the Centre and West Blocks on the Saskatchewan portion of the park and there is no finer way to appreciate the park than to take this tour. Key stopping points *en route* include: Lookout Point, offering a panorama of the prairies north to the Great Sand Hills; Bald Butte; the Conglomerate Cliffs and Adams Lake; and Fort Walsh National Historic Site. The road through 'the Gap' between the two Blocks of the park is unpaved, and may be impassable if wet.

## Fire-Dependent Pine Forests

The Lodgepole Pine forests of Cypress Hills are fire-dependent, relying on the heat of small fires that occur naturally to melt the resin covering the pine cones to release the seeds. The pine seedlings thrive in the burnt humus that results from the small fires and the natural life-cycle of the trees is maintained. However, there has been a long-standing practice in Cypress Hills of fire suppression that is threatening the survival of the forests. Fire suppression gives rise to a buildup of the forest litter layer, which is then susceptible to occasional fires that can subsequently rage out of control. While pine bark can withstand the heat generated by the smaller, less intense fires, it cannot survive the heat of occasional, intense fires. There is increasing concern that such a fire could devastate the forests of Cypress Hills.

# GRASSLANDS NATIONAL PARK

## A Work in Progress

*'Where the deer and the antelope play...'*
Dr. Breweter Highley, Home on the Range

The initial agreement to establish Grasslands National Park in southwestern Saskatchewan was signed in 1975 but insufficient funds have been committed for the purchase of critical lands in the area and the park is still only half complete. Any available funds for the Grasslands National Park are now set aside for land acquisition, and consequently there are no facilities or services in the park. However, the park, albeit incomplete, protects a number of endangered species, and offers Mule Deer and the Pronghorn Antelope a place to live in relative safety.

### Building Blocks

The existing, incomplete park is contained in two blocks, together comprising 420 square kilometres (168 square miles), though it is intended, that the completed park will be more than twice this size. The West Block, near Val Marie, is centered on the valley of the Frenchman River, and contains a dramatic eroded landscape, shaped first by glaciers, and subsequently by wind and water. The East Block, near the village of Killdeer contains the dramatic Killdeer badlands, a landscape unlike any other in Saskatchewan, and the site of one of the earliest discoveries of dinosaur fossils in 1874.

*Above, right: Gaillardia often blooms in profusion in drier upland areas.*

### Endangered Spaces, Endangered Species

No habitat in North America has been more thoroughly modified and tamed than the massive grasslands that once extended from west-central Canada south to Mexico. Hunting, land division, cultivation, and draining of wetlands has erased almost all the original prairies. However, although the original prairies have gone, visitors to the park can still expect a diverse and rewarding wildlife experience. There are nearly 300 species of birds, herptiles, and mammals present, some of which are found only in this park, including Pronghorn Antelope, Black-tailed Prairie Dog, Sage Grouse, Eastern Short-horned Lizard, and Ferruginous Hawk. Pronghorn Antelope and Mule Deer are the most commonly seen large animals, and elk, although still rare, are becoming more common in the East Block.

Among small mammals, Black-tailed Prairie Dogs are common in the West Block's Frenchman River Valley, the site of Canada's only colonies. Other small mammals include bobcat, coyote, badger, Striped Skunk, porcupine, mink, Long-tailed Weasel, White-tailed Jackrabbit, and Richardson's Ground-Squirrel. More than 190 bird species migrate through or breed in the park, including 20 species of raptor. Prominent species include Sharp-tailed and Sage Grouse, Prairie Falcon, Golden Eagle, Western Meadowlark, Sprague's Pipit, McCown's and

**Location:** West Block centres on the Frenchman River Valley; East Block centres on the Killdeer Badlands.

**Climate:** Hot summers, cold winters, frequent and strong winds, and low precipitation.

**When to Go:** Open year-round, though most visit from spring to autumn.

**Access:** Park administrative office in Val Marie is 125 km (78 miles) south of Swift Current on paved road. Park staff can advise on road access to the two blocks of the park. Nearest airport in Regina, 366 km (229 miles) distant by car.

**Facilities:** There are no facilities within the park. The Visitor Centre is in Val Marie, at the juntion of Hwy 4 and Center St. Restaurants, fuel and accommodations are in the towns of Mankota, Glentworth and Wood Mountain (for East Block), and Val Marie (for West Block). A municipal campground is in Val Marie, while Wood Mountain Regional Park near the East Block has a campground, swimming pool, laundry, and playground. Inside Grasslands National Park only no-trace tent camping is permitted, and only well away from roads and historic farm buildings.

**Watching Nature:** Mammals: Pronghorn Antelope, Mule Deer, Black-tailed Prairie Dog in West Block, elk in East Block. Birds: Sage Grouse, Golden Eagle, Prairie Falcon. Prairie Rattlesnake.

**Visitor Activities:** Hiking, horseback riding, and sight-seeing via an Auto-tour of the West Block. Landscape photography is particularly rewarding. Winter snow amounts are too slight for winter sports.

Above and below: *Black-tailed Prairie Dogs inhabit the grasslands in large communities, or 'towns'. They excavate elaborate underground burrows for shelter and protection from predators.*

Chestnut-collared Longspur, Baird's Sparrow, and the increasingly rare Burrowing Owl. The park protects a number of other species, including Loggerhead Shrike, Long-billed Curlew, Mountain Plover and Ferruginous Hawk.

The park also protects Eastern Yellow-bellied Racer Snake and hosts a small population of Prairie Rattlesnakes, including several of their winter denning sites in the West Block. There are also numerous wildflowers, such as Indian Breadroot, Prairie Buttercup, Prairie Crocus, Prickly Pear Cactus, and Sagebrush, which support a good selection of butterflies and other insects.

## Human Wanderings

Since the retreat of the continental glaciers 12,000 years ago, various nomadic groups of Canada's First Nations people have passed through this area, and many traces of their passage persist, particularly teepee rings. These people followed herds of bison (numbering more than 60 million animals) across the Great Plains, never staying in one place for very long. European expansion westward, both in the United States and Canada, resulted in the slaughter of all but a handful of

bison, with the effect that the First Nations people could no longer continue with their nomadic way of life. In the late 19th century the first European ranches began operation, and subsequent experience has taught that low key ranching is the only viable agricultural activity in this drought-prone area; dryland farming is not tenable, as failed attempts have proven.

## Replicating Fire and Grazing Regimes

The two major influences on the original grasslands were periodic (approximately annual) fires and grazing by ungulates, particularly bison (buffalo). However, now that the bison are gone and the orginal fire regimes have been disrupted, the vegetation that had adapted to the periodic regime is severely threatened. Three exotic perennial grasses, Smooth Broome, Crested Wheatgrass, and Russion Wild Rye, were used as hay/pasture species and now dominate the areas where they were seeded. The vegetation in the few remaining fragments of grassland can now be best maintained by mimicking both the original fire regime through controlled burns, and substituting Bison grazing for grazing by cattle (or other domestic ungulates), without over-grazing.

Above: *Foxtail Barley Grass brings a distinctive texture to the park's sweeping plains.*

Left: *Pronghorn Antelope, a quintessential grassland species, thrives in the park.*

# WATERTON LAKES NATIONAL PARK

## Land of the Shining Mountains

*'The Chinook be along any day now.'*

IAN TYSON, MILK RIVER RIDGE

Waterton Lakes National Park was the fourth national park to be established in Canada. It was set up in 1895 and although its size has altered over the years, it currently covers 505 square kilometres (195 square miles), much smaller than the neighbouring U.S. Glacier National Park, which covers 4,101 square kilometres (1,539 square miles). Together, the two parks comprise the Waterton/Glacier International Peace Park, established in 1932, the first such cooperative venture in the world.

The First Nations people of the area, the Blackfoot, called the Waterton Lakes area the 'Land of Shining Mountains', though the description favoured by park staff is 'Where the mountains meet the prairies'. Whereas along most of the Rocky Mountain chain a series of foothills separates the peaks from the prairies, at Waterton the foothills are absent, and the mountains rise abruptly from the vast plains to the west. The park preserves superb mountain habitat (Mount Blakiston, 2,942 metres/ 9,645 feet), as well as pristine fescue grassland.

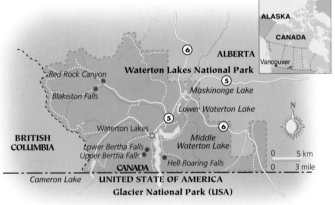

### Mountain habitat

Visitors can take one of three road systems into the mountains of the park and there are over 20 trails to explore the area on foot. It is comparatively easy to access alpine meadows, where wildflowers, including Avalanche Lily, Alpine Lupin, Mountain Arnica, and Subalpine Daisy, abound at the edge of the treeline. Clark's Nutcrackers frequently fly by, and Rocky Mountain Bighorn Sheep or Mountain Goats can be seen at times. Yellow-bellied Marmots favour the rocky areas. The rocks themselves are worth inspecting. A thrust fault, caused by an ancient earthquake, unearthed what is now the oldest, exposed sedimentary rock in the Canadian Rockies, 1,500 million years old. In some of the park mountains a 30-metre (100-foot) layer of black rock is visible, sandwiched between layers of white marble – the Purcell Sill – originally a layer of magma squeezed up between limestone deposits, 1,080 million years ago.

*Opposite, far left: Waterton Lakes is renowned for its magnificent displays of wildflowers. These include the Mountain Ladyslipper (top), and the Common Yellow Paintbrush (bottom).*

*Opposite: The valley to Red Rock Canyon may be explored by the hiker on a network of trails.*

*Above, right: Golden-mantled Ground-Squirrels are common, but they may hibernate for up to nine months of the year.*

**Location:** SW corner of Alberta, bordered to west by Akamina-Kishinena Provincial Park, and to south by Glacier National Park, Montana. Waterton townsite is 1,280 m (4,200 ft) above sea level. The park's highest peak, Mt. Blakiston, is 2,940 m (9,645 ft) above sea level.

**Climate:** Highly variable mountain weather. Brief, cool summers, mild snowy winters, possible extremes: high 35°C (94°F), and low -40°C (-40°F). 1,072 mm (42.2 in) of annual precipitation, more than half as snow. Strong winds — Daily winds average 32 km/h (20 mph), but 120 km/h (75 mph) gusts are not uncommon.

**When to Go:** Open year-round, but most facilities closed in winter. Year-round residential population of 80 people, increases in summer to about 2,000. Advance reservations for accommodations recommended in July–August.

**Access:** By road: 270 km (150 miles) south of Calgary, Alberta; 64 km (40 miles) northwest of St. Mary's, Montana. By air: international airport in Calgary. Vehicle rental in Calgary and Great Falls in Montana.

**Facilities:** Park: Visitor Centre ; on-site exhibits; campgrounds; picnic grounds; trails; cycle and horse trails, interpretive indoor theatre. Waterton townsite: commercial accommodations (motels, cabins); gas station; outdoor heated pool, groceries; restaurants, laundry, horseback and boat rentals (many closed in winter).

**Watching Nature:** Mountain Goats, Mule Deer, and Bighorn Sheep. Black and Grizzly Bears present, but elusive. Wildflowers.

**Visitor Activities:** hiking, backpacking, cycling, golfing, boat cruises, swimming, canoeing, horseback riding, Bison Paddock, and cross-country skiing.

Above: *Bison have been reintroduced, and may be seen from a road through the Bison Paddock.*

Below: *The underlying geology of the park is clearly exposed in Red Rock Canyon.*

Glaciers carved out the many lakes in Waterton, and Upper Waterton Lake, at 148 metres (493 feet), is the deepest lake in the Canadian Rockies. It supports some rare aquatic creatures, including the Deepwater Sculpin, the Pygmy Whitefish, and the Opossum Shrimp.

## Life on the Prairie

Waterton Lakes has 33 square kilometres (20 square miles) of fescue prairie, accessible via trail, or by road through the Bison Paddock. There are numerous wild-flowers (Wild Rose, Prairie Smoke, Shrubby Cinquefoil, Indian Paintbrush), birds (Western Kingbird, Savannah Sparrow, Yellow Warbler), and mammals (badger, Striped Skunk, and weasel).

## The Chinook

A Chinook is the Canadian name for the southerly or south-westerly wind that passes over the Rocky Mountains, drying and warming as it rapidly descends the lee slope. As the air flows down the slope waves are created, and the highest wave crest creates a distinct band of clouds lying parallel to the mountains, called a chinook arch. Such winds, which are particularly strong in southern Alberta, can occur throughout the year, but are more apparent (and welcome) in colder weather. They may last an hour or several days, though several can occur in one day. Waterton Lakes has one of the highest chinook frequencies in Alberta, resulting in the mildest winter climate in the province.

## Protecting a Varied Terrain

Waterton Lakes National Park protects elements of both the Prairie Grasslands and the Rocky Mountains natural regions. The park is too small in size to protect an entire ecosystem, even with the presence of the huge neighbouring Glacier National Park to the south. Lands to the east are subject to intensive agriculture, and the accessible valleys are showing signs of wear and tear from recreational use.

# RIDING MOUNTAIN NATIONAL PARK

## A Mountain Full of Devils

*'I dreamed of the devil, and waked in a fright.'*

CHRISTOPHER ANSTEY, THE NEW BATH GUIDE

Riding Mountain is actually an escarpment, rising above the surrounding plains to an elevation of 756 metres (2,480 feet). Although scarcely a mountain, it was, according to the early European explorer Henry Hind, imposing to local Indians, who refused to climb it, claiming it was 'full of devils'. Riding Mountain National Park was created in 1929 in order to attract tourism and bring economic growth to the area. The park has an area of 2,973 square kilometres (1,148 square miles).

### An Island of Diversity

Many national parks in Canada are becoming ecological islands, as agriculture and logging extend right to the park borders. Riding Mountain, surrounded by plains, has always been an inland 'island', separated by elevation and consequent differences in climate and vegetation. The park is varied, with elements of boreal forest in the upland areas, deciduous forest along the eastern edge of the escarpment, and meadows and grassland in the western areas. It is large enough to be ecologically self-contained, and has a nearly full complement of its original inhabitants. There are more than 55 species of mammals (including Northern Flying Squirrel and Silver-

*Above, right: Hiking the park's many trails is the only way to enjoy the diverse plant life, such as this Canada Goldenrod.*

haired Bat), 10 species of herptile (including Red-sided Garter Snake and Western Painted Turtle), 30 species of fish (including Burbot and Walleye), over 220 species of birds (including Golden-winged Warbler and Great Gray Owl) and more than 400 species of vascular plants (including Round-leaved Orchid, Canada Anemone, and Sarsaparilla).

### Islands within Islands

Inland, forested national parks can appear quite uniform and are often overlooked by travellers seeking the more immediate excitement provided by the mountains or the coast. Riding Mountain, as a result, is more favoured by local residents than visitors from afar. This is unfortunate, as a closer examination of the park reveals a diversity sure to please any visitor.

Leaving the roads, there are 30 or so excellent trails that enable you to explore all corners of the park on foot. Some backcountry trails require a commitment of time and sweat, but many of the park's secrets can be learned on one of the shorter frontcountry trails. The self-guiding Arrowhead Trail is an excellent introduction; the trailhead is near Wasagaming, and along its 1.7-kilometre (1-mile) length you'll pass through many of the habitats of Riding Mountain, including boreal forest, Aspen forest, grassland, marsh, and lake. Keep an eye out for flowers such as Wood Lily, birds such as Gray Jay and Blackburnian Warbler, and other animals such as Leopard Frogs and

**Location**: 95 km (59 miles) north of Brandon, Manitoba; 225 km (140 miles) north-west of Winnipeg.

**Access**: Hwy 10 north from Brandon or south from Dauphin. Hwy 16 from the south-east. International Airport in Winnipeg. Car rental agencies in Winnipeg and Brandon. Bus service from Winnipeg via Brandon, and from the north from Dauphin.

**When to Go**: Open year-round, but many park facilities only available May–October. Peak season July–August, when advance bookings for commercial accommodations are recommended.

**Climate**: Warm summers and cold winters. Mean daily max. and min. temperatures: July, 8.3 and 23.9°C (47 and 75°F); January, -13.8 and -27.3°C (7 and -17°F). Mean annual total precipitation is 48 cm (18.75 inches), one-third as snow. Summer thunderstorms common.

**Facilities**: Park: Visitor Centre; on-site exhibits; campgrounds; picnic grounds; trails; outdoor theatre. Wasagaming townsite: commercial accommodations; museum; police; gas station; groceries; outfitters; restaurants. Medical facilities in Brandon.

**Watching Nature**: Mammals (including moose, elk, and beaver) best seen at dawn or dusk. A small herd of bison is maintained at a paddock near Lake Audy. Frequent Black Bear sightings, and several packs of resident wolves.

**Visitor Activities**: Hiking, backpacking, cycling, tennis, lawn bowling, golfing, horseback riding, sailing, swimming, fishing, canoeing, snowshoeing, cross-country skiing.

**Special Notes**: Poison Ivy is common along the escarpment.

beaver in the marsh. The Burls and Bittersweet Trail, near the east entrance of the park, allows access to the Eastern Deciduous Hardwood Forest. Special trees here include Bur Oak, White Elm, Red Ash, and Manitoba Maple, while some of the flowers are Virginia Creeper, Bittersweet, Choke Cherry, Saskatoon Berry, Beaked Hazelnut, and Wild Plum. The buzzy song of Golden-winged Warblers is occasionally heard, and this is also a good area to find Eastern Towhee, Scarlet Tanager, and Indigo Bunting. The Brulé Trail is another rewarding trail that portrays the importance of fire in a healthy boreal ecosystem — the area experienced fires in 1929, 1957, and 1971, and the various stages of regrowth demonstrate that fire is necessary in a boreal ecosystem to promote diversity. Interesting trees here include Jack Pine and Black Spruce, and it is not surprising that Fireweed is one of the common wildflowers, along with Twinflower and Bunchberry. This can be a good trail for woodpeckers, and Black-backed, Three-toed, and Pileated can all be sighted.

## The Tenacious Wolf

The most impressive large predator in the park is the resilient Gray Wolf. As recently as the 1950s wolves were being culled by park staff, and in recent years population numbers have declined due to a mite that causes hair loss and skin lesions. Populations are closely monitored because wolves, in addition to their importance to the functioning of a healthy ecosystem, are excellent live barometers of the ecosystem's overall health, due to their position at the top of the food chain. Chances of seeing a wolf are slim, but, from August – once the young of the year are old enough – you might be lucky enough to hear howling at night as the wolves communicate with each other.

Above: *The bog at Moon Lake supports a variety of wetland fauna and flora.*

Right: *The self-guided Arrowhead Trail leads through a variety of the park's habitats, and visitors may encounter Gray Jays (near right), or plants such as the Dotted Gayfeather (far right).*

## Encircled by Farming

Riding Mountain National Park lies within the Southern Boreal Plains and Plateau Region of the national parks system. Riding Mountain, once surrounded by grassland, is now encircled by farms and ranches, and human influences are pressuring the park borders, and beyond. Hunting and poaching, especially of bears, is a particular concern, but other threats exist, including the drift of pesticides and herbicides from adjacent farms, the accidental introduction of non-native plants and animals, and the impact of pollution on Clear Lake, caused by the intense human development at Wasagaming.

Above: *Woodland Sunflower carpets the fenland near Wasagaming on the Arrowhead Trail.*

Below, left: *The Leopard Frog is a common and vocal inhabitant of the park's marshy areas.*

Below: *Water Arums are reflected in the still waters of the marsh.*

# DINOSAUR PROVINCIAL PARK

## The Wealth of the Badlands

'...and set me down in the midst of the valley which was full of bones.'

EZEKIEL, 37:1

Dinosaur Provincial Park covers an area of 73 square kilometres (28 square miles) of outstanding beauty, and contains dinosaur fossil deposits, resulting in the park's recognition by UNESCO as one of its first natural World Heritage Sites. The park was established in 1955 to preserve the Badlands of Alberta, but did not receive its present name until 1962. Red Deer River cuts through the valley, and its plains are the site where dinosaur bones, 75 million years old, are periodically released from their sedimentary prison by eroding wind and water.

the Red Deer River Valley was carved through the sediments, from which dinosaur bones are now found. Nearly 200 complete skeletons have been discovered, along with countless scattered remains of dinosaur bones, and some large disorganised congregations known as 'bone beds'. This is the only park in Canada with a Dinosaur Checklist, totalling 34 species, including Stegosauras, Albertosaurus, and Corythosaurus, all from the Late Cretaceous geological period, from which time all the fossils in the park have originated.

The variety of habitats within Dinosaur Provincial Park is accessed by a system of short trails: the Prairie Trail; the Coulee Viewpoint Trail; the Badlands Trail; the Trail of the Fossil Hunters; and the Cottonwood Flats Trail. For a quick introduction to the Badlands, take the self-guiding Badlands trail, a short 1.3-km (less than 1-mile) loop trail off the Public Loop Road, leading to the edge of the Natural Preserve. The only access into the Natural Preserve (the primary fossil area) is on a guided tour. Many visitors combine a visit to the park with a visit to the world-famous Tyrrell Museum in Drumheller, Alberta, where there are numerous displays on dinosaur excavations and research. Occasionally park visitors make fossil discoveries, as not all fossils are within the restricted area. If you are so

## The Badlands and the Bones

Millions of years ago, the Badlands area of the park was a swampy coastal plain, bisected by rivers. Resident dinosaurs foundered in the bogs, or were drowned by periodic floods, and their bones became entombed in the river and swamp sediment. Subsequent earth pressures turned the sediments into rocks, and after the last glacier period

Left: *Hoodoos and other unearthly sculpted rock formations may be seen near Drumheller and in the park.*

Above, right: *The Prickly-pear Cactus is one of the many botanical delights of the Badlands.*

**Location**: In SE Alberta, 48 km (30 miles) NE from the town of Brooks, on the Trans-Canada Hwy.

**Climate**: Hot and dry in summer (frequently 40°C+/104°F+ in the shade), cold and dry in the winter. Occasional violent summer thunderstorms.

**When to Go**: Open year-round, but some services available only April–September.

**Access**: By road: Hwy 544 then Hwy 551 from Brooks. Nearest major airport is Calgary, 226 km (141 miles) to the west.

**Facilities**: Campground park service centre (May–October, with laundry, store, showers); trails; on-site exhibits; picnic site; outdoor theatre; Tyrell Museum Field Station (open year-round, but not daily). Town of Brooks: full tourist services. When the Dinosaur Prov. Park campground is full, try Kinbrook Island Provincial Park, 15 km south of Brooks, a 45-minute drive from Dinosaur P.P. Reservations are recommended for the guided hikes and bus tours into the restricted-access Natural Preserve.

**Watching Nature**: Wildflowers (esp. in June), including cactus; birds (June–July) such as Say's Phoebe, Rock Wren, Mountain Bluebird and Prairie Falcon; Plains Spadefoot Toad and Prairie Rattlesnake. Mammals include Mule and White-tailed Deer, Pronghorn Antelope, and coyote.

**Visitor Activities**: Camping; picnicking; hiking; nature photography; canoeing; fishing; cross-country skiing.

**Special Notes**: Most of the area south of the Red Deer River (outside the main visitor area) is a natural preserve, with access by permission only. Daily tours of this area, numbers restricted. 50 per cent of spots reservable, the remainder first-come first-served, at 8:30 a.m. at the Field Station.

Above: *The Tyrell Museum in nearby Drumheller is open all year* (left). *Prairie Cottontail Rabbit* (centre) *and Eastern Kingbird* (right) *are among the local wildlife.*

Below: *Panorama from the Coulee Viewpoint Trail.*

fortunate as to find a fossil, do not disturb it, and report it to park personnel. If the find is significant, you will receive an official Fossil Finder Certificate.

Beyond the palaeontological wealth of the park there are many other visitor attractions. Some come to photograph the heavily eroded landscape, with its myriad unearthly, and constantly changing, land forms, while others come to see the variety of species that live in the unusual confluence of habitats. Prairie birds include Long-billed Curlew, Marbled Godwit, and Swainson's Hawk; in the river valley and Cottonwood groves are Eastern and Western Kingbird, Spotted Towhee, Yellow-breasted Chat, and Great Horned Owl; and in the Badlands are Prairie Falcon, Rock Wren, and Say's Phoebe. Botanical delights include Ball and Prickly-Pear Cactus, Prairie Sage, and a host of wildflowers, and keep an eye out for Bull Snake, Prairie Rattlesnake, Plains Spadefoot Toad (heard more often than seen) and Blotched Tiger Salamander.

# ELK ISLAND NATIONAL PARK

## Good Fences Make Good Neighbours

*'Oh, give me a home where the buffalo roam...'*

DR. BREWETER HIGHLEY, HOME ON THE RANGE

**Location**: 35 km (20 miles) east of Edmonton, Alberta.

**Climate**: Dry Continental. Average high temperatures in July/January: 25°C/-10° C (78°F/ 14° F).

**When to Go**: Open year-round, but many facilities only open June–September.

**Access**: By scheduled airlines or train to Edmonton. By paved Hwy 16 ('Yellowhead Highway') from Edmonton (35 km/20 miles)

**Facilities**: Visitor Centre (nature bookstore); on-site exhibits; campground (112 sites); picnic grounds; 100 km/60 miles of trails; interpretive outdoor theatre; playground.

**Watching Nature**: 44 sp. of mammal, including elk, Plains and Wood Bison, coyote, beaver, White-tailed Deer, and moose. 230+ bird species, best diversity in June–July – waterbirds are a speciality, with Common (Great Northern) Loon, Trumpeter Swan, Barrow's Goldeneye, Red-necked Grebe, Canvasback, Ruddy Duck, Redhead, Double-crested Cormorant, Black-crowned Night-Heron, Great Blue Heron – and numerous passerines present, including Black-backed Woodpecker, Western Meadowlark, Yellow Warbler, Common Yellowthroat, Black-throated Green Warbler, Ovenbird, American Redstart, Clay-colored Sparrow, and Yellow-headed Blackbird.

**Visitor Activities**: Summer: hiking; swimming; canoeing; sailing; auto-tour through Bison Paddock. Winter: snow-shoeing and cross-country skiing.

**Special Notes**: Although there is a fence, the mammals in the park are wild. Keep your distance from Bison and other large mammals, and don't frighten or approach them.

Elk Island National Park is a 194 square-kilometre (75 square-mile) wilderness 'island' that lies in the Beaver Hills. The park contains the second largest herd of Plains Bison in Canada and is surrounded by a 2.4-metre (8-foot) fence that acts as a buffer to the surrounding ocean of agricultural and industrial land. The Beaver Hills is an upland area that rises modestly to 30 metres (200 feet) above the encircling plains, and is a glacially modified mosaic of small lakes, ponds (called potholes), marshes, forest, and grassland. The park is a place for gentle reflection and investigation, where visitors have the opportunity to enjoy a protected remnant of a once-widespread landscape, 90 per cent of which has now disappeared from Canada.

### The Need for a Refuge

At the close of the 19th century, expanding European settlement nearly eradicated all large mammals from the Beaver Hills. Elk were particularly threatened, with fewer than 20 animals remaining. After local petitioning, and the posting of a bond to pay for fencing, the federal government created the protected area in 1905,

*Above, right: Beavers are regularly seen in the lakes and marshes of the park.*

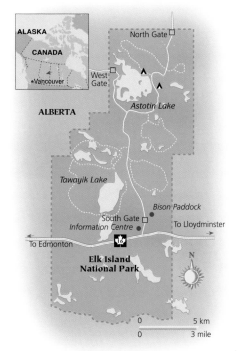

which became a full national park in 1913. A purchased herd of Plains Bison from Montana was temporarily quartered in Elk Island in 1907, en route to Buffalo National Park (since divested), and some animals escaped, forming the nucleus of the Plains Bison herd that roams the park today. Today, on average, there are about 1,600 elk and 1,000 bison living in the park.

### Where the Buffalo Roam

Although 44 species of mammal inhabit Elk Island, most visitors are interested in the hooved species: elk, moose, White-tailed Deer, and Plains and Wood Bison. All are wild and wary of humans, and are generally easier to see in winter when they are less mobile. However, any summer visitor willing to invest some time hiking the excellent trail system will certainly be rewarded with some sightings, and the animals can sometimes be seen from the road. Although the mammals are wild, their wilderness is incomplete as the original large predators, wolves and bears, were locally extirpated long ago, and the park is too small to support their reintroduction. Consequently, park staff play the role of the predator of the large mammals by striving to maintain a natural population and ensuring sustainable sex ratios and age groups. The staff will remove

*Right: The quiet visitor may encounter moose along the Amisk Wuche Trail.*

*Below, right: The Leopard Frog is at home in the aquatic habitats of Elk Island.*

*Below: While larger predators such as wolves and bears have disappeared from the park, coyotes are still present.*

excess animals, and either sell them at auction or send them elsewhere to establish new free-roaming herds.

## Look Beyond the Elk

While many visitors are understandably attracted to the large mammals, many discover the more subtle delights of this diverse landscape. Scattered among the Trembling Aspen, cattail marshes, grassy meadows, and small lakes, are hundreds of plants, birds, and insects. It is worth looking for smaller mammals, and beaver, Richardson's Ground-Squirrels (locally called gophers), and muskrats are regularly seen. The locally extirpated Trumpeter Swan, one of the largest waterfowl in the world, is being painstakingly reintroduced to the area, and there are numerous species of ducks, including Ruddy Duck, Canvasback, and Blue-winged Teal. Swainson's and Red-tailed Hawks nest in the trees and hunt the open country. Many songbirds breed, and in meadows in spring the buzzy song of Clay-coloured

Sparrows is easily submerged by the delicious aural whistling waterfall of the Western Meadowlark. The hills, with fields alternating with groves of aspen and conifers, support many flowering plants, including Yellow Lady-Slipper Orchid, Red-Osier Dogwood, Northern Bedstraw, and Silver Buffaloberry. The flowers in turn encourage visits from butterflies, among them Callipe Fritillary, Gorgone Checkerspot, and Spring Azure.

## Keeping it Natural

In the absence of large predators and where natural wild fires have been suppressed, constant effort is required to maintain as natural an ecosystem as possible. Human agricultural and housing developments surrounding the park are a negative influence, resulting in pesticide and herbicide drift, poaching, and the introduction of exotic species, such as escaped garden plants, agricultural grasses, and feral or free-roaming cats.

Above: *Sunset paints a tranquil scene on Lake Astotin in the north of the park.*

Below: *Canada Geese breed beside many of the park's lakes.*

# ONTARIO

Canada's largest province has the three smallest national parks (Georgian Bay Islands, St. Lawrence Islands, and Point Pelee), while its best-known and most visited wilderness 'national' park, Algonquin, is actually a Provincial Park. Almost all Ontarians live in the south, in the Temperate Boreal Ecological Region, leaving the immense Boreal and SubArctic Regions sparsely populated. And the boreal region is truly capacious, as anyone who drives the Trans-Canada Highway can attest. Although logging occurs widely and intensely, and other impacts of human activity are readily apparent, the image of the boreal landscape is still one of endless, primordial wilderness.

Ontario is physically dominated by the Canadian Shield, with its forests and countless lakes, and some of the wildlife typical of the Taiga is well known, including Common (Great Northern) Loon, Black Bear, moose, White-tailed Deer, Ruffed Grouse, Timber Wolf, Gray Jay, and White-throated Sparrow.

Southern Ontario, however, due to a long history of settlement and habitat destruction, tenuously harbours many of the country's rarest species, most associated with the St. Lawrence River Lowlands. The Carolinean Forest habitats, once more widespread, are now protected within only a few parks, including Point Pelee. There are species found nowhere else in Canada, including Hackberry, Tulip Tree, Sassafras, Burning Bush, Butterfly Weed, Five-lined Skink, Eastern Fox Snake, Prothonotary Warbler, Acadian Flycatcher, Northern Bobwhite, King Rail, Carolina Wren, and Southern Flying Squirrel.

In addition to the five National Parks in Ontario, there are many provincial parks, of which Algonquin is the largest. Others of note include Rondeau, Long Point, Catechu, Polar Bear and Rainbow Falls.

# POINT PELEE NATIONAL PARK

## Pilgrimage to Pelee

*'Rara avis in terris' (A Rare Bird on this Earth)*

JUVENAL

oint Pelee is the most southerly national park in Canada and is considered the top site in North America for viewing spring bird migration. The park is renowned for rarities and it has a total bird list that exceeds 350 species. Although Point Pelee is the second smallest national park in Canada—it covers just 15 square kilometres (6 square miles)—it is subject to more intense visitor pressures

*Opposite far left: Point Pelee, jutting south into Lake Erie, experiences periodic influx of migrant birds, especially in May. These may include the Yellow-billed Cuckoo (top), the Baltimore Oriole (middle), and a wealth of wood warblers, including the American Redstart (bottom).*

*Opposite left: Herring Gulls congregate on East Point Beach, the southernmost tip of Canada.*

Above right: *Thousands of Monarch Butterflies congregate at Point Pelee for a few days each autumn, awaiting suitable weather conditions for their departure to Mexico.*

Previous pages:

Page 82: *The trails, canoe routes and autumn colours of Algonquin Provincial Park hold great allure for many of the millions of people who live in close proximity. The White-tailed Deer (page 83), a familiar animal throughout Ontario, lives in the park's mixed-wood forests.*

than any other. Established in 1918, primarily because of its importance to migrant birds, the park also protects many other endangered plants and animals in the Carolinean Forest. Despite visitor pressure, it still retains a sense of wilderness today.

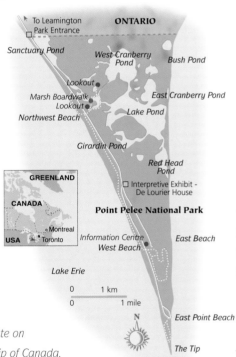

### Migration

Point Pelee is a 17-kilometre (10-mile) long, narrow peninsula that extends south into Lake Erie, and it is a conduit for migrations of birds, butterflies and dragonflies. Birds of all kinds, plentiful and rare, pass through Point Pelee on their way northwards or southwards. Each year, birders make their own Pilgrimages to Pelee (to quote native-Ontarian nature-writer Gerry Bennett), visiting the park in large numbers in the autumn migration period, from mid-August until November, and in spring. May is the most popular time for birders, when (particularly in adverse weather) many species, especially wood-warblers, pass through in colourful breeding plumage, occasionally in exceptional numbers. The migration can be a magnificent spectacle, and if you are lucky a true rara avis might appear among the more expected species.

### Monarchs

For a few days each autumn, Point Pelee is a staging area for thousands of migrating Monarch Butterflies

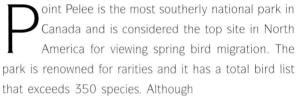

**Location**: 50 km (30 miles) south-west of Windsor, Ontario. Windsor is across the border from Detroit, Michigan, U.S.A. Point Pelee is the southernmost mainland in Canada.

**Climate**: Humid continental climate, with variable weather. Moderating lake effects: delayed leafing in spring, humid summers, warmer winters. Mean temperatures: January -3°C (27°F), July 23°C (73°F). Annual precipitation 81 cm (32 in).

**When to go**: Open year-round, but some facilities/services open only May through October, or with reduced hours in winter. Visitor Centre open year-round.

**Access**: Hwy 3 from Windsor; Hwy 401 from Toronto, take Exit 48. Daily commercial flights to Windsor, and international airports in Toronto and Detroit.

**Facilities**: Visitor Centre; trails; picnic sites; beaches; marsh boardwalk trail; canoe and bike rentals (April–October). Note: there is no camping permitted within Point Pelee National Park; private campgrounds are nearby, and at Wheatley and Rondeau Provincial Parks. Town of Leamington and City of Windsor: full facilities and services.

**Watching Nature**: Bird and Monarch Butterfly migration; many rare plants and animals.

**Visitor Activities**: Birding; walking; cycling; canoeing; swimming; picnicking; ice-skating; fishing; nature photography;

**Special Notes**: (1) Extensive trail reclamation is on-going. Please respect all signage accordingly. (2) The use of tape recordings to lure birds is not permitted. (3) The Black-legged Tick, one of the carriers of Lyme disease, occurs. (4) Poison Ivy is present, in both ground shrub and climbing-ivy forms.

Above: *The Marsh Board-walk allows comfortable access to one of the park's richest environments.*

Below: *The Painted Turtle is one of an exceptional number of herptiles present in the park.*

Mexico do not survive to return to Ontario, but their offspring do, later that same year.

## The Carolinean Zone

The Carolinean Forest is more typically found in the central United States, but due to the southern location, and the moderating lake effects, a thin band of Carolinean Forest historically occurred near the Great Lakes in extreme southern Ontario. Today, only 2 per cent of this forest remains, the rest having been cleared for agriculture. There are more rare species of plants and animals in the Carolinean Forest than in any other region of Canada, including 70 species of trees (Hackberry, Honey Locust, Tulip Tree, etc.), 47 different herptiles (such as Five-lined Skink and Fox Snake), birds such as Acadian Flycatcher, Carolina Wren, and Red-bellied Woodpecker, and many special wildflowers, including Prickly-Pear Cactus, Burning Bush, and Butterfly Weed.

## Reclaiming the Park

The park has been over-visited for decades, and determined attempts are now being made to reclaim as much as possible of this diminutive park, to maximise the chances of survival for its plants and animals. Nearly 40 per cent of the plants in the park are non-native, and some of these invaders pose serious and dominant threats to the native vegetation. It is impossible to eradicate every single non-native plant, but assaults have been made on the most aggressive species, such as Black Locust, White Mulberry, and Purple Loosestrife, and native species are being retransplanted into areas from where they disappeared. Only 11 per cent of the dry land area is now occupied by visitor facilities (including roads), a significant decline from earlier times, and many trails have been closed to allow regeneration. Southern Flying Squirrels, formerly extirpated, have been successfully reintroduced, and White-tailed Deer numbers are being maintained at manageable levels by culling, as their original predators were long ago wiped out in southern Ontario.

## Park Pressures

Point Pelee protects the West St. Lawrence Lowlands natural region. Despite the recent positive efforts to reclaim the park, this precious and fragile environment remains at risk from the pollution of Lake Erie, continued visitor pressures, and introduced flora and fauna.

seeking a shorter route across Lake Erie. During periods of colder weather the Monarchs roost, especially in early morning, in the tips of trees where they await warmer temperatures and tail winds. The Monarch's ultimate destination is 3,000 km (1,900 miles) south, to the evergreen forests high in the mountains of central Mexico. Here, they overwinter, breed, and then migrate north, laying eggs on Milkweed, the larval host plant, as they go. Most adults that overwinter in

# PUKASKWA NATIONAL PARK

## On the Shores of Lake Superior

*'On Pukaskwa River so early this morning, while mending my trumpline I hear the geese calling.'*

WADE HEMSWORTH, THE WILD GOOSE

Pukaskwa is one of the smaller national parks in Canada (1,878 square km/722 square miles), even though it is, by far, the largest National Park in Ontario, Canada's biggest province. It is also the wildest park in Ontario, lying, as part of the Precambrian Shield, along the northern edge of the largest lake in the world, Lake Superior. Many visit the park from Pukaskwa's small frontcountry area near Hattie's Cove, and venture along the wild shore of Superior, either along the Coastal Hiking Trail leading to North Swallow River, or by paddling along the coastline.

### Big Water

Lake Superior dominates the park, influencing the weather and vegetation of the lands that surround it, and it is fed by more than 800 streams and rivers. Known as 'Gitche Gumee' (Big Water) to the local First Nations people, Lake Superior is 82,100 square kilometres (31,577 square miles), stretches along 4,400 km (2,750 miles) of coastline, and holds one-tenth of the world's surface fresh water. The lake's water is cold, with an average year-round water temperature of 4°C (38°F) and it can be a formidable place. In 1975 the ore carrier *Edmund*

*Above right: Sanderling pass through the park on passage each year, searching for food along the shoreline.*

*Fitzgerald* foundered in a ferocious November storm, and sank with all hands only a few hours after passing the Otter Island lighthouse, off Pukaskwa. The Reverend George Grant wrote (in 1872), 'Superior is a sea. It breeds storms and rain and fog like the sea... It is wild, masterful, and dreaded'.

### Bordering on the Wilderness

Unlike most national parks south of the Arctic, Pukaskwa can only truly be explored at its edges, either along the Superior coast, or by canoe along the White River in the north and along the Pukaskwa River in the south. The interior of the park is dense forest, unbroken except for a few rivers and lakes. Anyone who attempts to 'bushwhack' their way into the expanse will quickly abort the task, and come to appreciate why everyone who has ever travelled in the 'bush', from the earliest First Nations people, through the first European trappers and explorers, to today's urban visitor, has limited their journey to following waterways or keeping to the few trails.

There are short trails emanating from the Hattie's Cove area, and for most visitors this glimpse into the park is sufficient. However, the coastal trail to the North Swallow River provides a true wilderness experience. The 60-km (38-mile) hike is difficult, and requires thorough

**Location:** On the northern shore of Lake Superior, northern Ontario, just south of the Trans-Canada Hwy.

**Climate:** Conditions change quickly, due to lake influences. Winters are long, snowy, and cold. Temperature range July–August 10–23°C (50–73°F), with 18 cm (7 in) of rain.

**When to go:** Open year round, but many services and facilities open only in summer.

**Access:** By road: from Heron Bay on Hwy 627, and Marathon on Hwy 626. There is regular bus service and daily commercial flights between Marathon and both Sault Ste. Marie and Thunder Bay.

**Facilities:** Park: campground (one, 67 sites); 10 backcountry camp sites; trails; picnic site; Visitor Centre. The nearby towns of Heron Bay and Marathon both have full modern services and facilities.

**Watching Nature:** As access to the park's interior is limited, wildlife sightings are less frequent than in most national parks. There are breeding boreal birds in the North Swallow river area, and coastal/Arctic plants along the shoreline and bays.

**Visitor Activities:** Hiking; canoeing; kayaking; camping; sailing; snowshoeing; swimming; fishing; nature photography.

**Special Notes:** All white-water trips, back-packing trips, and sailing excursions must be pre-registered with the park.

Map labels: To Thunder Bay · Information Centre · Marathon · 627 · Heron Bay · Hattie Cove · ONTARIO · GREENLAND · CANADA · USA · Montreal · Toronto · Oiseau Bay · White Gravel River · Simons Harbour · North Swallow River · Pukaskwa National Park · Cascade River · Pukaskwa River · Otter Cove · Lake Superior · 0 15 km · 0 10 miles · N

preparation and fitness. The route is well marked, there are bridges where necessary and a series of exquisite backcountry campsites near beaches and sheltered bays. Many birds breed in the area, including Gray Jay, Bay-breasted Warbler, White-throated Sparrow, and there are coastal plants with Arctic affiliations (due to the cooling influence of Lake Superior), including Franklin's Lady's Slipper, Alpine Blueberry, Northern Twayblade, and Encrusted Saxifrage.

## Making Names

Many consider the Pukaskwa area a land of mystery. It is still not understood exactly who built the shallow rock foundations on Pukaskwa's boulder beaches, and why. These stone circles were believed to have had spiritual significance to their creators, the Anishnabe First Nations people, who have been present along the shores of Lake Superior for thousands of years. Equally mysterious is the origin of the name 'Pukaskwa', for which there are different spellings and suggested ety-mologies. Some scholars trace the name to 'eaters of fish' or 'safe harbour', while Ojibway and Cree First Nations scholars have suggested that 'Pukaskwa' should be 'Pukasu'. The name 'Pukasu' is traced to a story regarding a native named Joe who killed his wife at a river's mouth, burned her body, and threw the cooked bones into the river. First Nations people usually named people according to their deeds, and as Joe was then given the name 'Opakasu', meaning 'cooker of marrow', and the river into which he threw the bones became the Pukasu, later anglicised as Pukaskwa.

## Logging, Development, and Fires

Pukaskwa National Park represents the Canadian Boreal Uplands of the Precambrian Shield. The Woodland Caribou are disappearing, for reasons not completely understood. Logging activities near the park, mineral explorations, and hydroelectric developments will have unpredicted impacts. A long history of fire-suppression in the park has altered the forest species balance, and the risk of a major forest fire is high.

Left, above: *The Gray Jay breeds in deep forest, but is often encountered along backcountry trails and near campsites, where it likes to scrounge for food.*

Left, below: *The coastal trail to the North Swallow River provides a true wilderness experience.*

Below: *The distinctive Belted Kingfisher is solitary, except during the breeding season, and may be seen near woodland streams and along the lakeshore.*

Above: *The Headland Trail leads along the lakeshore to Pulpwood Harbour.*

Left: *The cold and sometimes treacherous waters of Lake Superior dominate Pukaskwa's landscape.*

# GEORGIAN BAY ISLANDS NATIONAL PARK

## Fragments of Splendour

*'About these harsh barren islands there is an undeniable fascination ...'*

ANDREW Y. JACKSON, GROUP OF SEVEN ARTIST

The Georgian Bay Islands National Park protects the lowlands of Lake Huron's massive Georgian Bay and a group of islands that lie within the bay. Although there are more than 30,000 islands in the eastern end of the bay, only 59 (either whole or in part) are publically owned and come under the protection of the Georgian Bay Islands National Park. Beausoleil Island is the largest of these protected islands, and the total area covered by the 59 islands is 25 square kilometres (10 square miles). The park contains more herptiles than any other national park, and includes the infamous Massassauga Rattlesnake. The dramatic varied landscape of Georgian Bay and the countless rocky islands attract artists, tourists, explorers, and those seeking a weekend escape from the rigours of urban life.

Opposite: *The Fairy Lake Trail on Beausoleil Island traverses the exposed rock of the Precambrian Shield.*

Above right: *The Cardinal Flower is amongst a varied flora supported by the diversity of habitats on the islands.*

### Unexpected Diversity

To the casual observer, Georgian Bay is dominated by the rock of the Precambrian Shield, and the hardy species that thrive on it, such as Eastern White Pine. However, the reality is that in this region of transition between the coniferous forests of the Taiga and the hardwood forests of southern Ontario, an unexpected mix of habitats supports a high diversity of plants and animals. There are four main habitat types: exposed rock outcrops and sandy beaches; wetlands; mixed forest; and the outer islands.

In the exposed rock outcrops are a number of hardy plants, including Rock Polypody (a fern), Pink Corydalis, Creeping Juniper, and Eastern White Pine. Also, Prairie Warblers breed in this habitat and Fox Snakes are regularly encountered. The swamps, marshes, and bogs of Georgian Bay's wetlands support more herptiles than in any other national park (there are over 35 species), including Gray Tree-Frog, Musk Turtle, Mudpuppies, Water Snake, and the endangered Spotted Turtle. The abundant wetlands provide a habitat for many dragonflies and damselflies, such as the Canada Darner and the Jewelwing. The forests are primarily hardwoods, most notably Beech and Sugar Maple, although there are

**Location:** Southern Georgian Bay, Ontario. The park is three separate groups of islands along 64 km (40 miles) of Georgian Bay coastline, between Macey Bay and Moose Deer Point. All surrounding islands are privately owned.

**Climate:** Continental climate, moderated by the lake. Warm summers, cold winters, stormiest in spring and autumn. High waves with W or SW winds. 1,020 mm (40 in) precipitation annually, 60 per cent between November and April. Summer thunderstorms may develop quickly.

**When to go:** Open year-round, although full services are only available mid-May through September.

**Access:** By boat, either from Honey Harbour, Midland, or Penetanguishene. Private water taxies from Honey Harbour. Honey Harbour is a two-hour drive north from Toronto, the nearest international airport. Take Hwy 400 north from Toronto to Muskoka District Road 5 (Exit 156), then left on Muskoka Road 5 to Honey Harbour.

**Facilities:** Visitor Centre (nature store) on Beausoleil Island, 15 campgrounds (200 sites), trails. Town of Honey Harbour: commercial accommodations, marinas, boat rentals, and supplies and services.

**Watching Nature:** Mammals scarce, but birding good in June–July. Area famous for variety of herptiles, more than any other national park, with 33 species on Beausoleil Island alone.

**Visitor Activities:** Boating; sailing; swimming; hiking; fishing; cycling; picnicking; nature photography; birding; scuba diving; snorkeling.

Map labels: Goblin Lake; Georgian Bay Islands National Park; Fairy Lake; GREENLAND; CANADA; Montreal; USA; Toronto; Beausoleil Island; Cedar Spring Campground; Bruce Peninsula; Beausoleil Island; Georgian Bay; Owen Sound; Midland; 0 1 km; 0 1 mile; N

Above: *The sculpted lake-shore of Beausoleil Island is the work of glaciers.*

Below: *The distinctive head pattern of the Massassauga Rattlesnake precludes confusion with any other of the islands' snake species.*

several oaks, birches, poplars, and other maples. Due to the heavy leaf cover, most forest wildflowers bloom in late April and early May, before the trees have fully leafed. At this time of year, keep an eye out for Red and White Trillium, Corn and Wood Lily, Springbeauty, and more than 20 types of orchids, including Yellow Lady's Slipper. The outer islands occasionally support colonies of Herring Gulls and Common Terns.

### The Massassauga Rattlesnake

The Massassauga Rattlesnake lives in the swampy and marshy places of Georgian Bay's wetlands. Once found throughout Southern Ontario, this endangered species is now reduced to a few scattered populations on the tip of the Bruce Peninsula and the shoreline of Georgian Bay. Numbers are difficult to census, but there are at most only a few thousand left, and perhaps only hundreds. This rare snake may be found in areas where its favourite meals, frogs and other small amphibians and mammals, are abundant. It has a very confined range. On average, it travels a total distance of only 700 metres a year, and in one small area, the snake will eat, mate, breed and hibernate. The word 'Massasauga' comes from the Ojibwa word meaning Great River Mouth, perhaps in reference to the snake's preferred habitat.

The Massassauga is usually small, light to medium brown, with a dark-brown bow-tie pattern down its back, and has a triangular-shaped head and an obvious rattle. Contrary to popular belief, it is a retiring snake and will do its best to avoid people, only ever striking if severely harassed. It is important to remember that snakes are vital to the functioning of a healthy ecosystem and should be treated with respect. Only two people have ever died of the bite of a Massassauga, and neither received proper medical treatment. Many people mistakenly identify the more common Eastern Fox Snake as a rattler. The Fox Snake is a sleeker animal, with a straighter copper-coloured head, a tapered tail (which may vibrate, but never rattles), and a yellowish body, covered in irregular black blotches.

### Acquiring the Islands

By the 1920s almost all the islands were already privately owned, so that by the time the federal government was convinced of the importance of a national park in Georgian Bay, only a few were available for acquisition. Initially, 29 islands were requisitioned, including Beausoleil, and although further islands (or parts of islands) have been subsequently purchased, the park remains diminutive, and at constant threat from the surrounding 'summer playground'. Georgian Bay Islands National Park protects part of two natural regions, the Central Great Lakes/St. Lawrence Precambrian, and the West St. Lawrence Lowlands. The biggest threat is pollution of Georgian Bay caused by unrestrained recreational use of surrounding lands and waters. Motorboats are a major source, though industrial pollution from further afield and acid rain are also concerns.

# Algonquin Provincial Park

## Ontario's Accessible 'Wilderness'

*'And the wolf behowls the moon'*
SHAKESPEARE, A MIDSUMMER NIGHT'S DREAM

Algonquin is Canada's first provincial park and, as such, has been declared a National Historic Site. It was created in 1893 at the behest of logging companies who wanted a wildlife refuge to ensure good hunting in the area. The park's large size (7,725 square kilometres/2,971 square miles) and proximity to ten million people that live within a half-day's drive, have ensured its continued popularity. Some come to the park to relax in upscale hotels and resorts, while others seek tranquility and motivation in the wilderness. Canada's renowned Group of Seven landscape painters found inspiration here, as well as artist Tom Thompson, whose unexplained drowning in the park adds to Algonquin's mystique. Today the park is especially popular with canoeists, who explore Algonquin's 1,500 lakes and rivers, and hikers and cross-country skiers who enjoy the changing seasons of the wilderness.

### Algonquin Seasons

Perhaps the highlight of the year in the park is in autumn, when the changing colour of the deciduous trees covers the land with a palette of reds, yellows, greens, and oranges. The peak time to see the changing

*Above, right: Though Timber Wolves are seldom seen, their eerie howling is a potent symbol of Algonquin's wilderness.*

colours is typically late September through the second week of October, but the timing varies slightly each year. Autumn is a good time for canoeists when they can enjoy the park without the inconvenience of biting insects.

Algonquin has much to offer in winter. There are more than 80 kilometres (50 miles) of cross-country ski trails and all the hiking trails are available to snow-shoers. Highway 60 is ploughed and sanded all winter, and the Mew Lake Campground is available for winter camping. Commercial operators offer dog sledding as well.

In spring, Moose are more likely to be seen and wildflowers are at their peak, especially in deciduous forests. More than 250 species have been recorded in the park, including Black-backed Woodpecker, Spruce Grouse, Gray Jay, Boreal Chickadee, and Mourning Warbler.

Most people visit the park in Summer (July and August), when the greatest range of activities are possible, and many residents of the nearby urban areas of Toronto and Ottawa take their vacations. In the heat of a southern summer, the cooler lakes and forests of Algonquin are inviting.

### Enjoying the Wilderness

Typically, for convenience, most visitors to Algonquin remain close to the road corridor, picnicking, swim-

**Location**: In southern Ontario, 281 km (176 miles) north-north-east of Toronto, and 235 km (147 miles) north-west of Ottawa (halfway between Ottawa and Sudbury).

**Access**: By road: Hwy 60, from either Huntsville to the west, or Renfrew to the east.

**When to go**: Open year-round, although many facilities and services available only May–October. Advance campsite and accommodations reservations recommended for July–August, and on spring and autumn weekends.

**Climate**: Continental: cold winters, warm springs and autumns, hot summers. The ice normally leaves the lakes in late April.

**Facilities**: Visitor Centre (open year-round, daily from May–October, weekends and special holidays otherwise); trails; campsites. Nearby communities: typical visitor services, including commercial accommodations; licensed outfitters; equipment rentals; fuel.

**Watching Nature**: Moose (especially May–June), White-tailed Deer, Black Bear, and Beaver, Timber Wolves. Changing colour of trees best seen late September through the second week of October; weekly updates are given from the Visitor Centre each Friday through September and October.

**Visitor Activities**: Hiking; nature photography; canoeing; camping; picnicking; cross-country skiing; mountain biking; bicycle trails; dog sledding; horseback riding; wolf 'howls'; Algonquin Logging Museum; Algonquin Gallery (Canadian and international wildlife art).

**Special Notes**: Obey the speed limit; more than 30 moose are killed annually through collisions with vehicles.

ming, camping, and fishing, or taking part in the park's interpretive programs. Those with more energy hike the park's many trails, both those close to the highway, and those heading into the backcountry. There are two major hiking trails in the interior for those who wish to get off the beaten track. With over 1,500 lakes and rivers in the park, canoeing is very popular—so much so that all the backcountry campsites along the canoe routes are reserved long in advance. In winter fewer people are in the park, but they are rewarded by some of the finest cross-country skiing in southern Ontario.

## Wildlife Viewing

The easiest wildlife viewing is along the main Park Corridor on Highway 60, and the best times are early and late in the day. If you have a choice, go early, at dawn, when the temperature is cooler and there are fewer biting insects. The best areas for sighting wildlife are bogs, beaver ponds, and meadows. There are moose (especially in May and June), White-tailed Deer, Black Bear, and beaver (which are easier to see in September and October, otherwise at dusk). If you spot an animal from a vehicle, ensure that you pull over onto the shoulder of the road carefully, well off the pavement. You might also be able to see these animals if you hike some of the shorter trails that lead off from Highway 60, such as the Beaver Pond Trail, the Spruce Bog Boardwalk, and

*Above: Late September to early October is the best time to see the blaze of autumn colour.*

*Right: Opeango Lake in late summer offers the tranquility and beauty that draws so many visitors to the park.*

the Mizzy Lake Trail. Algonquin has one of the most southerly wolf populations in North America, and although they are exceptionally difficult to see, they can be relatively easy to hear, especially after mid-summer. The park authorities organize a summer park interpretive program, called the Wolf Howl, which is scheduled for August, after an 'accessible' pack of wolves is located. Naturalist staff, after dark, lead visitors near to a known rendezvous site (a location where a particular wolf pack gathers after the young are nearly full-grown), and imitate wolf howls in the hope the pack will respond. Not every such attempt is successful, but the experience can be very memorable.

## Exploiting Park Resources

Provincial Park legislation permits a wide range of resource exploitation within the park boundaries. Logging is permitted in nearly 80 per cent of the park, and is restricted only along the main road corridor, and within sight of selected backcountry trails and canoe routes.

Above: *Mizzy Lake may be reached on a short trail from Highway 60.*

Below: *The cry of the loon, another haunting emblem of Algonquin, carries across Joe Lake at night.*

# BRUCE PENINSULA NATIONAL PARK AND FATHOM FIVE NATIONAL MARINE PARK

## Wild Tracts of Land and Water

*'If the visitor delights in rough wild tracts of land and water . . .*
*he is ready to fall in love with the Bruce'*
W. SHERWOOD FOX, THE BRUCE BECKONS

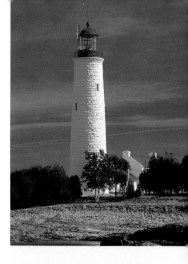

Bruce Peninsula National Park and Fathom Five National Marine Park are administered jointly to protect the terrestrial and aquatic environments of the Niagara Escarpment where it descends into Georgian Bay. The parks were established in 1987 and together cover an area of 154 square kilometres (59 square miles). Bruce Peninsula is the long and narrow projection that separates Lake Huron and Georgian Bay, and contains an array of habitats, including limestone cliffs, mixed forests, flat rock plains, wetlands, and beaches. The peninsula includes a section of The Bruce Trail, one of the finest hikes in the world that extends out of the park to Niagara Falls. Fathom Five is Canada's first national marine park and protects 20 of the Tobermory Islands at the mouth of Georgian Bay and the underwater ecosystem down to 200 metres (670 ft). It encompasses 112 square km (43 square miles) of crystal clear waters and is very popular for wreck diving.

*Opposite, above: The north shore of Bruce Peninsula forms part of the Niagara Escarpment.*

*Opposite, bottom left: Flowerpot Island in Fathom Five National Park is so named for its unusual limestone sea-stacks.*

*Opposite, bottom right: Sweepstakes is the best-known of many shipwrecks to be seen beneath the crystal clear waters of the park.*

*Above right: The lighthouse on Cove Island, built in 1856, has today been restored and opened to the public.*

**Fathom Five National Marine Park** — Echo Island — Cove Island — Flowerpot Island — Russel Island — Information Centre — Tobermory — Trails — Cyprus Lake — **Bruce Peninsula National Park** — Georgian Bay — Cabot Head — Emmett Lake — Trails — Singing Sands — Lake Huron — Picnic — 6

GREENLAND — CANADA — Montreal — USA — Toronto

0 — 15 km — 0 — 10 miles

### The Niagara Escarpment

The heart of Bruce Peninsula National Park is the Niagara Escarpment, a sedimentary rock wall that extends out of the park from Tobermory to Niagara Falls, nearly 800 kilometres (500 miles) long. The world-renowned Bruce Trail follows the escarpment for 782 kilometres (486 miles) from Little Tub Harbour to Queenston Heights. Virtually the entire length of the trail is monitored and maintained by volunteers. 35 kilometres (22 miles) of the trail run

**Location:** At the tip of Bruce Peninsula, near Tobermory, NW of Toronto. Bruce Peninsula N.P. spans the Niagara Escarpment between Georgian Bay and Lake Huron. Fathom Five National Marine Park encompasses 112 km2 of lake and includes 20 Islands.

**Access:** By road: from the south on Highway 6 or from the north via Ontario Northland Ferry M.S.Chi-Cheemaun, during the spring, summer, and fall—phone (519)596-2510. Toronto is three hours distant by road.

**When to Go:** Open year-round: many services not available in winter.

**Climate:** Continental, moderated by the lake. Cool springs, warm dry summers, pleasant but stormy autumns, and cloudy cold winters. (Mean temperatures: July 17.5°C (65°F), February -7°C (19°F).

**Facilities:** Park: Visitor Centre in Tobermory; campground; trails; picnic sites. Wharf, picnicking, and backcountry camping on Flowerpot Island. Tobermory: medical services, stores, private campgrounds, commercial accommodations, and groceries. Similar services also along Hwy 6. M.S.Chicheemaun Ferry between Tobermory to South Baymouth on Manitoulin Island.

**Visitor Activities:** hiking; picnicking; swimming (Singing Sands Area); fishing; canoeing; kayaking; scuba diving; snorkeling; glass-bottom boat tours; sailing; cross-country skiing; snowshoeing; winter camping.

**Special Notes:** (1) Divers in Fathom Five Nat. Marine Park must preregister in Little Tub Harbour in Tobermory. (2) Campfires are not permitted within the parks.

Above: *The limestone cracks and crevices on Russel Island provide good hunting for the Red Fox.*

Above, right: *The White-fringed Orchid is one of many species that thrive on the acidic soils of the island.*

Below: *The Red-sided Garter Snake is common in the St. Lawrence Lowlands.*

through the park, and there are two designated tenting areas (9 sites at each).

The acidic nature of the soil overlying the escarpment and the islands is ideal for orchids, and more than forty species have been found here, including Calypso Orchid, the rare Alaskan Rein Orchid, Showy Lady's Slipper, and Yellow Lady's Slipper. Other special plants are the Indian plaintain, the Dwarf Lake Iris, and Northern Holly Fern. The Eastern White Cedar has adapted to the harsh conditions at the edge of the Niagara Escarpment, and recent studies have suggested that some individual trees on the escarpment are more than 900 years old, nine times the typical age for the species; one tree on Flowerpot island is dated as being more than 1,800 years old.

## A Diver's Paradise

There are twenty-eight known shipwrecks within park waters, and as the underwater visibility is often very good the wrecks are very popular sites for divers and snorkelers. The lake bed of Fathom Five is limestone, too acidic for much life, so sediments are few and the water is very clear; light penetrates to 20 metres (66 feet) or more. A glass-bottom boat tour exists for those who wish to see the underwater world from the dry comfort of a boat. The best-known wreck is that of the *Sweepstakes,* a 36-metre (119-foot) schooner, which sank in Big Tub Harbour in 1885.

The frequent shipwrecks are the result of dangerous waters around the Bruce Peninsula. The wrecks occurred—notably between 1880 and 1920 when shipping activity was intense—despite the presence, since 1856, of the Cove Island Lighthouse. Today, this lighthouse is a restored historic site that is open to the public.

## A Heavy Tread

Bruce Peninsula National Park preserves part of the St. Lawrence Lowlands natural region. Heavy visitor use of some trails has led to trampled vegetation. Heavy recreational use outside the protected areas may also threaten park resources. Flowerpot Island, named for its limestone sea-stacks, was formerly part of Georgian Bay Islands National Park and has been protected since 1930.

# ST. LAWRENCE ISLANDS NATIONAL PARK

## The Garden of the Great Spirit

*'... for the people and their favourite islands'*

W.H. AUDEN

St. Lawrence Islands National Park was established in 1914 and is Canada's smallest national park, covering just 9 square kilometres (3½ square miles). There are 23 forested islands in the park, which are all part of the Thousand Islands region of Ontario. Most of the 23 islands in the park range in size from 4 to 12 hectares (10 to 30 acres), though the smallest, Mermaid, is only 2 hectares (5 acres), and the largest, Grenadier, is 155 hectares (385 acres). To the First Nations people of this area, the Thousand Islands region was 'Manitouana', the Garden of the Great Spirit, created when petals descended from the heavenly garden of the Great Spirit. The French, the earliest Europeans to live here, named the region 'Le Lac des Mille Îles', lake of a thousand islands. There are actually more than 1,700 islands and islets, lying in the flow of the mighty St. Lawrence River, one of the most beautiful riverine landscapes in the world.

The islands are the much-eroded peaks of ancient mountains that once linked the Adirondack Mountains of New York with the Canadian Precambrian Shield. The Mississaugas were the First Nations group that lived in this region. In the 1900s they ceded their land to the

*Above right: The elusive Least Bittern is one of many bird species that breed on the islands..*

government in trust; the government repaid that trust by selling off most of the islands for summer homes. In 1904 some local residents petitioned the government to keep the few remaining unsold islands for public use, and a decade later the National Park was formally established.

### Micro Park, Micro Habitats

The islands contain a remarkable diversity of plants and animals, sustained by different habitats that exist in close proximity. The islands are uniformly billion-year-old Precambrian rock, but subtle changes in relief and exposure have created distinct environments. Coniferous plants that have northern affinities are found on sheltered, cooler, wetter northeast-facing slopes, and hardwood forests of southern origin are found on sunnier, drier south-west-facing areas. There are many rare or unusual species in the area, including Pitch Pine, Shag Bark Hickory, Rue Anemone, Least Bittern, and Wild Turkey. The Black Rat Snake is found on some of the islands; it is the largest snake in Canada (it grows up to 2.5 metres (over 7 feet) long), and is an endangered and persecuted species.

Many birds breed on the islands, but fewer than on the mainland, as some species require large unbroken tracts of land to breed, which the fragmented islands do not offer. There are heron and tern colonies, and Osprey,

**Location:** In the St. Lawrence River, downstream of Lake Ontario, east of Kingston, Ontario, on the Canadian side of the Canada-U.S. border, which runs down the river.

**Climate:** Humid continental climate, moderated by water. River is frozen from late December through early April. Mean daily temperature: January -8°C/18°F; July 21°C/70°F.

**When to go:** Open year-round, but most visit from May–October. Many facilities and services unavailable outside this period.

**Access:** By road: off Hwy 401 east of Kingston, to Mallorytown Landing, the sole mainland component of the park. Nearest commercial airport in Kingston, Ontario. By water: boat tours and rentals in the towns of Rockport, Ivy Lea, and Gananoque.

**Facilities:** Campgrounds: one on mainland, 15 islands campgrounds; trails; picnic sites; Visitor Centre (nature store); beach; day-use docking. Abundant typical services and facilities in surrounding area, including at Gananoque and Kingston.

**Watching Nature:** Large mammals are scarce, but the park is ideal for birding and botany. Some of the special plants include Rue Anemone, Pitch Pine, and Deerberry. Least Bitterns breed in the park, as do many warblers and flycatchers. Many diving ducks overwinter along the river, such as Canvasback, Common Goldeneye, and Oldsquaw, and Bald Eagles are regular then.

**Visitor Activities:** Boating; hiking; camping; picnicking; swimming; cross-country skiing; scuba diving; sailing; kayaking; nature photography.

Above: *A fine view of the Thousand Islands may be had from the Lookout Tower.*

and a good variety of forest species, including Pine Warbler, Ovenbird, and Eastern Wood-Pewee. Waterfowl congregate along the river in winter where swift water leaves gaps in the ice; flocks include Canvasback and Common Goldeneye.

## Aquatic Superhighway

If lakes and rivers were the highways during early European settlement and exploration of Canada, then the St. Lawrence River was the multi-lane superhighway of the country. The First Nations people had always used the river, and the first fur traders similarly paddled up and down it. After the American Revolution, many United Empire Loyalists settled in the area, and both agricultural and industrial industries flourished. The area increased in strategic importance during the War of 1812, and later hundreds of thousands of new immigrants arrived in Canada after passing through the islands. The age of railroads in the 1850s diminished the importance of the river as a transportation corridor, (although it is still a vital cargo vessel route), but the trains opened the area up for tourism, and the Thousand Islands have been a summer playground of activity ever since.

Left: *Thousands of ducks, such as the Common Goldeneye, congregate along the unfrozen stretches of the river in winter.*

## Busy Waters

St. Lawrence Islands National Park represents the Central Great Lakes-St. Lawrence Precambrian region, and straddles the two separate St. Lawrence Lowlands regions. The park lies within one of the busiest commercial waterways in the world, with additional boat traffic provided by the thousands of people that pursue recreational activities each year. Pollution and overuse are a constant threat, and the physical nature of the park (scattered islands spread along 80 kilometres/50 miles of waterway) makes it difficult to monitor impacts on park lands.

Above: *In spring the Thousand Islands are carpeted with flowers.*

# QUÉBEC

La belle province, second largest in Canada (15% of the country), extends 2,000 kilometres (800 miles) south to north through four ecological regions: Temperate Boreal, Boreal, SubArctic, and Arctic. The three national parks, and most of the human population, are in the south, close to the St. Lawrence River, the largest river flowing into the Atlantic Ocean, and the outlet for the Great Lakes. The river flows into the Gulf of St. Lawrence, bordered and shared by five provinces, but two large island groups belong to Québec, Anticosti, and les Iles de la Madelaine. There is considerable faunal diversity, from Walrus in the far north to White-tailed Deer in the south, from Connecticut Warblers in the west to Bicknell's Thrushes in the east.

The Canadian Shield dominates northern Québec, and is the source of much of the province's wealth in minerals, wood, and hydroelectric power. The eroded mountains of the Appalachian chain form the backbone of the Gaspé Peninsula in the province's south-east. In Québec's far north, the forests give way to Tundra. Within Québec's immense area and geographic diversity there are numerous natural attractions: the concentration of Snow Geese at Cap Tourmente; the autumn colours of the southern deciduous forests; whales feeding off the Saguenay Fjord; and passerine migration on Mont Royal.

There are numerous provincial parks, but most with a southern focus, leaving much of the boreal region open to intensive clear-cut logging, and massive hydroelectric projects. Some of the more popular provincial parks include Gatineau, Gaspé, Mont Jacques-Cartier, Mont Tremblant, and Grands Jardins.

# La Mauricie National Park

## *Old Landscape, New Park*

*'The lone cry of a loon from an unseen lake. Peace, contentment.'*

Grey Owl (Wa-sha-quon-asin), Men of the Last Frontier

La Mauricie National Park lies in south-central Québec, protecting a section of the Laurentian Hills at the edge of the Precambrian Shield. It is a horseshoe-shaped, wild, but small park – covering only 536 square kilometres (207 square miles) – and although it has a foundation of one billion-year-old rock, it was established as a national park only in 1970. The Common Loon (known as the Great Northern Diver in Europe) is seen and heard regularly in the park. The nuances, subtlety, power, and variety of the cries of this boreal bird are symbols of the great northern forests of Canada.

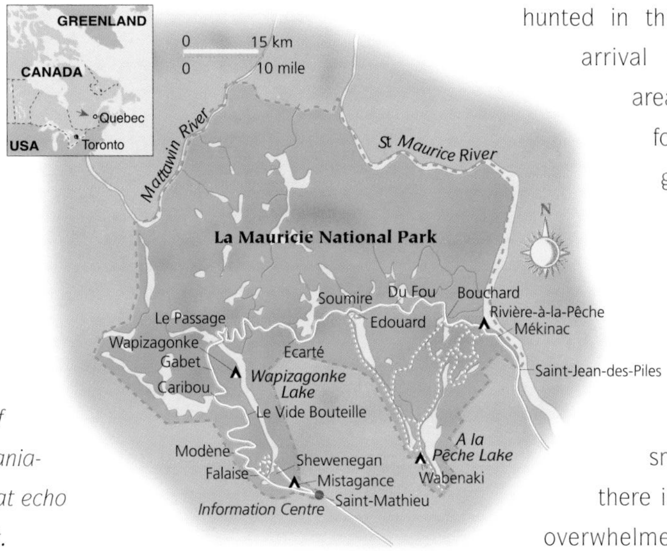
GREENLAND
CANADA
Quebec
USA
Toronto
0 15 km
0 10 mile
Mattawin River
St Maurice River
La Mauricie National Park
N
Le Passage
Wapizagonke
Gabet
Caribou
Ecarté
Wapizagonke Lake
Le Vide Bouteille
Soumire
Du Fou
Edouard
Bouchard
Rivière-à-la-Pêche
Mékinac
Saint-Jean-des-Piles
Modène
Falaise
Shewenegan
Mistagance
Information Centre
Saint-Mathieu
A la Pêche Lake
Wabenaki

The First Nations people of this area, the Algonquins, the Iroquois, the Hurons and the Attikameks, all hunted in this region, and, with the arrival of the Europeans, the area was ruthlessly exploited for hunting, trapping, logging, and mining. Although now protected, the park suffers from being so close to Montréal and Québec City – more than 300,000 people a year visit this relatively small wilderness park – and there is a risk of the park being overwhelmed by those innocently seeking peace and contentment through hearing the lone cry of the loon.

### *A Wilderness Flavour*

La Mauricie is an excellent location to learn the art of canoeing as there are numerous lakes, mostly small, and there is no white water (although there are some long portages). Cross-country skiiing is also very popular in the park where there are warming huts every 5 kilometres (3 miles) along the 80 kilometres (50 miles) of skiing trails. However, the great majority of visitors to the park stay in the frontcountry, away from the rigours of back-

Opposite above: *The Common Loon has an extraordinary repertoire of calls, including wailing, maniacal laughter, and hoots that echo through the forest at night.*

Opposite below left: *There is winter accommodation for cross-country skiers near Wabenake Lodge.*

Opposite below right: *Canoe rental is available at Shewenegan recreational area.*

Above right: *The confiding Red Squirrel is more easily seen than the larger mammals of the forest.*

Previous pages:
Page 102: *Les Cascades River tumbles through La Mauricie National Park.* Page 103: *The Willow Ptarmigan is found on rocky slopes and tundra in the north of the province.*

**Location**: 200 km (125 miles) north of Montréal, Québec.

**Climate**: Humid continental, with cold winters, hot summers, and pleasant springs and autumns.

**When to go**: Open year-round, but most services and facilities only open mid-May–mid-October.

**Access**: From Montréal or Québec City, take Hwy 40 to Trois-Rivières, then Hwy 55 north, taking exit 217 for the Saint-Gérard-des-Laurentides entrance to the park (west side), or exit 226 for the Saint-Jean-des-Piles entrance (east side). Park is 200 km (125 miles) from Montréal; 60 km (37 miles) from Trois-Rivières; 190 km (118 miles) from Québec City. International airport and train station in Montréal.

**Facilities**: Trails; on-site exhibits; Visitor Centres (nature bookshop); picnic sites; campgrounds; boat launch and mooring; commercial accommodations; playground; boat rentals. Nearby communities: all usual facilities and services.

**Watching Nature**: Wildlife is common in the park, but hunting has left animals wary of humans. Dawn and dusk are the best times for observation. Moose are often seen; beaver less frequently; loons are heard most often at night, but are regularly seen on lakes during the day. Lac-Étiénne, La Cache, and Lac-Gabet trails have blinds (hides) and telescopes to aid wildlife sightings.

**Visitor Activities**: Hiking; swimming; picnicking; scuba diving; fishing; canoeing; cross-country skiing; mountain biking.

Above: *Ile les Pins view-point affords panoramic views of the area.*

country travel. So, too, did the well-heeled clients of the numerous Fish and Game Clubs that were opened in this area as early as 1883. The exclusive member-ships conferred significant privileges, including exclu-sive access to large areas of land, for hunting and fishing in style and comfort. The Wabenaki and Andrew Lodges are historic artifacts of this period, and

Right: *The presence of beavers is often revealed by the distinctive manner in which they cut trees.*

still function as lodges, but without any attendant priv-ileges. The lodges did prevent over-exploitation of the animals being hunted and fished, but they also intro-duced many non-native fish (19 different species have been identified), which has had serious repercussions for the environment.

## The Loon Alone

Loons, often seen in the park, are one of the oldest birds on earth, having been around for more than 60 million years. They are powerful swimmers, strong fast fliers, but very ungainly on the ground. They lay two eggs, and are attentive parents. They breed in all provinces and terri-tories of Canada, and winter along both the Atlantic and Pacific coasts. Loons are best known for their repertoire of calls, including mournful wails, maniacal laughs, and echoing hoots. They frequently call at night, and an evening camping in the boreal forest is not complete without a loon chorus.

Left: *Autumn Maple leaves (both Sugar and Red are illustrated), are powerfully evocative of La Mauricie.*

Left: *The keen-eyed hiker may find Purple Trillium flowering on the forest floor.*

Below: *The Red Fox is a versatile predator that feeds primarily on small rodents.*

## Protecting the Loons and Pines

La Mauricie National Park protects a part of the Precambrian Shield and the Laurentian Boreal Highlands.

The Eastern White Pine was once the dominant tree in the area, but now accounts for only 1 per cent of the forest. Controlled burns are being used to gradually increase the amount of pine in the park, as pine is a fire-dependent species.

Recent studies suggest that numbers of the loon may be declining in the park. Historically, 25 of the park's lakes were suitable for nesting loons, but they seem to have abandoned ten of them, and often fail in their nesting attempts on the others. Park staff are working aggressively with park visitors to change visitor behaviour, so that the loons remained undisturbed. Canoeists are now prohibited from landing on islands during the loon nesting season, and access to some lakes is restricted when loons are present.

# FORILLON NATIONAL PARK AND BONAVENTURE ISLAND PROVINCIAL PARK

## Land's End and Seabirds

*'He watches seagulls fly, silver on the ocean,
stitching, through the waves, the edges of the sky.'*

JUDY COLLINS, ALBATROSS

Forillon National Park and Bonaventure Island Provincial Park lie at the eastern tip of the Gaspé Peninsula. They jut into the Bay of Gaspé to the south-west and the Gulf of St Lawrence to the north-east. The drive around the Gaspé Peninsula of Québec is one of the world's most scenic excursions. Forillon National Park was established in 1974 as Québec's first national park and covers an area of 240 square kilometres (94 square miles) of mainly forest. The park is bordered on three sides by ocean, and whales can be sighted from the park's south coast. Bonaventure Island Provincial Park is 4.2 square kilometres (1.6

square miles) and was first establshed as a provincial park in 1972. The island and adjacent Percé Rock (a magnificent sea-arch) are home to thousands of seabirds, and since 1985 the region has been established and maintained as a Conservation Park.

### Land's End

At the northern end of Forillon National Park, at Cap-Gaspé, lies the land's end of the Gaspé Peninsula. The park itself is at the northern end of the International Appalachian Trail (IAT), a 1,000-kilometre (625-mile) trail that begins at Mount Katahdin, Maine, U.S.A. The trail proceeds from northwards across the New Brunswick border, near Mount Carleton, into Québec via the Matapédia Valley, the Matane Reserve, and Gaspésie Provincial Park, and ends in Forillon National Park. From Maine, the IAT also links with the famous Appalachian Trail, which started construction in 1937, and runs for 3,455 kilometres (2,160 miles) between Maine and Georgia.

There is an unexpected diversity of plants within the park's relatively small area due to the diversity of habitats. Although 95 per cent of the park is forest, there are

*Opposite, above: The Northern Gannet colony on Bonaventure Island supports thousands of breeding pairs.*

*Opposite, below left: The coastal escarpment at Cap-Gaspé shows evidence of massive geological uplifting.*

*Opposite, below right: Percé Rock is home to many seabirds, including Common Murres and Black-legged Kittiwakes.*

*Above, right: Black Guillemots nest amongst boulders at the foot of the seacliffs.*

**Location**: At the eastern end of the Gaspé Peninsula. Forillon is near the town of Gaspé, about 700 km (438 miles) north-east of Québec. Bonaventure Island Provincial Park accessible from the town of Percé, 50 km (30 mi) south of Forillon.

**Climate**: Continental, but heavily modified by the sea. Mean temperatures: July 17°C/62°F; January -10°C/14°F. Annual precipitation 100 cm (39 in).

**When to go**: Open year-round, but most facilities and services only available from mid-May–mid-October. Boat trips to Bonaventure Island available June–mid-October.

**Access**: Via Hwy 132 from Québec. Nearest major airport in Québec. Bonaventure Island: by boat from Percé, which is 50 km (30 miles) south of Forillon, on Hwy 132.

**Facilities**: Campgrounds; trails; picnic sites; Visitor Centre; heated outdoor swimming pool; recreation centre; Grande-Grave National Historic Site. Typical facilities and services in Gaspé and Percé.

**Watching Nature**: Seabird colonies active May–July; seals and whales active May–September; whale-watching cruises early June–late September.

**Visitor Activities**: Hiking; picnicking; swimming; salt-water fishing; biking; salt-water boat cruise; whale-watching cruise; tennis; volleyball; scuba diving; snorkeling; sea-kayaking; cycling; horseback riding; cross-country skiing; snowshoeing.

Above: *La Chute waterfall is one of the park's many scenic attractions.*

pockets of alpine meadows, cliff faces, sand dunes, fresh- and salt-water marshes, fields, streams, and lakes, each supporting a different group of plants. There are 115 species of arctic-alpine plants. They are found on cliff edges, and on rock outcrops on the summits of highlands, where the rugged cliffs and cool maritime climate combine to provide a tenuous refuge. Examples include Tufted Saxifrage, Snowy Cinquefoil, Divided-Leaf Fleabane, Yellow Mountain Avens, and Small Flowered Anemone.

One of the main attractions of the park is the chance of seeing whales off the coast, between Grande-Grave and Cap-Gaspé. There are also guided two-and-a-half hour whale-watching cruises from Grande-Grave harbour. The common whales that are seen are Fin Whale, Humpback Whale, and Minke Whale, although as many as seven species of whale have been seen in these waters, including the Blue Whale, the world's largest whale. The park also contains an array of wildlife, including the smallest race of Black Bear in North America, moose, Red Fox,

Left: *Northern Gannets feed exclusively on fish which they catch with a spectacular plunge.*

Far right: *Unlike gannets, Double-crested Cormorants fish by diving from the surface.*

coyote, Snowshoe Hare, porcupine, groundhog, mink, ermine, Eastern Chipmunk, beaver, and Red Squirrel.

## Bonaventure Island Provincial Park and Percé Rock

Ocean currents, and the mixing of fresh and salt water, ensure that the waters off the eastern tip of the Gaspé Peninsula are very rich in sea life. This has meant that the secure nesting sites of the adjacent cliffs have been occupied by seabirds for thousands of years. On Percé Rock and Bonaventure Island there are huge colonies of seabirds, including Herring Gulls, Double-crested and Great Cormorants, Great Black-backed Gulls, Black-legged Kittiwakes and Black Guillemots. Bonaventure is also home to Razorbills and Common Murres, a few Atlantic Puffins, and an enormous colony of Northern Gannets, approachable to within a few paces. Many of the seabirds, though not the puffins or gannets, also breed in smaller numbers along the cliffs at Forillon National Park. Bonaventure Island is accessible only by boat; cruises depart all day and usually include a trip around the island.

In addition to seeing the seabird colonies, there are the several trails through the wooded centre of the island where you can see numerous forest breeding birds, including Bicknell's Thrush and Fox Sparrow.

## Park protection

Forillon National Park protects part of the Central St. Lawrence Lowlands Region. This heavily visited park is at risk from surrounding activities, including commercial fishing, water pollution, logging, and wildlife poaching.

Above: *A magnificent sea-arch is the most distinctive feature of Percé Rock.*

Left: *The Snowshoe Hare loses its white coat in summer.*

# SAGUENAY–ST. LAWRENCE MARINE PARK

## Marine Greyhounds and Sea Canaries

*'See the Leviathan in vastness is lying, making the ocean her sumptuous bed,*
*While high overhead the seabirds are flying, combing the billows that break o'er her head.'*

TRADITIONAL WHALING SONG

The Saguenay – St. Lawrence Marine Park was created in 1997 as a joint undertaking between the governments of Canada and Québec, although the park has yet to be gazetted. It is the first national marine park in Canada, established to protect whales and all the other flora and fauna that are determined to lie within its boundaries. The park covers an area of 1,139 square kilometres (438 square miles) at the mouth of the Saguenay River where it flows into the mighty St. Lawrence, the largest Canadian river flowing into the Atlantic Ocean.

The waters at the confluence of the Saguenay and the St. Lawrence are particularly nutrient-rich, because of their respective currents colliding and swirling around a submerged, curved, raised mound of gravel (known as a 'glacial moraine') off the mouth of the Saguenay Fjord. The glacial moraine forces the water of the Saguenay River upwards, circulating rich bottom sediments, forming the first link in a nutritious food chain. This food chain has attracted whales to the region since the end of the last glacial period.

*Opposite, above: The Pointe de L'islet projects into the Gulf of St. Lawrence, where heavy fogs and autumn storms are frequent and whales may be sighted.*

*Opposite, below: Steep vegetated sand dunes stretch along the shore of the Baie du Moulin à Baude.*

*Above, right: The old church in Tadoussac looks out over the St. Lawrence River.*

## Watching Whales

The marine park is very close to the large population centres of central Canada and is a popular site for whale watching. In all, 10 species of cetacean have been sighted in the area, though the Fin Whale and the Beluga Whale are the most common.

The Fin Whale, known as the marine Greyhound for its speed, is the second-largest whale on the planet, after the Blue Whale. The Fin Whale is a baleen whale that obtains its food by squeezing large volumes of water through hundreds of fibrous plates on the upper jaw, filtering out krill and small fish in the process. Fin Whales are massive, growing up to 23 metres (75 feet) long, and weighing up to 50 tonnes. The Fin Whale is the only asymmetrically coloured animal in the world – its lower right jaw and front baleen are white rather than blue.

**Location:** On the north shore of the St. Lawrence River, at the mouth of the Saguenay Fjord.

**Climate:** Maritime climate, heavily modified by the Gulf of St. Lawrence. Ocean water temperatures range only from 10°C (50°F) in summer to 0°C (32°F) in winter. Summer air temperatures may reach 24°C (75°F) during the day, falling to 10°C (50°F) at night. Fog is frequent on southerly winds, and autumn storms are common.

**When to go:** All year-round, but whale-watching (and Saguenay fjord) tours operate only from mid-June–mid-October.

**Access:** By boat, from the town of Tadoussac, on the east side of the mouth of the Saguenay Fjord, and Baie Sainte-Catherine on the west side; a car ferry crosses the fjord throughout the day. Baie Sainte-Catherine is 210 km (131 miles) north-east of Québec via route #138. From the south shore of the St. Lawrence River car ferries cross from Trois-Pistoles to Les Escoumins (north-east of Tadoussac), and from Rivière-du-Loup to Saint-Siméon (south-west of Baie Sainte-Catherine).

**Facilities:** Facilities in town of Tadoussac. Campgrounds, picnic sites, trails in Saguenay Provincial Park.

**Watching Nature:** Common sightings of whales: Beluga, Fin, Minke and sometimes Blue. Seabird watching: Black-legged Kittiwakes, Northern Gannets, Common Eider, Scoters, and Jaegers. Also sight-seeing tours of the Saguenay Fjord.

**Visitor Activities:** Whale watching (June–October); seabird watching; photography; scuba diving.

Above, top: *The tall colum-nar blow of a Fin Whale is a useful identification pointer.*

Above: *The Minke Whale is considerably smaller than the Fin Whale.*

dive. Each summer, approximately 40 Fin Whales return to the Saguenay area and are seen on almost every whale-watching trip.

Beluga Whales are much smaller than Fin Whales – Belugas are (5 metres/16 feet) long, and are toothed. Belugas are also white (though juveniles are gray, until six years of age), and have been nick-named 'Sea Canaries' for their constant underwater chattering. In the 1930s, in an effort to protect the dwindling numbers of codfish, the government placed a bounty on the cod-eating Belugas with the result that thousands of Belugas were killed. By 1983, when the St. Lawrence Belugas were declared an endangered population (isolated from the more numerous Belugas in the Arctic), the number of Belugas that annually visited the St. Lawrence area had fallen from over 5,000 to fewer than 500. Despite the protection since the 1970s, the population has not grown, and might still be shrinking. Given the precarious status of the population, whale-watching boats are now not allowed to approach Belugas any closer than 1 kilometre (⅔ mile) – a much safer distance from which it is still possibile for visitors to view these magnificent creatures.

## Whales under Threat

Parks Canada does not yet have legal jurisdiction over the waters of the park, and so is unable to control the activities of the whale-watching companies. There is concern that too many boats now ply the waters in search of whales, and that harassment occurs. Pollution of the Saguenay and St. Lawrence Rivers is an ongoing problem, and the St. Lawrence is one of the busiest commercial waterways in the world, with thousands of oceangoing vessels moving past the park annually, posing a constant risk of oil spills.

Whales may be identified by their relatively small dorsal fin that lies two-thirds of the way down the animal's back, and by its very tall, columnar blow, that appears immediately after the whale resurfaces. Also, unlike other whales that can be seen in the area, Fin Whales are less demonstrative in their behaviour: they do not breach, lunge, spy-hop, slap, or even show their tail when they

Right: *Beluga Whales are toothed whales, and are more closely related to dolphins than to the larger baleen whales.*

# MINGAN ARCHIPELAGO NATIONAL PARK RESERVE

## The Islands of the Sea Parrot

*'The fair, frail palaces, the fading alps and archipelagoes...'*

THOMAS BAILEY ALDRICH, MIRACLES

Mingan Archipelago National Park Reserve is a group of 49 islands that stretch for 175 kilometres (109 miles) along the Québec shore of the Gulf of St. Lawrence between Aguanish and Longue-Pointe. Parks Canada acquired 40 of the islands from a petroleum company in 1983 and the park was established a year later, though it remains a reserve pending negotiations between the government and the local First Nations people, the Attikamek-Montagnais. There are some compelling landforms on the islands, including monoliths, arches, caves and grottos, which have formed from eroding sedimentary rock. The islands are otherwise fairly flat and the cliffs and headlands attract nesting seabirds, including the Atlanctic Puffin, which nests on three of the islands.

*Above, right: The Atlantic Puffin is known locally as the Sea Parrot because of its outlandish and comical bill during the breeding season.*

### Monk Puffins, Sea Parrots and Calculators

In French, the Atlantic Puffin is known as the *Macareaux moine*, the Monk Puffin, in reference to its monk-like habit of keeping its feet together when standing, as monks do in prayer. In Canada, Atlantic Puffins are known as *perroquets de mer* (Sea Parrots) because during the breeding season they have a colourful beak and take on a comical theatrical appearance. Another local name is the *calculot* (calculator) in reference to its frequent head-nodding, as if it were counting its neighbours in the colony.

The puffins favour the Mingan islands for the good nesting areas, the abundant food in the nearby oceanic waters, and the relatively few predators, of which the Great Black-backed Gull is the most determined. The Atlantic Puffin is related to penguins, but is much smaller, only about 30 cm (12 in) tall. Unlike penguins, it flies well, and with its short, streamlined wings and webbed feet, is a superb swimmer. On land, however, it is clumsy, and is then most vulnerable to predators. Puffins nest in steep grassy banks inside deep burrows. Pairs mate for life, and return to the islands in mid-April,

*Map: Mingan Archipelago National Park Reserve. To Sept-Îles, Longue-Pte, Mingan, Île Quarry, Havre-St-Pierre, Île Nue de Mingan, La Grande Île, Île Niapiskau, Île du Havre, Grosse Île au Marteau, Île à la Chasse, Île du Fantôme, Petite Île au Marteau. GULF OF ST LAWRENCE. 0–10 km / 0–5 mile. Inset: GREENLAND, CANADA, Quebec, USA, Toronto.*

**Location:** On the north shore of the Gulf of St. Lawrence, near Havre-Saint-Pierre. About 860 km (538 miles) from Québec City.

**Climate:** Maritime climate, heavily modified by the Gulf of St. Lawrence. Ocean water temperatures range only from 8°C (46°F) in summer to 0°C (32°F) in winter. Summer air temperatures may reach 20°C (68°F) during the day, falling to10°C (50°F) at night. Fog is frequent on southerly winds, and autumn storms are common.

**When to go:** Open year-round, but no facilities outside the June-September period. Weather conditions generally limit functional visits to June–September.

**Access:** Highway 138 from Québec City. By bus: bus service links Baie-Comeau to Havre-Saint-Pierre via Sept-Îles. By plane: regional service links Québec City to Havre-Saint-Pierre. By boat: Ferry service links Rimouski, Sept-Îles, Port-Meunier, Havre-Saint-Pierre and the Lower North Shore.

**Facilities:** Visitor Centre at Havre-Saint-Pierre; campgrounds (backcountry sites on six islands; advance reservations required); hiking trails (24 km/15 miles) on four islands; picnic sites. Havre-Saint-Pierre and nearby communities: frontcountry campground; fuel; commercial accommodations; boat rentals; water taxis; medical clinic; marina.

**Watching Nature:** Main attractions are botany, birds, cetaceans, and geology. The peak time for flowers and birds is the latter half of June. Whale watching is best in July–August.

**Visitor Activities:** Boating; sea kayaking; hiking; camping; nature photography; scuba diving.

**Special Notes:** From May 1 to August 1 many islands, in whole or in part, have no public access to avoid disturbing nesting birds.

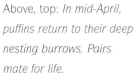

Above, top: *In mid-April, puffins return to their deep nesting burrows. Pairs mate for life.*

Above: *The Great Black-backed Gull is a significant predator of puffins.*

using the same burrow year after year. A single egg takes 40 days to hatch, and the chick is fed small fish (Capelin and Sand Eels) until it fledges, usually in early August. The birds depart the islands in late August, and their wintering grounds are unknown, although they are thought to be on the open sea, perhaps on offshore fishing banks. The park's puffin population is around 500 pairs, scattered between three colonies, on Île à Calculot des Betchouanes, Île aux Perroquets, and Île de la Maison.

## Sea Wolves

There are three species of seals, locally known as *loups de mer* (Sea Wolves), that live in Mingan: Grey, Harbour, and Harp. The Grey Seal is the largest and most common, and can be identified by its large head with a distinctive Roman nose, almost horse-like in

shape – which is the reason for its nickname, *tête-de-cheval* (horse head). The Harbour Seal is much smaller and less common in the islands. It has a more rounded head with a small nose. The local name is *loup-marin d'esprit* (intelligent Sea-Wolf), in reference to the cow Harbour Seal's clever strategy of encouraging newly borne pups to enter the sea to avoid land predators. Harp Seals, identified by their yellow coats, are not permanent residents of the archipelago, but they do feed in the area from April to June, before heading further north along the coast of Labrador.

Nine species of whales have been sighted near the park, of which Inshore Minke Whales and Harbour Porpoise are the most frequently seen. Further out, in the deeper water of the Gulf of St. Lawrence, there have also been sightings of Humpback, Fin, and even Blue Whales.

## An Unsettled Coast

There is a long history to human use of the Mingan area, going back more than 2,000 years to when the area was visited seasonally by the Attikamek-Montagnais, who call themselves the 'Innu' or 'the people'. The Attikamek-Montagnais still live in the area today, although their lifestyle has been persistently disrupted by new arrivals. The first Europeans to the region were the Basque whalers from northern Spain (remains of their oil rendering sites have been found on two of the islands) and they were closely followed by The Hudson Bay Company, which did not permit settlement along the coastline. However, following 1850, when the Hudson Bay Company's monopoly was terminated, permission was granted for settlement along the coast, and settlers came from Jersey, Québec, Îles-de-la-Madeleine, and Acadia.

## A Fragile Sea

Mingan Archipelago National Park Reserve protects an important part of the St. Lawrence Lowlands. It is at potential risk from rising sea levels due to global warming, from pollution in the Gulf of St. Lawrence, and from overuse of its fragile landscape by visitors.

Above: *The distinctive limestone monoliths on Île Quarry have been created by the erosive power of wind and wave.*

Left: *The Harbour Seal may be distinguished from the Grey Seal by its smaller size and more rounded head.*

# ATLANTIC CANADA

Atlantic Canada comprises the four eastern-most provinces of New Brunswick, Prince Edward Island, Nova Scotia, and Newfoundland and Labrador. The first three taken together are referred to as the Maritimes. There are no national parks in Labrador, which lies both in the SubArctic and Arctic Ecological Regions. The island of Newfoundland is entirely within the Boreal Region, while the Maritimes are in the Temperate Boreal Region. The region's national parks are proportionately large, and all seven border salt water; the ocean's influence is pervasive in the area's history, culture, economy and natural history.

New Brunswick's northern boreal forests meld into lush southern valleys and the dynamic coast of the Bay of Fundy, which it shares with Nova Scotia. Mount Carleton is the gem of its provincial park system. The Nova Scotia coastline, straightened, would extend to Europe and back, and special Provincial Parks include Chignecto, McNab's Island, and Blomidon.

Naturalists come for the whales and seabirds in the Bay of Fundy off Brier Island, the seabird colonies off Cape Breton, the millions of southbound shorebirds, and the winter concentrations of Bald Eagles. Everyone enjoys the scenery, from Cape Sable Island in the south to the Cabot Trail in the north. Prince Edward Island is Canada's smallest province, with a gentle landscape, heavily modified by agriculture. The province's beaches attract the endangered Piping Plover, as well as sun-seeking humans.

The waters surrounding Newfoundland's Avalon Peninsula are rich in life, supporting enormous seabird colonies. The island's interior is hilly and forested, while the western backbone is the ancient Long Range Mountains, part of the Applachians, offering the province's finest scenery, as well as the famous site of the Viking settlement at L'anse aux Meadows, the first such European enterprise in North America.

# GROS MORNE NATIONAL PARK

## The Rocky Road to Fame

*'That one might read the book of fate, and see the revolution of the times make*
*mountains level ... and the continent melt itself into the sea!'*

SHAKESPEARE, HENRY IV

Gros Morne National Park lies on the west coast of Newfoundland and has some of the most spectacular scenery in eastern Canada. The park covers an area of 1,805 square kilometres (694 square miles) and has a stunning diversity of land forms, including the Long Range Mountains, fjords, basalt cliffs, and uplifted mantle. Although the park is well-known for its magnificent landscapes and the wildlife it supports, it gained recognition as a World Heritage Site in 1987 for the many rare rock formations found in the park. The rocks are of great importance to earth scientists as they provide compelling evidence for the theory of plate tectonics – the theory that continents drift around the earth. The abundance and variety of the rare rock formations in the park is unparalled. Many date from Cambrian to Middle Ordovician times (570–475 million years ago); some are twice as old. The positions of these different rocks provides strong evidence that the continents have moved, and are still doing so. The most striking example is The Tablelands, a piece of sub-mantle rock, lying beside a mountain comprised of lithosphere (ocean floor) lying on top of continental crust.

Opposite: *The shoreline at Green Point reveals ancient rocks worn smooth by the sea.*

Above, right: *Common Terns display an elegant mastery of flight as they twist and hover over the water in search of food.*

Previous pages:
Page 118: *Sunset illuminates the rocky shelves along the shoreline of Bonne Bay.* Page 119: *The Least Chipmunk inhabits a variety of terrain, where it makes its home in ground burrows.*

### Gros Morne Mountain

The Long Range Mountains run the length of the park and are at the northeastern end of the ancient Appalachian Mountains of North America. Rising above them is Gros Morne Mountain, 806 metres (2,650 feet) high and the centrepiece of the park. The hike to the summit of Gros Morne via the James Callaghan Trail is strenuous but rewarding, and in addition to memorable vistas, offers the chance to see caribou, Rock Ptarmigan, Arctic Hare, and a variety of alpine flowers. Some serious and well-prepared hikers traverse the Long Range Mountains between Western Brook Pond and Gros Morne on a rigorous multi-day adventure.

**Location**: The west coast of the island of Newfoundland, NW of Cornerbrook

**Climate**: Maritime influenced, unpredictable. Mean temperatures: summer 15°C (60°F), winter -7°C (19°F). 400 cm (160 in) snow, 1,000 mm (40 in) rain. Frequent strong winds.

**When to go**: Open year-round, but many facilities only June–September.

**Access**: By scheduled airlines to Deer Lake. By paved highway from Deer Lake (one hour drive).

**Facilities**: Visitor Centres (nature bookstore); on-site exhibits; campgrounds (5); picnic sites; trails; historic buildings; swimming pool. Park enclave communities: commercial accommodations (motels, cabins, B&B, hostel); museums, hospital; restaurants.

**Watching Nature**: Moose; caribou; whales (Bonne Bay, summer); Harbour Seals (St. Paul's Bay). Rock Ptarmigan (alpine plateau); Boreal Chickadee (widespread); Bald Eagle (Bonne Bay); shorebirds (St. Paul's Bay); warblers (James Callaghan Trail). Arctic/alpine flora on alpine plateau; bog plants on the Coastal Plain.

**Visitor Activities**: Boat tours; hiking (22 trails); backcountry camping; kayaking; swimming; fishing (permit required); sightseeing by car. Numerous maps, trail guides, and other references may be purchased in the park.

**Equipment**: Clothing: be prepared for diverse weather, including wind and precipitation.

**Special Notes**: (1) Rock collecting by permit only. (2) Drive carefully; collisions with moose occur regularly, especially dawn or dusk. (3) Mosquitos and Black Flies are abundant in summer.

Above: *Hikers may encounter moose on some of the more remote trails in the park.*

## The Tablelands

The effect of continental drift can be seen at The Tablelands, a flat-topped, golden hill that was formed when molten magma was uplifted by colliding plates millions of years ago. This plateau is really a section of the earth's mantle, or peridodite, that usually lies 16 kilometres (10 miles) below the earth's crust. The striking, unearthly landscape does not support much wildlife as the mantle's mineral composition is poisonous to most vegetation. The road between the communities of Woody Point and Trout River offers an arresting contrast between the yellow Tablelands to the east and the grey forested cliffs of the Lookout Hills to the west. An exhibit and trail introduce visitors to this special landscape.

## Fjords and 'Ponds'

During the last ice, glacial erosion carved a series of fjords into the western face of the Long Range Mountains. Gros Morne contains six fjords, five of which are now cut off from the sea by the rising Coastal Plain, and are locally called 'ponds', a name which belies their size – they are up to 16 kilometres (10 miles) long, 165 metres (500 feet) deep, and their bordering cliffs can be as high as 660 metres (2,000 feet). Boat tours on Western Brook Pond and Trout River Pond are popular. The Western Brook Pond tour is accessible via a 3-kilometre (2-mile) level walk across the Coastal Plain, while the Trout River Pond tour can be reached by road.

*Right: The Arctic Tern is a record-breaking migrant, returning to the region every year from the Antarctic to breed.*

## Coastal Plain and Bonne Bay

The flat, albeit boggy, terrain of the Coastal Plain, and the ocean accessibility of Bonne Bay (the only true fjord in the park) encouraged human settlement, and people have lived in this area for more than 5,000 years. The British have had a presence in this region for centuries, and today's local residents continue their traditional harvest of certain resources of the sea and forest. A permit even allows activity within the park's boundaries. (Glimpses of this rich history are available at the Lobster Cove Head Lighthouse and in the preserved fishing buildings at Broom Point.) Virtually all the park's facilities and services are located around the bay and along the plain, and most visitors stay within these areas, venturing out only on established trails. Most visit in the summer for the camping, beaches, picnics, hiking, and wildlife watching, though skiing and winter camping entice a few hardier souls from December through to March.

## Hiking

Gros Morne's 180 kilometres (110 miles) of trails are the best way to see and understand the park. It is wise to not veer off the well-constructed trails, though the presence of the thick impenetrable coastal coniferous forest (locally called 'Tuckamore', a type of krummholz), as well as numerous bogs, encourage hikers to keep to established routes. A relatively easy level trail is at Berry Head Pond (a 2-kilometre/1¼-mile circular walk), and two moderate level return walks are at Western Brook Pond (a 6-kilometre/4-mile walk) and at Baker's Brook Falls (a 10-kilometre/6-mile walk). The Green Gardens Trail is a moderately strenuous 9-kilometre/5½-mile return walk, while the hike up Gros Morne Mountain is the most strenuous of the trails in the park, on which walkers cover 16 kilometres (10 miles), and climb 806 metres (2,650 feet).

## Encroaching on the Boundaries

Gros Morne protects a representative sample of the Western Newfoundland Highlands. Over-fishing of local waters has greatly reduced much of the local fishery, and logging is poorly controlled within park area communities. Logging outside the park has encroached to the park boundaries, making the remote backcountry more accessible, increasing poaching. The impact of local use of snowmobiles in the park during winter has yet to be established.

Right: *No visitor forgets a visit to The Tablelands; the golden, barren, flat-topped mountain of mantle rock, thrust to the surface by the forces of continental drift.*

Above: *Caribou* (top) *may be seen on the hike to the summit of Gros Morne* (bottom). *In addition to fjords, the coastal plain is dotted with shallow lakes* (middle).

Right: *Imposing cliffs rise hundreds of metres above Western Brook Pond.*

# Cape Breton Highlands National Park

## From Headlands to Highlands via the Cabot Trail

*'My heart's in the Highlands, my heart is not here;*
*My heart's in the Highlands a-chasing the deer...'*

ROBERT BURNS

Cape Breton Highlands National Park, established in 1936, is the oldest national park in Atlantic Canada and the second largest national park in Canada east of Ontario and south of 60° North. The Cabot Trail, one of the world's most scenic roads, winds along both sides of the park, framing an outstanding varied wilderness that includes lush valleys, exposed rocky coastlines, and windswept boggy barrens. The park covers an area of 948 square kilometres (366 square miles) and within its boundaries there are numerous opportunities for

recreation, including walking, whale watching, swimming, fishing, and birdwatching. There are also many cultural opportunities in communities surrounding the park, where the visitor can experience traditional Acadian or Gaelic activities, including music, meals, dances, and ceilidhs.

### The Cabot Trail

The Cabot Trail is an integral part of the Cape Breton Highlands National Park, and whether you drive the route quickly, stopping at only the 'obligatory' viewpoints, or use the road as a jumping-off point for exploration, you will appreciate its moods, vistas, and leisurely speed limit. Cabot Trail is named after the Italian explorer Giovanni Cabotti, who explored for the British and was known by them as John Cabot. This region of Nova Scotia has attracted the dispossessed for centuries, first the Acadians, most of whom were expelled by the British, and later the Scots, expelled from Scotland during the 'Clearances'. Both cultures are still represented in local park communities and many of the local names, such as Chéticamp and Ingonish, reflect these origins. There are some interesting diversions off the Cabot Trail that can be taken by drivers wishing to explore the park. From

Opposite, above: *The Cabot Trail winds around the park, and is considered one of the world's most scenic drives.*

Opposite, below left: *The long wings and tail of the Northern Hawk-Owl give it a hawk-like appearance.*

Opposite, below right: *Birds are a common sight along the coastlines of the park.*

Above, right: *The Bog Trail boardwalk allows visitors to observe the specialised flora of a highland plateau bog.*

**Location**: The northern tip of Cape Breton Island between the Gulf of St. Lawrence and the Atlantic Ocean.

**Climate**: Complex, variable, and unpredictable, with maritime and altitudinal influences. Cold winters with heavy snowfall, cool springs, warm summers, and pleasant autumns. The climate on the plateau is the most severe in Nova Scotia. The Cheticamp coast experiences strong winds – 'La Suete' – from the south-east.

**When to go**: Open year-round, but most services and facilities only open from mid-May–mid-October.

**Access**: Via the Cabot Trail. From Trans-Canada Hwy (105) take either Exit 7 for Cabot Trail west to Chéticamp, or Exit 12 for Cabot Trail east to Ingonish. From Sydney, take Hwy 125 to Hwy 105, then Exit 11 to the Cabot Trail. Nearest airport in Sydney. Ferry service to Newfoundland from North Sydney.

**Facilities**: The most extensive nature bookstore in Atlantic Canada is at the park's Visitor Centre, just north of Chéticamp; campgrounds (six frontcountry sites; backcountry sites require reservations); picnic sites; trails; on-site exhibits; viewpoints; Lone Shieling Historic Site; golf; tennis; beach; commercial accommodations. Local communities: all services and facilities.

**Watching Nature**: Birdwatching (May–June); whale watching (Pilot Whales) (June–August); autumn colours (late-September–mid-October); moose.

**Visitor Activities**: Hiking; picnicking; scenic drives; whale watching; fishing; golfing; nature photography; camping; tennis; cross-country skiing; downhill skiing; swimming; cycling.

Right: *Black Brook Bay is a popular picnic site along the Cabot Trail.*

Pleasant Bay a narrow, dead-end, winding road leads along the coast of the Gulf of St. Lawrence to Red River, and provides access to quiet woods, an area where there are few tourists. At Big Intervale, a side road heads into the park to Beulach Ban Falls, which is a particularly impressive sight in spring when the snow begins to melt. At Cape North a paved road leads north to Bay St. Lawrence, and from there a gravel, all-weather road clings to the cliffs en route to Meat Cove, the end of the road, and the most northerly commu-

Below: *The Grande Anse Valley, incised deeply into the highlands, shelters lush forested hillsides.*

nity in Nova Scotia. Between South Harbour and Neil's Harbour, you can take either the Cabot Trail (and a side trip into the park to the Glascow Lakes), or a slower scenic route along the coast via White Point. However, if time and ability allow you to leave your vehicle, and explore the park on foot, many more possibilities become available.

## Hiking Trails: 'Winding Roads to Mystery'

Although Cape Breton Highlands National Park has the renowned Cabot Trail, the park is best explored on foot. Grey Owl spoke of the trail as '...the stage on which all the drama, the burlesque, the tragedy and the comedy of the wilderness are played', and indeed only by taking several of the 27 trails (that have a total length of more than 200 kilometres/125 miles), can the visitor begin to appreciate the diversity and nature of the park. It will take many visits to hike all the trails, but a worthwhile cross-selection can be undertaken in a three-to-five day visit. The following, from west to east, are some recommended trails: Trous de Saumon Trail is a walk along the Chéticamp River through an Acadian Forest, where there is a variety of breeding birds, including Blackburnian Warbler and White-breasted Nuthatch. Skyline Trail is a walk through highland plateau forest, where there are Mourning Warblers and Lincoln's Sparrows singing, and regular moose sightings. The walk leads to outstanding views at 390 metres (1,300 feet) above the ocean below. Bog Trail is a

boardwalk trail through a highlands plateau bog, where there are Pitcher Plants, Sundews, Rhodora, and Bicknell's Thrush. MacIntosh Brook Trail is renowned for its mature Sugar Maples and Yellow Birch. Lone Shieling Trail is an easy walk through mature Acadian Forest, where many trees are more than 350 years old. Jack Pine Trail is a good introduction to a Jack Pine Forest and to Cape Breton's Atlantic shoreline. Warren Lake Trail is a circular walk around Warren Lake through mixed forest, where breeding Common Loons are regularly seen. Middle Head Trail is an energetic hike to the tip of Middle Head and extends east into Ingonish Bay, where there are wonderful views. The Freshwater Lake Trail is a fully accessible short hike that passes a lake, a pond, the ocean, and forest, and is excellent for bird-watching and watching loons and beaver.

## Resource Extraction

Cape Breton Highlands National Park represents the Maritime Acadian Highlands natural region. As with so many parks, it is threatened by intensive resource extraction at its borders, especially logging and hydro-electric dams.

Left: *The bogs on the Highland Plateau are carpeted with a rich variety of wetland flora, including Bladderwort, a carnivorous plant.*

Below: *Beavers may be seen from a short hike along the Freshwater Lake Trail.*

# FUNDY NATIONAL PARK

## A Pocket Wilderness

*'Fundy's long and Fundy's wide. Fundy's fog and rain and tide,*
*Never see the sun or sky, just the green waves going by.'*
GORDON BOK, BAY OF FUNDY

Fundy National Park, despite its small size, is a critically important pocket of wilderness. It was established in 1948, and is the only intact piece of wilderness left in the southern half of New Brunswick. The park extends over an area of 206 square kilometres (79 square miles) of forest, meadow, river and bog inland from the Bay of Fundy. Although the park is mostly inland forest and meadow, the Bay of Fundy is a constant influence on the park's plants and animals, and has a great impact on visitors. The tides of the Bay of Fundy are the world's highest – the difference between high and low tides can be as much as 16 metres (53 feet) – and, at low tide, the large area of exposed intertidal zone is a fascinating habitat.

Opposite, far left: *Visitors to Fundy's inland forests and meadows may find the Yellow Dog Lily (above) and Swamp Candle (below).*

Opposite: *The attractive Dickson Falls may be reached by one of the many trails into the interior of the park.*

Above, right: *Great Blue Herons feed in the salt-marsh at the mouth of the Upper Salmon River, a habitat kept fertile by tidal inundation.*

## Fundy's Coast

The amplitude of the tides at the Bay of Fundy increases as one moves inland from the mouth of the bay, and reaches an extreme at the inner end of the Minas Basin at the head of the bay on the Nova Scotia side. Fundy's tides have only been this extreme since the last glaciation. Three factors have combined to produce the current high tides: Fundy's seiche (natural water rocking motion), is 13 hours, which is close to the 12.5-hour tidal change, and thus reinforces it; Fundy Bay narrows and becomes shallower near its head, further amplifying the tidal wave; and the mouth of the bay faces south, directly into the northward moving tidal wave. If any of these three influences change, due to rising ocean levels, earthquake, or continental drift, the tides will become less pronounced. Fundy's tides are impressive not just for their amplitude, but for the volume of water involved; the twice-daily tidal change equals the daily discharge of all the rivers of the world combined, roughly 100 cubic kilometres (24 cubic miles) of water.

The intertidal zone appears a harsh environment, battered by waves, alternately exposed and flooded, hot in summer, crushed with ice in winter, yet there is an abundance of life. Fundy National Park's easy shore access at Alma Beach, combined with the enormous

**Location:** Near the Village of Alma, New Brunswick, on provincial Highway 114. On the west shore of the Bay of Fundy.

**Climate:** Warm continental climate, except tempered near the Bay of Fundy. Inland: warm summers (average temperature 22°C/72°F) with little fog, cold winters with more snow. Coastal: cool summers (average temperature 16°C/6°F) with frequent fog, milder winters with less snow.

**When to go:** Open year-round, but some services and facilities open only May–October.

**Access:** No public transportation to the park. Nearest bus terminals in Sussex and Moncton. Airports in Moncton, Saint John, and Fredericton. By car: from Moncton, take exit 432 on Trans-Canada Hwy (Hwy 2), then southwest on Hwy 114 (one hour drive). From Saint John take Hwy 1 and 114 (two hour drive). Nearest commercial airport in Moncton.

**Facilities:** Visitor Centre (nature store); trails; campgrounds (four frontcountry sites, reservations accepted); on-site exhibits; picnic sites; commercial accommodations; restaurant. Adjacent communities (Alma, Riverside-Albert, Hopewell Hills): commercial accommodations.

**Watching Nature:** Moose and White-tailed Deer; birdwatching: excellent spring and autumn migration along coast; fine opportunities to view intertidal life.

**Visitor Activities:** Hiking; camping; canoeing; picnicking; bowls; golf; swimming (heated saltwater pool); cross-country skiing; tennis; scenic drives; mountain biking; fishing; children's playground; nature photography.

**Special Notes:** (1) Be careful when exploring intertidal areas, and check local tide schedules. (2) Intertidal shellfish are frequently toxic and harvesting is illegal.

The map shows: GREENLAND, CANADA, Quebec, USA, Toronto, NEW BRUNSWICK, To Moncton, To Saint John, Wolfe Lake, Tracey Lake, Laverty Lake, Bennett Lake, 114, Fundy National Park, Alma, Information Centre, Point Wolfe River, Herring Cove, Marven Lake, Point Wolfe, Bay of Fundy, 0 5 km, 0 3 miles

Above: *The covered bridge at Point Wolfe is popular with visitors; historically, bridges were covered to keep the wood protected from the elements.*

Below: *Along the coast at The Hopewell Rocks, just north of the park, the soft cliffs have been eroded by massive tides into bizarre stacks and columns.*

intertidal zone (the exposed muddy bottom of the bay at low tide may extend out for more than a kilometre ($\frac{2}{3}$ mile)) makes the park's coastline the main attraction to many visitors. The mudflats might appear barren, but many odd animals live there, such as Mud Shrimps, clams, and worms, including the Blood Worm (named for its colour), Clam Worm (an iridescence of colours from green through to pink), and Bamboo Worm, which lives in a vertical mud tube. These worms, and other invertebrates, are a vital food source for southward-bound shorebirds, which stop in the millions in the Bay of Fundy to refuel before continuing their flight to South America. At nearby Mary's Point, New Brunswick, hundreds of thousands of Semipalmated Sandpipers congregate on a rising tide in early August, and provide an unforgettable acrobatic show.

Rock outcrops along the shore or on the flats provide an anchor for seaweeds and barnacles, and a wide variety of animals live among the boulders and in tidal pools, including Dog Whelks, Sea Slugs, Periwinkles, and crabs. Salt marshes are not covered by daily high tides, but the highest tides each month inundate them and so their fertility is maintained. The most accessible Salt Marsh is at the mouth of the Upper Salmon River. Herons and waterfowl feed in the marshes here and American Black Ducks nest, as do Nelson's Sharp-tailed Sparrows and Willets. Grand seaside cliffs harbour many hardy plants and animals, including the hardy Roseroot and the dashing Peregrine Falcon. The cliffs are formed from 300 million-year-old sedimentary rock, and often contain well-preserved plant fossils which are exposed by coastal erosion.

## Reintroducing the Wilderness

The Fundy National Park has experienced a number of lamentable extirpations, plants and animals no longer present that once were an important part of the ecosystem. Wolves are high profile absentees, though other species have gone as well. To redress the balance, the park authorities have begun restoration projects to bring at least some of these species back. The American Marten has not fared well anywhere, victim of intensive trapping for fur, and the loss of the mature spruce forests, its preferred habitat. Between 1984 and 1991 38 martens were reintroduced, and subsequent surveys have suggested that a small population has become tenuously established, though numbering only about 15.

Atlantic Salmon are vanishing from New Brunswick's rivers, due to dams, silted spawning beds, global warming, overfishing, and pollution. Attempts to rehabilitate Fundy's Wolfe River, and reintroduce salmon, have so far met with failure. Better success has been achieved with Peregrine Falcons. Perched precariously at the top of its food chain, this dashing bird was nearly wiped out in the 1960s by the accumulation of the insecticide DDT in the environment. In 1982 Fundy National Park began work with the Canadian Wildlife Service to reestablish Peregrines in the upper Bay of Fundy. One of the two original hacking sites was on a cliff above Point Wolfe Cove. Fifty-five birds were released between 1982 and 1988. Currently as many as ten pairs now breed along the Bay of Fundy's cliffs, including one pair that breeds in Fundy National Park.

## Forest Management

Fundy National Park represents the Maritime Acadian Highlands region. The park is bordered by intensively managed forests, which often comprise monocultural tree plantations, or non-native species. To alleviate the potential harmful impacts of such land use, the park has initiated the Greater Fundy Ecosystem Project, in concert with private landholders and lumber companies, to try to manage the forests both within and outside the park.

Above: *At Point Wolfe there is a dramatic daily fluctuation in water level, amplified by the extreme tides of the Bay of Fundy.*

Right: *Despite the loss of other large predators from the area, most notably the wolf, Black Bears may still be found in Fundy National Park.*

# KEJIMKUJIK NATIONAL PARK

## Petroglyphs, Plovers, and Pennyworts

'Los buenos pintores initan la naturaleza.'
(Good painters imitate nature)

MIGUEL DE CERVANTES

Kejimkujik National Park is an important riverine wilderness in the heart of southwestern Nova Scotia. Established in 1967, the main park area covers 404 square kilometres (146 square miles) of island-dotted lakes, stillwater streams and mixed woodlands. The park is bordered by provincial crown land, some in a protected area of Special Significance, and the rest in the Tobeatic Management Area, which help buffer resource extraction activities. The First Nations People of the area, the Mi'kmaq, were keen artists, and evocative petroglyphs representing their life, art, and perception can be seen carved in slate.

In 1988, 22 square kilometres (8½ square miles) of the tip of a peninsula, the Seaside Adjunct, was added to the park to protect the nesting grounds of the endangered Piping Plover along a stretch of Atlantic shoreline.

Opposite, above: *Kejimkujik Lake is popular with canoeists, despite the long portages encountered.*

Opposite, below: *The Mersey River flows through the mixed woodlands in the heart of the park.*

Above, right: *The Purple-fringed Orchid occurs in the park's damp meadows.*

Kejimkujik takes its name from the lake, which was so named by the Mi'kmaq, in reference to the arduous portages required to reach it – Kejimujhik means 'swollen parts'. Despite the long portages, Kejimkujik is popular with canoeists, and its distance from the popular coastal areas has meant that the park is much less visited than many other Canadian parks.

### A Refuge for Rarities

Along the park's lakeshores, the Mi'kmaq's petroglyphs, now faint through erosion, show stylised people, animals, activities, and outlines of objects, including hands. Due to their fragility, these petroglyphs are off-limits, but some can be observed on guided interpretive walks in summer months.

Park staff hope protection of the Seaside Adjunct will improve the breeding success of the Piping Plover. Up to ten pairs of Piping Plover nest on St. Catherine's River beach, and the authorities fence off nests to keep out predators and close the beach to the public during nesting season to prevent disturbance.

One of the rarest plants in the Kejimkujik is Water Pennywort (Hydrocotyle umbellata), a coastal plain plant. The plant occurs only in two localities in Canada, both in south-west Nova Scotia, and is considered an endangered species. Other rare species include the

**Location:** Main park in south-central Nova Scotia. Seaside Adjunct on Atlantic coast, south of Liverpool.

**Climate:** Kejimkujik is a warm pocket: warm, dry weather in summer, winter short and cool, with little snow accumulation. Average daily temperatures: winter -5°C (23°F); spring 10°C (50°F); summer 18°C (65°F); autumn 8°C (46°F). Precipitation at any time of year, 1,400 mm (55 in) annually. Shallow park lakes have warm summer water temperatures. The Seaside Adjunct has air temperatures a few degrees cooler than inland in summer, warmer in winter.

**When to go:** Open year-round, including Visitor Centre, but most facilities and services open May–October. Seaside Adjunct beach areas are closed during Piping Plover nesting season.

**Access:** Main park is accessible off Route 8, by travelling 160 km (100 miles) from Halifax via Hwy 103, or 190 km (118 miles) from Yarmouth via Hwy 101, or 90 km (56 miles) from Digby via Hwy 101. The Seaside Adjunct is 100 km (62 miles) south of the main Park, and is accessible from Highway 103, 25 km (15½ miles) south-west of Liverpool.

**Facilities:** Main park: Visitor Centre; campgrounds concession; playground; supervised beach; canoe and bicycle rentals. Seaside Adjunct: none.

**Watching Nature:** Herptiles: snakes, turtles, salamanders, frogs and toads. Plants: Purple-fringed Orchid and Pitcher Plant. Birding.

**Visitor Activities:** Hiking; camping; picnicking; cycling; canoeing; swimming; fishing; nature photography; cross-country skiing.

Above: *Deciduous trees spread in a wide upper canopy to maximise the capture of sunlight.*

Below, right: *The Scarlet Tanager is one of several bird species found at the northern limit of their range in the park.*

astonishingly loud peeping is heard everywhere there is standing water.

### The Seaside Adjunct

The Seaside Adjunct was an important acquisition for the park, as little of Nova Scotia's coastline remains in public hands. The sole access to the adjunct is via two main hiking trails, which are rough and frequently wet. From Southwest Port Mouton, the old gravel road leads to Black Point 8 kilometres/5 miles away, and the (mostly) boardwalk trail leads from St. Catherine's River, 3 kilometres/2 miles away. Harbour Seals are common on offshore rocks and points, as are Double-crested Cormorants and Common Eiders. Shorebirds are common on the beaches and mudflats, especially in August. The Purple-fringed Orchid occurs in damp meadows, as does the Pitcher Plant.

### Conservation Issues

Kejimkujik National Park is an outstanding example of the Atlantic Coast Uplands natural region. More than most other parks in Canada, the park seems to be especially threatened by acid rain, perhaps due to its southerly location, and being on the receiving end of weather systems travelling from more industrial areas to the west and south.

Northern Ribbon Snake (in Canada it is only found in this region and in extreme southern Ontario), and the Southern Flying Squirrel. Some bird species in the park are at the northern limit of their range in Nova Scotia, such as Scarlet Tanager, Great Crested Flycatcher, and Wood Thrush. Kejimkujik's climate is also conducive to many species of ferns, some with a limited range in Nova Scotia, including Oak Fern, Dwarf Chain Fern, Bog Fern, and Curly-grass Fern.

### Herptile Heaven

Kejimkujik is the most important national park for herptiles in Atlantic Canada. There are five species of snakes, three species of turtles, five species of salamanders, one species of toad, and seven species of frogs. This cornucopia is due to the hot summers and clement winters in this region combined with an abundance and diversity of water, slow-moving rivers and streams, shallow lakes, bogs, and marshes. Of the three species of turtles, Blanding's is the rarest, with an estimated 150 adults in all of Nova Scotia, 95 per cent of which live in the park. The most commonly seen snakes are the Maritime Garter Snake and the Northern Red-bellied Snake, and none of the species of snakes in the park is poisonous. The frogs and toads are usually easier to hear than see, whether the trilling of the American Toad, or the deep voice of the Bullfrogs. Green Frogs are often seen along streams, but the diminutive Northern Spring Peeper is almost never viewed, even during spring, when its

# KOUCHIBOUGUAC NATIONAL PARK

## Of Beaches and Bogs

*'They are the sea made land, to come to the fisher town,*
*And bury in solid sand the man she could not drown.'*
ROBERT FROST, SAND DUNES

Kouchibouguac National Park was established in 1969 and covers an area of 239 square kilometres (92 square miles) of bog, beach and forest. Most of the land is covered in a mixture of forest, both coniferous (Eastern White Cedar, Red Spruce, and Balsam Fir) and deciduous (Red Maple, Yellow Birch, and Trembling Aspen). The park's sheltered coastline is popular with visitors, as it stretches for 25 kilometres (16 miles), and is primarily sand dunes and barrier beaches that protect the salt marshes and lagoons from the full force of the Gulf of St. Lawrence and make the park a popular destination for visitors in the summer. The remainder of the park is flat, with poor drainage, and extensive deep bogs, with sphagnum moss more than 5 metres (16 feet) thick in places.

### Beaches for All

The sandy beaches are very popular because the ocean waters are relatively sheltered and the temperature of the water in summer rises to pleasant levels. However, the high visitor numbers puts pressure on other animals that make it their own temporary home. Common Terns prefer to nest on low-lying sandy islands, where they are safer from ter-

*Above, right: The park's self-guiding interpretive trails enable visitors to learn more about the park environment.*

restrial predators. However, most tern colonies have disappeared from eastern Canada, having been displaced (or predated) by larger, more aggressive, and more adaptable gulls, whose numbers have grown with every garbage dump, sewage pipe, or boatload of discarded fish offal. One of the largest remaining Common Tern colonies (about 5,000 pairs) has remained in the park, but is still vulnerable to disturbance, and is off limits to visitors in nesting season. The Piping Plover is one of the rarest shorebirds in the world, with fewer than 2,500 pairs remaining in North America. They breed exclusively on sandy beaches strewn with small rocks, and must compete for these favoured places with people. To date, the plovers have lost the competition, but in Kouchibouguac their nesting sites are protected, and access is forbidden to these beaches during the nesting season. With such protection the birds' future is not guaranteed, but there is at least hope. Grey and Harbour Seals also enjoy the barrier beaches, and their pups can be seen along the shoreline. Hundreds linger in the park area through the summer.

### A Question of Ownership

To the Mi'kmaq (the First Nations people who first lived along coastal New Brunswick) the main river in the park

**Location:** In Kent County, New Brunswick, on the eastern coast, 100 km (60 miles) north of the city of Moncton.

**Climate:** Humid continental, with warm summers, cold winters, and frequent storms, especially in autumn and winter. Annual precipitation 106 cm (19 in), 40% as snow.

**When to go:** Open year-round, but many facilities and services only available May through October.

**Access:** Either Hwy 126 north from Moncton and Hwy 480 east to the park, or Hwy 15 from Moncton to Shediac, and 11 north along the coast. Nearest airport (daily commercial air service) in Moncton.

**Facilities:** Visitor Centre (nature store); campgrounds; trails (hiking, biking, cross-country skiing); picnic sites; on-site exhibits; outdoor theatre; playground; restaurant; supervised beaches; canoe rentals. Nearby communities: commercial accommodations; medical services; fuel; laundry; restaurants; museums; stores.

**Watching Nature:** Osprey are common in the park; they fish over lagoons. Watch for migrating shorebirds in the Kelly's Beach mudflats in August. Common Terns are a constant sight over water June–August.

**Visitor Activities:** Hiking; nature photography; swimming; canoeing; mountain biking; cross-country skiing; birding.

**Special Notes:** (1) The nesting areas of Piping Plovers are off-limits during breeding season (April–early August). Please obey warning signs.

Above, top: *Black-eyed Susan is a distinctive flower of damp meadows.*

Above: *The Pitcher Plant is a carnivorous species, thriving in damp areas in the park.*

Above, right: *The park's rivers and protected lagoons offer an excellent opportunity for canoeists.*

area was Pejeboogwek, the 'river of the long tides'. This was altered by Europeans to Kouchibouguac (pronounced 'Koosh-uh-boog-oo-whack'). The Mi'kmaq never signed away their rights to the land through treaties, and the matter is still under legal negotiation. European settlers cut the forests (especially White Pine), cleared land for agriculture, and harvested the salt marsh grasses. None of the park's forests are virgin, but are in various stages of successional growth. Kouchibouguac was perhaps the last park in Canada to be established via expropriation, the forced selling of private holdings for the public good. This was understandably an emotional and provocative issue, especially for the local residents, primarily of Acadian descent, whose ancestors had suffered a previous

expulsion at the hands of the then British government. The park was established in 1979 after a decade of expropriation and conflict, but resentments linger, and the issue is not forgotten. The beauty and special nature of the park have, however, created a significant tourism economy, much needed in an area of high unemployment.

## Rising Sea Levels

Kouchibouguac National Park protects a portion of the Appalachian Maritime Plain natural region. The park is under threat from the effect global warming may have on the sea level; the highest point in the park is only 30 metres (100 feet) above sea level. Poaching of animals is also an ongoing concern.

Above: *The park shelters one of the largest colonies of the Common Tern in Canada.*

Left: *Visitor facilities include a boardwalk with a raised viewing platform across the bog.*

Left: *Birds to be seen in the park include the Ruffed Grouse* (far left), *inhabiting the woodlands, and the Killdeer* (left), *along the coastline.*

# Terra Nova National Park

## Sounds, Arms, Reaches and Tickles

*'gaze upon the glory of the Sunset and . . .*
*see an eagle, high above me, flying far.'*

Grey Owl (Wa-sha-quon-asin)

Terra Nova is Canada's easternmost national park and was established in 1957, less than a decade after Newfoundland and Labrador joined the Confederation of Canada. While it is not as large as the federal government had originally hoped, it covers an area of 400 square kilometres (154 square miles) and protects an important landscape in eastern Newfoundland. The park is the only area of protected land along the Atlantic coast of Newfoundland. Unlike other National Parks that border the sea, Terra Nova is dominated by neither forest nor ocean, but is an equal mix of the two, unique among Canada's parks. The forests and bogs are best explored on the park's fine system of hiking and interpretive trails.

### The Island Life

During the last ice age, glaciers scoured the island of Newfoundland, and following the retreat of the ice, only a few mammals colonised the island. However, while there are not many indigenous animal species, many have been introduced to Newfoundland and have thrived, often at the expense of the native species. One species, the

*Above, right: Bald Eagles hunt for fish along the shores of the park.*

Newfoundland Wolf, was wiped out by hunting, and it has not been reintroduced, but coyotes have recently arrived on Newfoundland across the ice from Labrador, and have spread across the province. Snowshoe Hare, Masked Shrew, Red Squirrel, Least Chipmunk, and moose have all been introduced and have flourished. Moose have done especially well, and are more easily seen in Terra Nova than any other national park in Canada. They are so common that collisions between moose and vehicles are a serious problem, with more than 20 such accidents a year. Obey posted speed limits, and be particularly alert at dawn and dusk, when moose are more often near the road.

Mammals are not the only introduced species. Ruffed and Spruce Grouse were brought in as game birds, and several different frog species have been introduced. And as with most of North America, many plants have arrived, either deliberately, through gardens, or inadvertently (as seeds) carried by visitors from the mainland.

### The Ocean Life – Icebergs, Bergy Bits, Slob Ice, and Growlers

Boat tours of Terra Nova's sounds, arms, and reaches are very popular. There is a small Atlantic Puffin

**Location:** On the east coast of the island of Newfoundland.

**Climate:** Continental, but with maritime influences. Cold, snowy winters, cool springs, warm in summer and autumn.

**When to go:** Open year-round, but many facilities and services only open May–early October.

**Access:** From the Trans-Canada Highway, 240 km (150 miles) north-west of St. John's, and 80 km (50 miles) south-east of Gander. Nearest commercial airport is Gander.

**Facilities:** Visitor Centre (nature store); trails; picnic sites; on-site exhibits; campgrounds; playground; outdoor theatre; boat launch; wharf. Nearby communities (Glovertown, Clarenville, Port Blandford, Gander): all facilities and services.

**Watching Nature:** Moose, along roadsides at dawn or dusk. Whales and icebergs on saltwater boat tours.

**Visitor Activities:** Hiking; picnicking; canoeing; ocean-going boat tours; scenic driving tours; golfing; scuba diving; cross-country skiing; fishing.

**Special Notes:** (1) Drive carefully; collisions with moose occur regularly, especially at dawn or dusk. (2) Mosquitos and Black Flies can be abundant in summer.

*Map labels: GREENLAND; CANADA; Quebec; USA; Toronto; To Gander; Glovertown; Broad Cove; Louil Hills; Terra Nova River; Newman Sound; Swale Island; Mount Stamford; Information Centre; Lion's Den Bay; Bread Cove Hills; Terra Nova National Park; Terra Nova; Ochre Hill; Platters Beach; Cannings Cove; Clode Sound; Information Centre; To St John's; 0 5 km; 0 3 miles*

colony, Humpback Whales are regularly sighted, and at the right time of year there are some spectacular icebergs. Glaciers retreated long ago from Newfoundland, but they still exist in northern latitudes, especially in Baffin Island and Greenland where massive glaciers

move slowly downslope eventually meeting the sea where pieces break off ('calve') and drift with the ocean currents. The numbers of icebergs formed each year varies, but 1,000 or more will break off in an average year, of which 400 or so will survive the several-year journey on arctic currents to Newfoundland's waters. A true iceberg is a deep blue-green colour, the result of minute particles of bedrock scraped by the glaciers. Quite distinct from this is the white sea ice (known as 'slob ice') that forms on the Arctic Ocean in winter, and is carried southward by currents along with the icebergs. As the ice gradually melts, icebergs frequently break apart into smaller pieces, called 'bergy bits' or 'growlers'.

The best time to view the icebergs is from May through to mid-July and local boats may be chartered for a closer inspection. Although the boat captains are experienced there is an element of danger in viewing icebergs. As much as 75 per cent of the ice lies below water level and underwater ice shelves can cause a lot of damage to a boat. Icebergs can also suddenly calve at any time, and can cause waves and whirlpools that can be treacherous. If conditions do not allow an approach by boat, there is a telescope on the viewing tower on either Blue Hill or Ochre Hill that enables a closer view of the massive icebergs drifting southward to their destruction.

## Too Small for Security

Terra Nova National Park protects the Eastern Newfoundland Atlantic natural region. Had the park been established with the originally intended 1,000 square kilometres (400 square miles), it would be more secure than it is today, but the province retained areas considered valuable for timber or hydroelectric resources, and so the park is coming increasingly under threat from heavy logging at its borders. Trapping and poaching are also concerns, and island-nesting birds may be disturbed by too-close approaches by boats, and are adversely affected by the over fishing in coastal waters.

Above: *Sunrise illuminates an impressive panorama across the hills and waters of Newman Sound and Eastport Bay.*

Left: *The striking Blue Flag Iris grows in the park's wetland areas.*

Left: *Jellyfish thrive in the nutrient-rich waters of the park.*

# NORTH OF 60°

'And the North, silent, eerie and primordial, filled with magic, peopled with...spirits, and things mentioned only in a legend, now comes into its own, and swallows up the little camp, immersing it in the loneliness of a thousand leagues of Wilderness, engulfing it in the vastness of immeasurable and unimaginable Distance'. Grey Owl (Wa-sha-quon-asin)

Nowhere else in Canada do the First Nations and Aboriginal cultures so dominate life. And nowhere else does winter so dominate the climate. The Yukon Territory, Northwest Territories, and Nunavut stretch west to east across Canada's Arctic, difficult to access, and unvisited by most Canadians or anyone else. The landscape is vast, and so are the parks. And so are the economic problems, as the Aboriginals' lifestyles shift from mobile to sedentary, with attendant adjustment problems. But their culture, and their pride, persist.

The Yukon is mostly mountainous, with lower flatter areas towards the Arctic Ocean. The Northwest Territories are immense, with the MacKenzie Mountains in the west, the Tundra Hills along the Arctic Ocean, the islands of the Western Arctic Lowlands, and Boreal Uplands to the Southeast. Nunavut, Canada's newest autonomous territory, holds the icy, mountainous islands of the High Arctic, an extensive tundra region on the mainland, Baffin Island, and all of Hudson Bay. Northerners love their land, and are eager to share it with those who take the time, trouble, and expense of reaching there. The northern National Parks are nonpareil, and if but one is accessible by road, all are accessible to the spirit. This is, unarguably, Canada's true wilderness.

# KLUANE NATIONAL PARK RESERVE

## Canada on High

*'...and snowy summits old in story'*

ALFRED, LORD TENNYSON

N one of the mountains and glaciers in British Columbia and Alberta can rival the height of the St. Elias Mountains in the western Yukon, the heart and soul of Kluane National Park Reserve. The highest mountain in Kluane, Mt. Logan, is 5,959 metres (19,545 feet) high, and is the highest peak in Canada and the second-highest in North America. Established as a National Park Reserve

Opposite above: *Seen from Haines Junction, the mighty St. Elias Mountains form an impressive backdrop to the vast wilderness of Kluane.*

Opposite, below left: *In summer Grizzly Bears move up from the lowland valleys into alpine meadows.*

Opposite, below right: *Dall Sheep are the commonest large mammal in the park.*

Above right: *The wolverine is a nomadic predator, travelling great distances in search of food.*

Previous pages:
Page 146: *From Summit Lake, the Weasel River Valley winds deep into the glacial interior of Auyittuq National Park.* Page 147: *Arctic Poppies thrive in the almost constant sunlight of the brief northern summer.*

in 1972, Kluane covers a vast area of wilderness (22,015 square kilometres/8,467 square miles) and contains the greatest array of large mammals in North America, including moose, caribou, Grizzly Bears, Black Bears, Dall Sheep and Mountain Goats. Eighty-two per cent of the park is mountain and ice, with the remainder a narrow band of valleys and lakes where most of the plants and animals occur.

### A Quick History

Kluane National Park Reserve is the homeland of the Southern Tutchone First Nations people. Over thousands of years these people (known as 'Dan') have developed effective methods for coping with the extreme conditions of this wilderness land. Their remarkable knowledge of seasonal variations and periodic fluctuations in animal and plant populations over many years has been passed on through oral tradition from generation to generation and has ensured that their culture remains potent today.

Kluane is named after Kluane Lake (which the Southern Tutchone called 'Lu'An Mün', meaning 'lake with many fish'), the largest in the Yukon. The Southern Tutchone traded first with the Tlingit First Nations of the Pacific coast, and later with the Europeans, who moved into the area in search of wealth. The wealth came from

**Location:** In the south-west corner of the Yukon Territory, bordering St. Elias Park and Glacier Bay National Park in Alaska, and Tatshenshini-Alsek Wilderness Park in British Columbia. Nearest town: Haines Junction, Yukon.

**Climate:** Dry, cold continental climate, volatile, with mountain and oceanic influences.

Extreme temperatures 33°C (91°F) and -50°C (-58°F). Mean temperatures: June (11°C/52°F); January (-21°C/-6°C). Hours of daylight: 19 in June, 4 in December. Frost or snow can occur at any time.

**When to Go:** Open year-round, but most park access and tourist facilities and services, late May–September.

**Access:** Via the Alaska Hwy from the east (160 km/100 miles to Whitehorse), or the Haines Road from the south (249 km/156 miles to Haines, Alaska). Commercial airport in Whitehorse with daily flights from Vancouver. The Alaska Marine Highway ferry system services Haines or Skagway.

**Facilities:** Trails; two Visitor Centres; campgrounds. Haines Junction: commercial accommodations; campgrounds; fuel; stores; medical services.

**Watching Nature:** Mountains and glaciers; Grizzly Bears; Dall Sheep; birds.

**Visitor Activities:** Hiking; cycling; mountain biking; horseback riding; fishing; white-water rafting; mountaineering; boating; canoeing; cross-country skiing; snowshoeing; dog sledding.

**Special Notes:** All backcountry travel requires pre-registration.

*Map labels:*
ALASKA
CANADA
Vancouver
YUKON TERRITORY
Burwash Landing
Kluane Lake
Destruction Bay
Mt Steele
CENTENNIAL RANGE
ST ELIAS MOUNTAINS
Kluane National Park
Mt Queen Mary
Mt Logan
5950m
(19522ft)
ICEFIELD RANGE
Mt Elias
5488m
(18006ft)
KLUANE RANGE
Beer Creek
Haines Junction
Dezadeash Lake
Kathleen Lakes
0  25 km
0  15 miles
ALASKA
BRITISH COLUMBIA

furs initally, though later from minerals, particularly gold. There was, however, little gold in the Kluane area, and the famous Klondike gold rush largely passed the area by. The area was not so fortunate to evade the effects of World War II, and the risk of an invasion prompted the Americans to pay for the construction of the world-renowned Alaska Highway in 1942, which is now one of the few major access routes to the park.

## Ice on the Move

The St. Elias Mountains would dominate any landscape, but in Kluane their presence is augmented by the proximity of the largest icefields in the world south of the Arctic Circle. Moist air from the Pacific Ocean deposits large amounts of snow on the glaciers, which in turn move downslope in fits and starts, usually 5 to 10 metres (15 to 30 feet) a year (though occasionally they can surge ahead as much as 1 kilometre (¾ mile) in a year). Around 1725, the 65-kilometre (40-mile) long Lowell Glacier moved downslope and blocked the Alsek River valley, forming an ice-dam that created an enormous lake that covered the site where the town of Haines Junction now stands. The dam gave way 125 years later, and the lake drained in the space in just two days. The effects of the resulting massive flood (an estimated 41 cubic kilometres/10 cubic miles of water flooded into the area) are visible today, as water scoured the landscape, depositing gravel in its wake and removing all vegetation and soil.

The Southern Tutchone First Nations have always had a healthy respect for glaciers, especially the Lowell (which they call Naludi), as they believe them to be living creatures that can swallow a person whole. A lake still lies at the foot of Lowell Glacier, though is now much smaller, and a boat can be taken to approach the inland 'icebergs' that have calved from the glacier.

## Flora and Fauna

Kluane, though south of the Arctic Circle, is still considered by Canadians as being 'north'. However, its relatively 'southerly' position and its proximity to the moist climatic influences of the Pacific Ocean have resulted in a greater diversity of plant and animal species than elsewhere in Canada's 'north'. The greatest variety is below the tree line where it is warmer, although more than 200 types of alpine plants grow in the harsh zone above the trees (but below the ice zone). There are not as many trees this far north as there are at Point Pelee National Park in Ontario, but Trembling Aspen and Balsam Poplar are the common deciduous trees, while White Spruce is the dominant conifer.

Many species of large mammals live in Kluane National Park. The most common large mammal is the Dall Sheep, which is most readily viewed (albeit at a distance) on the sides of Sheep Mountain. The sheep are easiest to spot in spring or autumn and there is a viewing telescope at the Sheep Mountain Visitor Centre to give you a better chance of spotting them. Keep an eye out also for Mountain Goats. In the lower areas, especially near water, you might see a moose – the local race is the largest in the world. Both Grizzly and Black Bears live in Kluane; the larger Grizzly Bears move between pine meadows and lowland valleys, whereas Black Bears live in the forests. Other mammals that live in Kluane are the elusive wolverine, Hoary Marmot, River Otter, and Arctic Ground Squirrel. There

are not as many birds in this park as there are in more temperate areas, but there are some interesting species, including White-tailed Ptarmigan, Golden Eagle, Gyrfalcon, Golden-crowned Sparrow, and Brewer's (Timberline) Sparrow.

## People and Poaching

Kluane National Park Reserve represents the Northern Coast Mountains natural region. Poaching is one of the more serious problems facing the park, and there are pressures to allow more visitor access away from the highway corridor.

Above: *The sparse deciduous forests in this northern latitude include Birch, Trembling Aspen and Balsam Poplar.*

Opposite, above: *Mount Alsek is permanently covered in snow.*

Opposite, below: *The Kaskawulsh Glacier forms part of the largest icefield in the world south of the Arctic Circle.*

Left: *Wolves can range over vast distances in search of prey.*

Overleaf: *Fireweed brings a blaze of colour to the alpine meadows of Kluane.*

# Auyuittuq National Park

## *The Land That Never Melts*

*'The Arctic trails have their secret tales...'*
Robert Service, The Cremation of Sam McGee

Canadians consider themselves people of the north, but only a small number have ever travelled north of 60°, and fewer have ventured to Auyuittuq to walk the exhilarating Aksayook Pass, ski across the Highway glacier, or admire the defiant cliffs of Mount Thor. Auyuittuq was set aside in 1972 and established as a national park in 1976, and covers a huge area of land (19,707 square kilometres/8,588 square miles). It does take some effort to reach the park, but with determination, preparation, and time visitors will be rewarded with stunning scenery of fjords, serrated mountains, and glacially carved valleys that are crowned by an immense ice sheet, the Penny Ice Cap. Rivers of ice extend outward from the cap, carving steep-sided valleys in the mountains, and, during the brief arctic summers, creating cold, fast rivers that race to the Arctic Ocean.

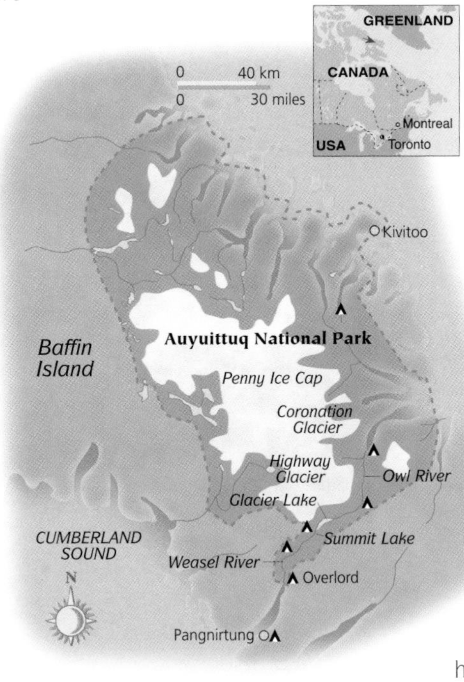

GREENLAND
CANADA
Montreal
Toronto
USA
0 40 km
0 30 miles
Kivitoo
Auyuittuq National Park
Baffin Island
Penny Ice Cap
Coronation Glacier
Highway Glacier
Owl River
Glacier Lake
Summit Lake
CUMBERLAND SOUND
Weasel River
Overlord
N
Pangnirtung


Opposite: *The precipitous cliffs of Mount Thor loom over a dramatic landscape, where the well-prepared and determined visitor can enjoy a memorable wilderness experience.*

Above, right: *There are few visitor facilities in the park, although emergency shelters have been erected at the campsite by Windy Lake.*

### *Aksayook Pass*

Most visitors to Auyuittuq hike across the Aksayook Pass (formerly known as Pangnirtung Pass), a peak-encircled valley that connects North and South Pangnirtung Fjords. The high point of the pass is only 400 metres (1,312 feet) high and is ice-free during the short summer. A popular walk is from the head of South Pangnirtung Fjord along the Weasel River to Summit and Glacier Lakes (the half-way point of the pass), a return distance of 103 kilometres (61 miles). It is possible to walk the entire length of the pass (over 100 kilometres/60 miles), and most who do this begin from the head of North Pangnirtung Fjord, having flown first to Qikitarjuaq. Departures from either Pangnirtung or Qikitarjuaq are dependent upon sea-ice conditions. Boats are used, but when the ice is firm snowmobiles are used, and during the break-up of the ice no access is possible.

The hike up Aksayook Pass provides views of the stunning landscapes of the Penny Highlands, including Mount Overlord (Pangniqtup Qingua to the Inuit), Mount Asgard (Sivanitirutinguak), Turner Glacier (Auyuittuit), and especially the imposing Mount Thor (Qaisualuk). At 1,500 metres (4,920 feet), these are

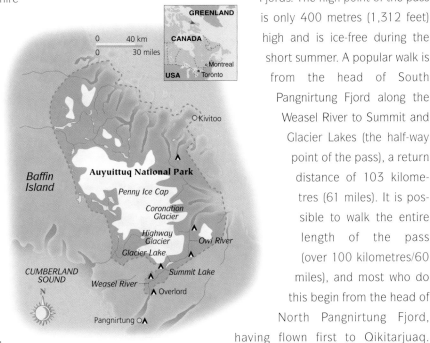

**Location:** On Baffin Island, on the north shore of the Cumberland Peninsula. Almost all the park is above the Arctic Circle.

**Climate:** Arctic, combined with unpredictable mountain effects. High temperatures: July 11°C (50°F), winter -23°C (-11°F). 36 cm (14 in) of precipitation annually, mostly snow. Snow possible anytime. Frequent strong winds.

**When to Go:** Park offices are open year-round, and the park itself never 'closes', though the latitude and climate combine to restrict most visits late May–mid-October. Most visit mid-July–mid-August.

**Access:** By jet to Iqaluit, NWT, from Montréal, Ottawa, and Yellowknife, and from Nuuk, Greenland. Then charter flight from Iqaluit to Qikitarjuaq, Broughton Island or Pangnirtung, Baffin Island. Use local outfitters to travel from the park to Pangnirtung or Qikitarjuaq, using boat (when fjord is ice-free, mid-July–mid-October) or snowmobile. To arrange outfitters, consult Visitor Centre in Pangnirtung, or staff in Qikitarjuaq.

**Facilities:** Park Administration and Visitor Centre in Pangnirtung. Warden office in Qikitarjuaq (April–September). No facilities in the park, except emergency shelters.

**Watching Nature:** Marine mammals: seals, whales, walrus. Land mammals: Arctic Fox, caribou, wolf. Birds: Rock Ptarmigan, Snowy Owl, Gyrfalcon. Plants: Arctic Poppy and Lapland Rosebay.

**Visitor Activities:** Hiking, mountain and cliff climbing, Nordic skiing, snowmobiling, dog-sledding, fishing.

**Special Notes:** (1) Personal safety is the visitor's responsibility. Be provisioned with the proper equipment, knowledge, skills and physical fitness. Consult Park staff throughout your trip planning. (2) Never approach Polar Bears.

## The People of the North

The Inuit have inhabited Baffin Island for thousands of years, almost always near the coast, as marine mammals and birds provided most of what they needed to survive. The Thule, the ancestors of the modern Inuit, built stone houses along Baffin's coast, and many of the foundations are still visible. Europeans first visited in 1585, and reports of whales enticed a community of Scots to establish a settlement at Kivitoo, near Qikitarjuaq (Broughton Island). Evidence of whaling activity remains at Kivitoo and at Kekerten Island Territorial Park in Cumberland Sound.

## Be Prepared

This immense park poses a challenge to every prospective visitor, at any time of year. It is possible to charter outfitters from Pangnirtung or Qikitarjuaq to take a day-trip visit to the edge of the park, but many prefer a more enduring experience, venturing into the park for days at a time. Such visits should never be undertaken lightly, and require a great deal of preparation and provisioning. Park Staff, and prospective outfitters, should be consulted before and during all preparations. However, even with all the advice sought beforehand, once you are in the park you are on your own, and you should not anticipate any easy or swift rescue if you encounter difficulties. Auyuittuq is pure wilderness, and should be treated with respect.

Above: *The Arctic Fox is a versatile predator that will often scavenge from the kills of larger animals.*

Below: *In summer a torrent of glacial meltwater rushes down the Weasel River Valley.*

some of the highest cliffs in the world. An equally impressive sight is the Schwartzenbach Falls (Qulitasaniakvik) which descends 600 metres (2,200 feet) to the Weasel River. Harder sections of the Aksayook Pass are marked with inukshuks (stone cairns), to indicate the safest routes across glacial moraines and rivers, and to minimize damage to arctic vegetation. Most hikers view the overhanging glaciers from a distance, though it is possible to venture up side valleys to view the ice cap more closely.

Left: Remnants of winter pack ice are stranded, and melt along the rocky shores of Cumberland Sound.

Bottom left: *Male caribou boast massive antlers during the rutting season; females bear smaller antlers.*

## The Fragile Arctic

Auyuittuq protects part of the Eastern Baffin Island Shelf marine region, and the Northern Davis natural region. Although visitors do contribute to local economies, the driving force for the establishment of the park was the need to protect these areas of Arctic wilderness. Even though there are only a few hundred visitors a year, the fragile arctic ecosystem can withstand little impact, and special care must be taken to avoid damaging the delicate landscape.

Left: *Moss Campion is a distinctive flowering plant of the tundra.*

Below: *A pod of Beluga Whales stands out amongst the broken sea ice.*

# NAHANNI NATIONAL PARK

## The Inaugural World Heritage Site

*'The Northern Lights have seen queer sights...'*
ROBERT SERVICE, THE CREMATION OF SAM MCGEE

In 1978 Nahanni National Park was made one of the first UNESCO World Heritage Sites. The park protects 300 kilometres (186 miles) of the South Nahanni River, roughly 80 per cent of this Canadian Heritage River, and approximately 800 visitors make the trip down the river each summer. Those who paddle the river see an array of remarkable sights, including unusually high hotsprings, and a waterfall that is twice the size of Niagara Falls. Hell's Gate, Funeral Range, Deadman's Valley, Headless Creek, Sunblood Mountain and Twisted Mountain are just some of the ominously-named places paddlers pass along the route, beneath the shimmering watch of the northern Aurora.

Opposite, above: *Colossal cliffs enclose the Nahanni River, most of which flows through the park, offering an adventurous trip for experienced canoeists and kayakers.*

Opposite, below left: *Trumpeter Swans are rare breeders in the park.*

Opposite, below right: *The raven, a bird of proven intelligence, is an opportunist, and takes advantage of seasonally available foods, including carrion.*

Above, right: *Park access is usually by chartered floatplane from Fort Simpson, landing upstream of Virginia Falls.*

### Hotsprings and Waterfalls

Along the river, there are two venues that have a unique appeal. The first is the Rabbitkettle Hotsprings, at the north-western edge of the park. It is a zone of special preservation and access can only be made under the supervision of a park warden. The hot springs, filled with calcium carbonate that has been building up since the last glaciation from deeply buried sedimentary rock (at a rate of 2 mm per year/$^1/_{10}$ in per year), rise from 2,000 metres (6,600 feet) below the surface. The springs bubble up through cracks in the rock and when they reach the surface they cool down, depositing impressive 'Tufa' mounds of calcium.

The second venue is the site of one of the finest waterfalls in the world, the Virginia Falls. The waterfall is 125 metres (416 feet) high and 200 metres (656 feet) wide, and flows around an enormous slab of rock. The Falls are the pivotal section of the river. Upstream from the Falls, the river descends gradually through a gentler landscape, meandering as it flows, whereas downstream from the Falls the river descends quickly, cutting an erratic course through narrow, steep-sided canyons and offering an unparalled white-water challenge to river-runners that have to navigate whirlpools, rapids, and eddies. Beyond the Falls, the river contin-

*Map labels:* Rabbitkettle Hotsprings · Hell Roaring Creek · South Nahanni River · ALASKA · CANADA · Vancouver · Virginia Falls · Figure-8 Rapids · Nahanni National Park · Third Canyon · Yukon Territory · Wildmint Mineral Springs · Second Canyon · First Canyon · Northwest Territories · 0 40 km · 0 20 miles · To Fort Liard

**Location:** In the south-west corner of the Northwest Territories, south-west of Fort Simpson.

**Climate:** Short warm summers and long cold winters.

**When to Go:** The park is 'open' year-round, but river travel is only practical in summer, and commercial trips are only offered at that time.

**Access:** Visitors usually take commercial flights to Fort Simpson, NWT, and then charter a float plane or helicopter into the park. No motorised craft permitted in the park, other than warden patrol craft. The majority of visitors are overnight river trippers. All visitors must register in advance at the Parks Canada office in Fort Simpson, north-east of the park. The Laird Hwy, from Fort Nelson, British Columbia, provides road access to Blackstone Territorial Park, 64 km (41 miles) from the eastern park boundary.

**Facilities:** A few trails and portages, and several backcountry camp sites. Basic services in Fort Simpson.

**Watching Nature:** Wildlife frequently allow close approach by canoes, kayaks, or rafts. Moose are seen, and occasionally Dall Sheep. Trumpeter Swans are rare breeders, but you are more likely to see Osprey, Golden Eagle, or Bald Eagle overhead, and Peregrine Falcons nest on the canyon cliffs.

**Visitor Activities:** Canoeing, kayaking, rafting, and hiking short trails. Nature photography.

**Special Notes:** Know your limits, especially if travelling independently. Many careless visitors have lost their lives along the South Nahanni River.

Right: *Virginia Falls is twice the height of the better-known Niagara.*

ues its descent through four canyons and leaves the park upstream from Nahanni Butte.

### Enduring Mysteries

The river and the park are named after the ancient inhabitants of the region, known by the nearby Athapaskan First Nations people as the Naha Dene (or Nahande), meaning 'people of the west'. The first European traders called them 'Nahanies'. The Naha Dene were an aggressive people, frequently raiding others from their remote home in the MacKenzie Mountains. A local story relates how the victimised tribes eventually took it upon themselves to retaliate, but when they reached the main Naha Dene encampment they found it deserted, and no sign of the Naha Dene has been discovered since. Intriguingly, however, the Navaho Indians of Arizona, 3,000 kilometres (1,875 miles) to the south, believe their ancestors came

from northern Canada, and the Slavey First Nations people, who currently reside in the Nahanni area, can understand the Navaho language, but not that of the First Nations in between. Are the Navahos the descendants of the missing Naha Dene?

Although many of the early European explorers sought furs, others chased gold, especially in the aftermath of the great gold rush in the Klondike in the neighbouring Yukon Territory. Two such prospectors were Willie and Frank McLeod, brothers of Métis heritage, who explored the Flat and Nahanni Rivers in approximately 1905. There are reports that the brothers were seen with gold after their first exploration, but sometime later their headless bodies were found in 1907 near a creek mouth flowing into the Nahanni River. The cause of their demise, and the source of their purported gold, has never been determined, but the story has endured through the naming of places such as Headless Creek, Deadman's Valley, and Funeral Range. The search for the source of the legendary gold continues to this day.

### Restricting River-Runners

Nahanni National Park protects a portion of the MacKenzie Mountains natural region. The park is long and narrow, and it is hoped that negotiations with nearby First Nations groups will increase the park's size. The park's popularity with river-runners requires that park staff impose strict quotas on use of the river. Potential mining developments outside the park may also pose a risk.

Below: *Ospreys feed exclusively on fish, and are widespread along the rivers of the park.*

# Wapusk National Park

## Land of the 'White Bear'

*'...a monstrous blot on a swampy spot, with a partial view of the frozen sea.'*
R. Ballantyne 1846

Wapusk was established in 1996 and is the largest national park in Canada that lies completely south of 60 degrees north. The park is mostly tundra and covers an area 11,475 square kilometres (4,413 square miles). The park protects the Polar Bear, and takes its name from a Cree Indian word for 'white bear'. The Churchill area west of the park is often touted as the 'Accessible Arctic', although as it lies at only 58 degrees north, it is not technically in the true Arctic. However, due to the cooling influence of Hudson Bay the landscape, climate, plants, and animals are all typical of landscapes normally found much further north.

Wapusk National Park is a low-lying, poorly drained plain sloping gently towards Hudson Bay. It is underlain by continuous permafrost, and blanketed by the most extensive cover of peat in North America. Half the land is lakes, bogs, fens, streams and rivers. With the retreat of the glaciers and the removal of the great weight of ice, the land is rebounding 1 metre (3 feet) per century, forming prominent beach ridges that protrude through the flat landscape. Inland from the treeless coast, the tundra mixes with ele-

*Above, right: Arctic plants such as the Stemless Raspberry grow in the thick layer of peat that blankets the continuous layer of permafrost beneath.*

ments of boreal forest, especially Tamarack and Black Spruce. In addition to Polar Bears, the park protects hundreds of thousands of breeding waterfowl and shorebirds, especially Snow Geese; the colony near La Perouse Bay exceeds 100,000 birds.

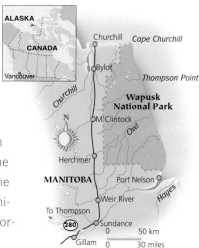

## 'Wapusk'

Polar Bears (Ursus maritimus) are the largest land carnivores in North America. Adult males weigh 300–450 kilogrammes (660–1,000 pounds) and adult females weigh 160–275 kilogrammes (350–610 pounds). The population in northern Manitoba is the most southerly in the world, and more accessible to visitors than any other. The bears favour the park area for denning sites. Summer dens, 6 metres (20 feet) deep, are dug into the permafrost and are used to escape summer heat. Some dens are centuries old. Pregnant females use dens in winter to hibernate and give birth, while males and non-pregnant females hunt seals on the ice of Hudson Bay. All Polar Bears, except young cubs still with their mothers, are exceptionally powerful, and capable of speeds of over 48 kilometres per hour (29 miles per hour), though they are usually seen resting or strolling. Polar Bears are consumate hunters. They are the most predatory of any bear species, and feed largely on seals, which they capture with stealth and speed: they are strong swimmers, run well up- or downhill, have an acute sense of smell, good hearing,

**Location:** East of the town of Churchill, in northern Manitoba.

**Climate:** In summer, temperatures range from 35°C–0°C (95°F–32°F), while in autumn it is stormy with temperatures 25°C–15°C (80°F–58°F). In winter, expect severe Arctic conditions: temperatures can be below -40°C (40°F) for weeks at a time. It is almost always windy along the shores of Hudson Bay.

**When to Go:** Polar Bear tours in September and October. Visits for other wildlife and plant life June–August.

**Access:** Churchill is accessible by daily air service from Winnipeg, via Thompson. Passenger train service is available from Winnipeg in summer. Those wishing independent travel into Wapusk must contact park authorities.

**Facilities:** There are no facilities within the park. A Visitor Centre is located in Churchill. Churchill also hosts commercial accommodations (motels, B&Bs); museum; gas station; restaurants; other stores.

**Watching Nature:** Most nature exploration is done in the Churchill area. Birdwatching in June; wildflowers, butterflies and Beluga Whales in July; autumn colours in August; Polar Bears in September and October. It is popular in winter to view the Northern Lights.

**Visitor Activities:** Hiking, canoeing, organised tours on 'Tundra Buggies' to view Polar Bears.

**Special Notes:** Treat Polar Bears with the utmost respect.

Above: *In autumn, the yellow leaves of the Arctic Willow provide a striking contrast to those of the Bearberry, known to natives as Kinnikinik.*

Right: *Fall comes early in the Arctic; the tundra is a blaze of colour in August, when leaves of the diminutive perennial plants and dwarf trees turn to an autumn palette.*

Opposite: *The Polar Bear, 'Nanook' to the Inuit, fasts during the short Arctic summer, and though it is often seemingly docile and approachable during this time, it is capable of surprising speed and agility.*

and good vision. Visitors should be in no doubt that Polar Bears are dangerous animals and must be treated with the utmost respect. They are most common in Wapusk National Park between July and November, though they may be encountered at any time of the year, anywhere in the park. In the Churchill area, the number of Polar Bears is approximately 1,200, and many congregate near Cape Churchill in autumn as they await the freezing of Hudson Bay.

### Other Tundra Attractions

Most visitors to Churchill do not venture beyond the coastal edge of the park proper, but still experience the wonders of the tundra landscape. Birdwatchers come in June, the nesting season, and seek out Ross' Gull, Harris' Sparrow, Smith's Longspur, and Gray-cheeked Thrush, among many other species. In July and early August the Arctic wildflowers put on a tremendous show (Lapland Rosebay, Mountain-Avens, Purple Saxifrage), and hundreds of Beluga Whales feed in the mouth and estuary of the Churchill River. Northern Butterflies are also a speciality, including White-veined Arctic, Theano Alpine, and Cranberry Blue. Mammals other than Polar Bears are also seen, including caribou, Arctic and Red Fox, and muskrat.

### An Ancient Settlement

The area around Churchill, Manitoba, has been occupied by Dene and Cree tribes, and used by the Inuit, for thousands of years. The first Europeans arrived in 1619, and the rivers flowing in Hudson Bay were the conduit for the exploration of Canada. The Agreement establishing Wapusk National Park provides for the traditional subsistence use of the land by First Nations and other local residents (particularly Métis), for fishing, trapping, gathering, and hunting.

### Hazards of Independent Travel

In and around Churchill, independent travel is feasible, although many visitors come to the area as part of a nature tour. Away from the Churchill area, however, independent exploration must be very carefully planned, and most visitors view autumn Polar Bears through commercial tour operators. For those preparing to go it alone, there are a number of hazards to bear in mind: unpredictable weather (including frequent storms); frostbite; hypothermia and snowblindness caused by snowstorms; 5-kilometre (3-mile) wide soft tidal mud-flats and no shelter for boats; unstable sea, lake, and river ice; swift, cold, deep river crossings; abundant biting insects in summer; rabies in foxes and wolves; the presence of Polar and Black Bears, and occasionally Grizzly Bears.

### The Regulation of Resources

Wapusk National Park protects a significant portion of the Hudson Bay-James Bay Lowlands natural region. Threats could include improperly regulated local use of park resources, and the unpredictable effects of global warming.

# Ivvavik National Park and Vuntut National Park

## Under the Northern Lights

*'The Arctic trails have their secret tales...'*
ROBERT SERVICE, THE CREMATION OF SAM MCGEE

The northern Yukon is a land removed from the daily lives of Canadians, and it long seemed unnecessary to protect the seemingly endless Arctic landscape within the borders of a National Park. However, by 1984, oil exploration and mineral prospecting convinced the local native people, the Inuvialuit, to insist that the creation of a national park be incorporated into their land claim settlement. Vunut National Park arose similarly from the settlement with the Vuntut Gwitchin First Nation people. The two parks are contiguous, but are administered separately. Ivvavik (which means 'a place for giving birth', in reference to the caribou in the park) protects 10,168 square kilometres (3,926 square miles)

and Vuntut (which means 'among the lakes') protects 4,345 square kilometres (1,671 square miles). Both parks are co-managed by park staff and the representatives from each First Nations group.

*Opposite, above: Ivvavik National Park was created as part of the land settlement with the local native people, the Inuvialuit.*

*Opposite, below: Vuntut National Park is contiguous with Ivvavik. Together the two parks shelter the world's largest single caribou herd.*

*Above, right: The Red-necked Phalarope migrates north to Vuntut from as far south as Argentina, to breed in the food-rich tundra summer.*

### Wildlife

The Porcupine Caribou herd ranges over an enormous area, migrating through Vuntut en route to their calving grounds in Ivvavik. The herd, numbering 180,000, is one of the largest in the world, and is a tenth of the world's caribou population. Arctic Wolves can be seen in the park following caribou, and Grizzly Bears and Polar Bears also inhabit the region, the latter closer to the coast. Musk Oxen spend most of their time in the tundra at lower elevations, and in the British Mountains Dall Sheep roam at the northern limit of their range. Almost every breeding bird in the area is a migrant, for the winters are too harsh for all but a few. Waterfowl and shorebirds thrive in the insect-rich long summer days, and the Old Crow Flats of Vuntut are visited by hundreds of thousands of breeding birds. Some of the migrants travel staggering distances; for example, Red-necked Phalaropes overwinter in Argentina, and Arctic Terns fly all the way to Antarctica. Snowy Owls and Gyrfalcons, Arctic specialities, breed here, as do other raptors, including Peregrine Falcons and Long-tailed Jaegers.

**Location:** Vuntut: the north-west of the Yukon Territory, bounded by Ivvavik National Park to the north, Alaska and the Arctic National Wildlife Refuge to the west, Black Fox Creek to the east and the Old Crow River to the south. Ivvavik: the extreme north-west corner of the Yukon, bordered to the south by Vuntut National Park, to the west by Alaska, and the north by the Arctic Sea.

**Climate:** Volatile and unpredictable. Temperatures can fluctuate wildly: in July, they can range from just below freezing to 25°C (80F).

**When to Go:** May–October.

**Access:** Vuntut: From Old Crow, itself accessible by air from Whitehorse, Dawson or Inuvik. From Old Crow, access park by air or river. Ivvavik: From Inuvik, itself accessible via the Dempster Highway, or from commercial air service to southern Canada. From Inuvik, access park by air or coastal boat charter.

**Facilities:** Vuntut and Ivvavik National Parks: no facilities or services in either park. Standard services in Inuvik, limited services in Old Crow: contact park officials in advance.

**Watching Nature:** Caribou; Arctic Wolves; Grizzly Bears; Polar Bears (closer to the coast); Musk Oxen; Dall Sheep; migrant birds.

**Visitor Activities:** Hiking, camping, rafting (Firth River), nature photography, canoeing.

**Special Notes:** (1) Independent travellers must be entirely self-sufficient and able to handle any emergency on their own. (2) Landing permits required for all aircraft in the park. (3) The use of Personal Locator Beacons is strongly recommended.

Above: *Dall Sheep are found in the British Mountains at the northern limit of their range.*

Below: *The thick coat of the Musk Oxen protects against winds in winter and insects in summer.*

winter solstice – as the parks are above the Arctic Circle – there are many days that are dark throughout. Peculiarly, there are two 'springs': the first, from late March through April, is characterised by snow, long hours of daylight and good travelling conditions; the second, in May and June, is the time of snow melt and ice breakup, and travel can be difficult, if not impossible. Summer begins in mid-June when there are 24 hours of sunlight, rapid plant growth, and the first biting insects. Autumn begins in early to mid-August, with the onset of frosts, and ends in September.

## The 'Refuge'

Vuntut and Ivvavik National Parks represent the Northern Yukon Natural Region and the Mackenzie Delta Natural Region. Depite their remoteness, pollutants from elsewhere still manage to drift to these parks, and have been measured in significant quantities in the plants and animals. The critical coastal plain of Ivvavik National Park extends into Alaska's Arctic National Wildlife Refuge where the Porcupine Caribou herd moves after calving. The U.S. Congress is considering opening up a 'refuge' to oil and gas development, despite entreaties from Canada and other interest groups to protect the refuge under the American Wilderness Act. In the absence of such protection, the Porcupine Caribou herd will be at risk.

## Climate

The weather in Ivvavik and Vuntut National Parks is volatile and unpredictable. Winds are modified by coastal effects and the mountains, and can suddenly change direction or quickly become dangerously strong. Temperatures fluctuate wildly and fog is common, especially along the coast. Snow can fall any day of the year, although annual precipitation amounts are low. Winter persists from October through to March, and around the

# AULAVIK, TUKTUT NOGAIT AND QUTTINIRPAAQ NATIONAL PARKS

## An Arctic Wilderness Trio

*'And the North, silent, eerie and primordial, filled with magic...and spirits, and things mentioned only in a legend, now comes into its own...'*
GREY OWL (WA-SHA-QUON-ASIN), TALES OF AN EMPTY CABIN

Tuktut Nogait National Park was established in 1996 to protect the calving grounds of Bluenose Caribou herd and covers an area of 16,340 square kilometres (6,285 square miles). Aulavik National Park (12,200 square kilometres/4,721 square miles) was established in 1992 and contains the world's most northerly navigable river, The Thomsen River. The vast Quttinirpaaq (Ellesmere Island) National Park Reserve was established in 1988 and is the second largest national park in Canada, covering 37,775 square kilometres (14,586 square miles). All three parks were created with the participation of the longtime residents of Canada's high north, the Inuvialuit and the Inuit, and are operated through co-management agreements. The agreements all provide for the right of the Inuvialuit and Inuit to carry out traditional activities within the park, including subsistence harvesting of park resources. The three parks are all remote, relatively inaccessible and fragile environments.

Above, right: *Snow Geese breed near the Thomsen River, and, in summer, congregate along the river for their moult.*

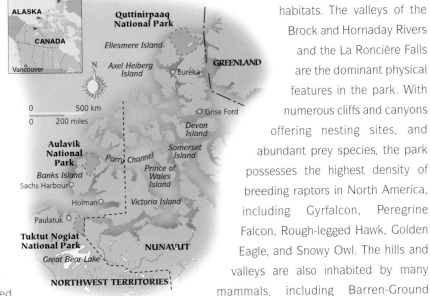

Tuktut Nogait National Park (Tuktut Nogait is Inuvialuktun for 'young caribou') is the the southernmost of the three parks and consists of tundra, rolling hills, and incised river canyons. By Arctic standards there are a considerable variety of plants and animals, the result of many micro-habitats. The valleys of the Brock and Hornaday Rivers and the La Roncière Falls are the dominant physical features in the park. With numerous cliffs and canyons offering nesting sites, and abundant prey species, the park possesses the highest density of breeding raptors in North America, including Gyrfalcon, Peregrine Falcon, Rough-legged Hawk, Golden Eagle, and Snowy Owl. The hills and valleys are also inhabited by many mammals, including Barren-Ground Grizzly Bear, caribou, Musk Ox, and Arctic Wolf.

Aulavik National Park (Aulavik is Inuvialuktun for 'the place where people travel') is a land of wide river valleys, hills, and badlands that contain many archaeological sites of the Inuvialuit and the Europeans. The Thomsen River is suitable for canoeing, kayaking, and rafting and is generally only navigable in early summer, during the period of high water runoff. There is no whitewater on the river, but strong winds can be a hazard. There are

**Location:** Aulavik National Park; on northern Banks Island, Northwest Territories (NWT). Tuktut Nogait National Park; 45 km (28 miles) east of Paulatuk, NWT, and 425 km (265 miles) north-east of Inuvik, NWT. Quttinirpaaq National Park; on northern Ellesmere Island, north-ernmost Canada.

**Climate:** Arctic desert climate, with cool short summers, and long cold winters. Maximum daily temperatures for June–August less than 10°C (50°F).

**When to go:** Practical travel only possible from June–August.

**Access:** Aulavik; air charter services from Inuvik, NWT (Commercial air service to Inuvik). Tuktut Nogait; by private boat from Paulatuk, by charter aircraft from Inuvik, or by hiking from Paulatuk. Commercial air service to Paulatuk from Inuvik (not daily). Quttinirpaaq; air charter services from Resolute Bay, Nunavut (Commercial air service to Resolute Bay).

**Facilities:** None of the three parks has any facilities or services. For available services in Inuvik, NWT, Paulatuk, NWT, and Resolute Bay, Nunavut, contact the parks.

**Watching Nature:** Musk Ox, caribou, wolf, Polar Bear, marine mammals, Long-tailed Jaeger, Gyrfalcon, Ivory Gull.

**Visitor Activities:** Hiking; nature photography; canoeing (Aulavik and Tuktut Nogait); fishing.

**Special Notes:** (1) Campfires are not permitted in any of the parks. (2) All visitors must pre-register with park authorities. (3) Only No-Trace Camping is permitted. (4) If travelling independently, all necessary equipment must be transported in to the park; local availability is limited or non-existent. Personal Locator Beacons (PLB) are recommended.

Above: *Great shelves of pack-ice blanket the ocean around Aulavik National Park.*

Below: *The Snow Bunting is one of many migrant birds that breed in the tundra.*

more than 150 tundra wildlowers, which have a peak flowering in early July, and are best viewed on south-facing hillslopes. More than 70,000 Musk Oxen – the world's largest population of these animals – live on Banks Island. Many are resident in the park area. There are also Peary Caribou (although the population is declining), Arctic Fox, wolf, hare, and Polar Bears. On the coast, Beluga Whales and Ringed Seals visit. Among the 40 bird species that nest in the park, there are many shorebirds, as well as birds of prey, whose numbers fluctuate with the density of lemmings, their primary prey. The lower section of the Thomsen River is a designated migratory bird sanctuary, to protect Brant and Lesser Snow Geese during their summer moult.

Quttinirpaaq (Ellesmere Island) National Park Reserve (Quttinirpaaq is Inuit for 'top of the world') protects the most northerly lands in North America. Glaciers 900 metres (3,000 feet) thick cover the mountains in the northern part of the park, and nunataks, including Mount Barbeau (2,616 metres/8,633 feet) – the highest peak in eastern North America – poke through the glaciers. The park's coastline contains glacial valleys and fiords, and in the north 80-metre (266-feet) thick sea-ice shelves blanket huge areas of the ocean. Lake Hazen, an Arctic 'thermal oasis', lies in the south of the park and supports most of the park's plants and animals. Quttinirpaaq is a polar desert, with 6 centimetres (2½ inches) of precipitation annually, yet there is sufficient plant life to support insects and in turn a few breeding birds, including Common Ringed Plover, Ruddy Turnstone, Red Knot, Ivory Gull, and Arctic Tern. There

are some land mammals, including Peary Caribou, Polar Bear, Musk Ox, and Arctic Wolf. Open coastal waters support walrus, Bearded Seal, Narwhal, Northern Fulmar, Thick-billed Murre, and Glaucous Gull. Remote Fort Conger, on the northeast coast of Ellesmere, has been the base for Arctic expeditions, including that of Robert Peary in his 1909 trek to the North Pole.

## Arctic Travel

Travel in the Arctic is not a trivial matter, and thorough preparation is essential. It is easier, and often not much more expensive, to utilise the services of approved commercial outfitters. Take every precaution to keep

yourself, and prospective rescuers, out of danger. However, despite sensible planning, accidents can still occur. Parks Canada has some basic capability for Search and Rescue Services, but these are constrained by lack of park facilities, remote geographical location, challenging weather conditions, and the small number of available staff. There can be lengthy delays due to weather and availability of aircraft and boats. Individuals who do not comply with National Park Regulations or fail to take responsibility for their actions may be held responsible for the full cost of their Search and Rescue operation.

## Thinning Ice Packs

The parks represent the following natural regions: Tuktut Nogait the Tundra Hills; Aulavik the Western Arctic Lowlands; and Quttinirpaaq the Eastern High Arctic Glacier. All three parks are relatively pristine, although measurable amounts of pollutants of distant origin have already been detected in plants and animals. The landscapes are incredibly fragile and so access to them is strictly controlled. Of more recent concern is the potential impact of global warming. The consequences of this are still unknown, but ice packs are thinning and declining rapidly, with potentially severe repercussions.

Above: *Ellesmere Island protects the most northerly land in North America.*

# SUMMARY OF CONSERVATION AREAS

The following is a brief summary of the major conservation areas known to be currently functional in Canada. Many of them are covered in this book. Some have been established primarily for research and are not generally accessible to tourists. A number of areas proposed as parks by differing authorities have been included in the list, and these are at varying stages in the process of creation. When planning a trip, check the 'Visitor Information' panels given for each area described in the book and contact the appropriate authority (see page 172).

## BRITISH COLUMBIA

**Pacific Rim National Park Reserve** (286 km²/110 miles²) Agreement in Principle 1970. Three park sections: Long Beach; West Coast Trail; Broken Group Islands.

**Kootenay National Park** (1,406 km²/543 miles²) Established 1920. 'Accessible' mountain park, bisected by Banff-Windermere highway. Sights include Marble Canyon, Paint Pots and Stanley Glacier.

**Yoho National Park** (1,313 km²/507 miles²) Established 1886. Icefields straddling the Continental Divide, in the Rocky Mountains.

**Glacier National Park** (1,349 km²/520 miles²) Established 1886. Protects some of the Columbia Mountains, as well as 400 glaciers. Contains the Rogers Pass, key to the country's transportation.

**Mount Revelstoke National Park** (260 km²/100 miles²) Established 1914. Features the Columbia Mountains, and road to the summit of Mount Revelstoke.

**Garibaldi Provincial Park** (1,950 km²/750 miles²) Established 1920. Close to Vancouver, but offering mountain peaks, glaciers, alpine meadows, and pristine lakes.

**Gwaii Haanas National Park** (1,495 km²/577 miles²) Agreement in Principle 1987. Includes an adjacent National Marine Park (3,400 km²/1,630 miles²). Protects 15% of the Queen Charlotte Islands, and heritage of the Haida First Nation.

## PRAIRIE PROVINCES

**Waterton Lakes National Park** [Alberta] (505 km²/195 miles²) Established 1895. Northern half of International Peace Park with Glacier National Park in Montana. Prairie grasslands and the Rocky Mountains.

**Banff National Park** [Alberta] (6,641 km²/2,656 miles²) Established 1885. Canada's first national park, and the most heavily visited. In Rocky Mountains, with Cave & Basin Hot Springs, Lake Louise, extensive visitor facilities, and access to alpine areas.

**Jasper National Park** [Alberta] (10,878 km²/4,200 miles²) Established 1907. Columbia Icefields, and the Continental Divide. Also Maligne Canyon, and Icefields Parkway – the world's most scenic drive.

**Elk Island National Park** [Alberta] (194 km²/75 miles²) Established 1913. The only Canadian National Park enclosed by a fence, protecting bison, elk and moose.

**Wood Buffalo National Park** [Alberta/Northwest Territory] (44,802 km²/17,299 miles²) Established 1922. Largest park in Canada, a World Heritage Site. Protects Whooping Crane, bison, and Peace-Athabasca Delta, largest freshwater delta in the world.

**Grasslands National Park** [Saskatchewan] (420 km²/162 miles²) Established 1975. Protects mixed-prairie grasslands, an endangered habitat in North America. Prairie Dogs, Sage Grouse, Prairie Rattlesnakes, Pronghorn Antelope.

**Prince Albert National Park** [Saskatchewan] (3,875 km²/1,496 miles²) Established 1927. 'Accessible' boreal wilderness. Rich diversity of mammals, plants, and birds. Final home of naturalist writer Grey Owl.

**Riding Mountain National Park** [Manitoba] (2,973 km²/1,148 miles²) Established 1929. A boreal 'island' on the Manitoba Escarpment, surrounded by plains.

**Cypress Hills Interprovincial Park** [Saskatchewan/Alberta] (250 km²/96 miles²) First interprovincial park in Canada. Highest point of land east of the rockies and south of the Arctic. A forested oasis surrounded by grasslands.

**Dinosaur Provincial Park** [Alberta] (73 km²/28 miles²) One of the first World Heritage Sites, so named in 1979. Badlands, extensive fossil resources.

## ONTARIO

**Pukaskwa National Park** (1,878 km²/725 miles²) Agreement in Principle 1971. On the northern shore of Lake Superior, in the heart of the Canadian Shield.

**Bruce Peninsula National Park** (154 km²/59 miles²). Protects part of the Niagara Escarpment. Ongoing land acquisition program to expand park.

**Fathom Five National Marine Park** (112 km²/43 miles²) Established 1987. First Canadian National Marine Park, protecting islands and lake at the mouth of Georgian Bay.

**Georgian Bay Islands National Park** (25 km²/10 miles²) Established 1929. Transition between Pre-Cambrian Shield and St. Lawrence lowlands.

**St. Lawrence Islands National Park** (9 km²/3.5 miles²) Established 1914. Canada's smallest national park, protects some of the Thousand Islands in the St. Lawrence River.

**Point Pelee National Park** (15 km²/6 miles²) Established 1918. Southernmost Canadian National Park, and second smallest. Diverse plantlife with southern affiliations. Renowned for viewing migrating birds in spring and autumn.

**Algonquin Provincial Park** (7,725 km²/2,971 miles²) Established 1893. One of the first provincial parks in Canada. Boreal Forest accessible to large population centres. Wolves, moose, Wood-Warblers.

## QUÉBEC

**La Mauricie National Park** (536 km²/207 miles²) Established 1977. Hills, lakes and forests of the Laurentians.

**Forillon National Park** (240 km²/94 miles²) Established 1974. Protects the eastern extension of the Gaspé Peninsula, as well as seabird nesting colonies.

**Bonaventure Island Provincial Park** (4.2 km²/1.6 miles²) Established 1972. Site of large seabird colony, including Northern Gannets, Razorbills, Great Cormorants and Black-legged Kittiwakes.

**Mingan Archipelago National Park Reserve** (150 km²/58 miles²) Established 1984. Limestone islands off the north shore of the St. Lawrence River. Many spectacular rock formations.

**Saguenay – St. Lawrence Marine Park** (1,138 km²/438 miles²) Established 1997. Protects the rich water at the mouth of the Saguenay Fjord. Fin Whales, Beluga Whales, seabirds.

## ATLANTIC CANADA

**Gros Morne National Park** [Newfoundland] (1,805 km²/722 miles²) Agreement in principle 1970. Largest park east of Manitoba and south of the Arctic. World Heritage Site due to park's geology, the 'Galapagos of Plate Tectonics'.

**Terra Nova National Park** [Newfoundland] (400 km²/154 miles²) Established 1957. The boreal forest meets the Atlantic Ocean. Whale-watching.

**Kejimkujik National Park** [Nova Scotia] (403 km²/155 miles²) Established 1974. Wild heartland of Nova Scotia, favoured by the Mi'kmaq First Nation. Adjunct on the Atlantic Ocean, protecting Piping Plover.

**Cape Breton Highlands National Park** [Nova Scotia] (948 km²/366 miles²) Established 1936. Ringed by the Cabot Trail, one of the world's top ten scenic drives. Where highlands meet the sea. Oldest national park in Atlantic Canada.

**Prince Edward Island National Park** [Prince Edward Island] (22 km²/9 miles² + new Greenich component) Established 1937. Beaches, coastal dunes, salt marshes, woodland.

**Kouchibouguac National Park** [New Brunswick] (239 km²/92 miles²) Established 1979. A land of bogs, forest, rivers, salt marshes, and offshore sand barrier islands.

**Fundy National Park** [New Brunswick] (206 km²/80 miles²) Established 1948. Preserves Acadian forest, and borders Bay of Fundy, with the world's highest tides.

## NORTH OF 60°

**Nahanni National Park** [Northwest Territories] (4,765 km²/1,840 miles²) Established 1976. Protects most of the South Nahanni River and its tributaries. Virginia Falls, Rabbitkettle Hot Springs, Nahanni River Canyon.

**Kluane National Park Reserve** [Yukon Territory] (22,013 km²/8,500 miles²) Established 1976. St. Elias Mountains, massive glaciers. Only northern national park accessible by road (Alaska highway). Grizzly Bear and Dall Sheep. A World Heritage Site.

**Wapusk National Park** [Manitoba] (11,475 km²/4,413 miles²) Established 1996. Tundra and taiga on the edge of Hudson Bay. Southernmost Polar Bear population in the world. Critical breeding area for waterfowl and shorebirds.

**Ivvavik National Park** [Yukon Territory] (10,168 km²/3,926 miles²) Established 1984. The northern part of the Yukon Territory, including the Firth River and the British Mountains. Calving ground for caribou.

**Aulavik National Park** [Northwest Territories] (12,000 km²/4,710 miles²) Agreement in principle 1992. Remote Arctic wilderness, centered on the Thompsen River basin, important for Musk Ox.

**Auyuittuq National Park** [Nunavut] (21,470 km²/8,588 miles²) Established 1976. Arctic mountain park, with glaciers, valleys, and fjords.

**Quttinirpaaq** (Ellesmere Island) **National Park** [Nunavut] (37,775 km²/14,586 miles²) Established 1988. Canada's northernmost and second largest national park. Protects Lake Hazen, an Arctic oasis.

**Tuktut Nogait National Park** [Northwest Territories] (16,340 km²/6,285 miles²) Established 1998. Canada's newest national park, protecting tundra and rare Arctic unglaciated terrain. Calving ground for Bluenose Caribou herd.

**Vuntut National Park** [Yukon Territory] (4,345 km²/1,671 miles²) Agreement in principle 1993. Protects the Old Crow Flats, an immense plain of vital wildlife importance.

# USEFUL ADDRESSES

**BRITISH COLUMBIA**

**Pacific Rim National Park Reserve**
Box 280, 2185 Ocean Terrace Rd.,
Ucluelet, British Columbia V0R 3A0.
Phone (250) 726-7721, Fax:
(250)726-4720.

**Kootenay National Park**
Box 220, Radium Hot Springs, British
Columbia V0A 1M0. Phone: (250)
347-9615; T.D.D.: (250) 347-9615;
Fax: (250) 347-9980.
E-mail: Kootenay_reception@pch .gc.ca

**Yoho National Park**
Box 99, Field, B.C., British Columbia
V0A 1G0. Phone: (250) 343-6324,
Fax: (250) 343-6330.
E-mail: yoho_info@pch .gc.ca

**Mount Revelstoke and Glacier
National Parks**
Box 350 Revelstoke, British Columbia
V0E 2S0. Phone: (250) 837-7500,
Fax: (250) 837-7536.
E-mail: revglacier_reception@pch.gc.ca.

**Garibaldi Provincial Park BC Parks**
c/o Alice Lake, Provincial Park, Box
220, Brackendale, British Columbia
V0N 1H0. Phone: (604) 898-3678.
Fax: (604) 898-4171. OR BC Parks
Head Office, 1610 Mount Seymour
Road, North Vancouver, B.C., V7G
1L3. Phone: (604) 924-2200.

**Gwaii Haanas National Park
Reserve/Haida Heritage Site**
Box37, Queen Charlotte, British
Columbia V0T 1S0. Ph: (250) 559-
8818 (year-round). FAX: (250) 559-
8366.
e-mail: gwaiicom@qcislands.ne

**PRAIRIE PROVINCES**

**Waterton Lakes National Park**
Waterton Park, Alberta T0K 2M0.
Phone: (403) 859-2224. TDD: (403)
859-2224. Fax: (403) 859-2650.
E-mail : waterton_info@pch.gc.ca

**Banff National Park**
900, Banff, Alberta T0L 0C0. Phone:
(403) 762-1550; Fax: (403) 762-1551.
E-mail: banff_vrc@pch.gc.ca

**Jasper National Park**
Box 10, Jasper, Alberta T0E 1E0
Phone: (780) 852-6176; Fax: (780)
852-5601.
e-mail: jasper_info@pch.gc.ca

**Elk Island National Park**
Site 4, RR 1, Fort Saskatchewan,
Alberta T8L 2N7. Phone: (780) 992-
2950.
E-mail: elk_island@pch.gc.ca

**Wood Buffalo National Park**
Box 750, Fort Smith, NWT X0E
0P0. Phone: (867) 872-2349, Fax:
(867) 872-3910. TDD: (867) 872-
3727.
E-mail: wbnp_info@pch.gc.ca

**Grasslands National Park**
Box 150, Val Marie, Saskatchewan
S0N 2T0. Phone: (306) 298-2257;
Fax: (306) 298-2042; TDD: (306)
298-2217.
E-mail: Grasslands_Info@pch.gc.ca

**Prince Albert National Park**
Box 100, Waskesiu Lake,
Saskatchewan S0J 2Y0. Phone: (306)
663-4522; Camping Reservations:
306-663-4513; Fax: (306) 663-
5424.
E-mail: panp_info@pch.gc.ca

**Riding Mountain National Park**
Wasagaming, Manitoba R0J 2H0.
Toll Free Information and Reservations: 1-800-707-8480 (toll free
for North America only). Phone:
(204) 848-7275. Fax: (204) 848-
2596. TTY/TDD: (204) 848-2001.
E-Mail: RMNP_info@pch.gc.ca

**Cypress Hills Interprovincial Park**
Box 850, Maple Creek,
Saskatchewan S0N 1N0. Phone:
(306) 662-4411. Alberta: Cypress
Hills Provincial Park, General Delivery,
Elkwater, Alberta, T0J 1C0. Phone:
(403) 893-3777.

**Dinosaur Provincial Park**
Box 60, Patricia, Alberta T0J 2K0
Phone: (403) 378-4342;
Toll-Free (Alberta only) 310-0000;
campsite reservations (403) 378-
3700; tour reservations of
restricted dinosaur area: (403)
378-4344.

**ONTARIO**

**Pukaskwa National Park**
Heron Bay, Ontario P0T 1R0. Phone:
(807) 229-0801; Fax: (807) 229-
2097.
E-mail:ont_pukaskwa@pch.gc.ca

**Bruce Peninsula National Park/
Fathom Five National Marine Park**
Box 189; Tobermory, Ontario N0H
2R0. Phone: (519) 596-2233; Fax:
(519) 596-2298; TDD (519) 596-
2283; to reserve at Cypress Lake
campground phone: (519) 596-2263.
E-mail: bruce_fathomfive@pch.gc.ca

**Georgian Bay Islands National Park**
Box 28; Honey Harbour, Ontario P0E
1E0; Phone: (705) 756-2415; Camp-
site reservations: (705) 756-5909;
Fax: (705) 756-3886.
E-mail: info_gbi@pch.gc.ca.

**St. Lawrence Islands National Park**
2 County Road 5, RR 3, Mallorytown,
Ontario, K0E 1R0. Phone: (613) 923-
5261; Fax: (613) 923-1021;
TTY/Voice: (613) 923-5261.
E-mail: ont_sli@pch.gc.ca

**Point Pelee National Park**
1118 Point Pelee Dr., R.R. #1; Leamington, Ontario N8H 3V4. Phone and
TDD: (519) 322-2365; Recorded
park info line: (519) 322-2371, daily
updates during bird migration. Fax:
(519) 322-1277.
E-mail : Pelee_Info@pch.gc.ca

**Algonquin Provincial Park**
Box 219, Whitney, ON, K0J 2M0.
Phone: (705) 633-5572. Campground
reservations: 1-888-668-7275.
E-mail: info@algonquinpark.on.ca.

**QUÉBEC**

**La Mauricie National Park**
794 5th Street, P.O Box 758,
Shawinigan, Quebec G9N 6V9.
Phone: Information: (819) 538-3232;
Camping Reservations: (819) 533-
7272; TDD (819) 536-2638; Fax
(819) 536-3661.
E-mail: parcscanada-que@pch.gc.ca

**Forillon National Park**
22 boul Gaspe, CP 1220, Gaspe,
Quebec G0C 1R0. Phone: (418) 892-
5951; Fax: (418) 892-5572.
E-mail: webinfo@sunqbc.risq.net.

**Mingan Archipelago National Park
Reserve** Parks Canada Mingan Dis-
trict, 1303 De la Digue Street, Box
1180, Havre-Saint-Pierre, Quebec
G0G 1P0. Phone: (418) 538-3285 in
season, (418) 538-3331 off-season.
Fax: (418) 538-3595.
E-mail: archipel_de_mingan@pch.gc.ca

**Saguenay – St. Lawrence Marine
Park**
182, rue de l'Église, P.O. Box 220
Tadoussac, Quebec G0T 2A0.
Phone: (418) 235-4703; Fax: (418)
235-4686.
E-mail: parkscanada-que@pch.gc.ca

**ATLANTIC CANADA**

**Gros Morne National Park**
Box 130, Rocky Harbour, Newfoundland A0K 4N0. Phone: (709) 458-
2417,
E-mail: grosmorne_info@pch.gc.ca

**Terra Nova National Park**
Glovertown, Newfoundland, A0G 2L0.
Phone: (709) 533-2801. Fax: (709)
533-2706.
E-mail : atlantic_parksinfo@pch.gc.ca

**Kejimkujik National Park**
Box 236, Maitland Bridge, Nova Scotia, B0T 1B0. Phone: (902) 682-
2772. Fax: (902) 682-3367.
E-mail: Kejimkujik_Info@pch.gc.ca

**Cape Breton Highlands National Park**
(902) 224-3403 or (902) 224-2306.
Fax: (902) 285-2866. TDD: (902)
285-2691.
E-mail: atlantic_parksinfo@pch.gc.ca

**Prince Edward Island National Park**
2 Palmers Lane, Charlottetown, PE
C1A 5V6. Phone: (902) 672-6350;
Fax: (902) 672-6370; TTY: (902)
566-7061.
E-mail: peinp_pnipe@pch.gc.ca.

**Kouchibouguac National Park**
Kent County, New Brunswick E0A
2A0. Phone: (506) 876-2443; Fax:
(506) 876-4802.
E-mail : kouch_info@pch.gc.ca.

**Fundy National Park**
Box 40, Alma, New Brunswick E0A
1B0. Phone: (506) 887-6000; TDD:
(506) 887-6015; Fax: (506) 887-
6008.
E-mail: Fundy_info@pch.gc.ca

**NORTH OF 60°**

**Nahanni National Park**
Box 348, Fort Simpson, Northwest
Territories X0E 0N0. Phone: (867)
695-3151; Fax: (867) 695-2446;
TDD: (867) 695-3841; Travel
information: GNWT Parks -

# FURTHER READING

403-695-7230 Nahanni-Ram Tourism Association Box 177 Dept. VG Fort Simpson, NWT, X0E 0N0. E-mail : Nahanni_Info@pch.gc.ca.

**Kluane National Park Reserve**
Box 5495, Haines Junction, Yukon Y0B 1L0. Phone: (867) 634 7250; Fax: (867) 634 7265. E:mail address: kluane_info@pch.gc.ca

**Ivvavik National Park**
Western Arctic District, Parks Canada, Box 1840, Inuvik, Northwest Territories X0E 0T0. Phone: (867) 777-3248; Fax: (867) 777-4491. E-mail: whitehorse_info@pch.gc.ca.

**Wapusk National Park**
P.O. Box 127, Churchill, Manitoba R0B 0E0. Phone: (204) 675-8863, or 1-888-748-2928 (toll free within North America). Fax: (204) 675-2026. E-mail: wapusk_np@pch.gc.ca

**Aulavik National Park**
Box 29, Sachs Harbour, Northwest Territories X0E 0Z0; Phone: (867) 690-3904; Fax: (867) 690-4808. E-mail: Gerry_Kisoun@pch.gc.ca

**Auyuittuq National Park** P.O. Box 353, Pangnirtung, Nunavut X0A 0R0. Phone: (867) 473-8828; Fax: (867) 473-8612. E-mail: Nunavut_Info@pch.gc.ca

**Quttinirpaaq (Ellesmere Island) National Park**
Box 353 Pangnirtung, Nunavut X0A 0R0. Phone: (867) 473-8828; Fax : (867) 473-8612. E-mail : Nunavut_Info@pch.gc.ca.

**Tuktut Nogait National Park**
General Delivery, Paulatuk, Northwest Territories X0E 1N0. Phone: (867) 580-3233; Fax: (867) 580-3234. E-mail: Gerry_Kisoun@pch.gc.ca.

**Vuntut National Park**
Box 390, Dawson City, Yukon, Y0B 1G0, Canada. Phone (403) 993-5462 OR Community Liaison Officer, Box 19, Old Crow, Yukon Y0B 1N0. Phone: (867)966 3622; Fax: (867)966 3432. E-mail: margret_njootli@pch.gc.ca

**Websites:**

**Parks Canada**
http://www.parkscanada.gc.ca/np/np_e.htm

**Canadian Heritage Rivers System**
http://www.chrs.ca/Main_e.htm

**Canadian Important Bird Areas**
http://www.bsc-eoc.org/Iba/canmap.html

**RAMSAR sites in Canada (wetlands of international importance)**
http://www.ramsar.org/profiles_canada.htm

**Canadian Wildlife Service**
http://www.cws-scf.ec.gc.ca/cwshom_e.html

**Provincial Parks of British Columbia**
http://www.env.gov.bc.ca/bcparks/explore/explore.htm

**Provincial Parks of Alberta**
http://www.gov.ab.ca/env/parks/parkinfo/index.html

**Provincial Parks of Saskatchewan**
http://www.serm.gov.sk.ca/parks/

**Provincial Parks of Manitoba**
http://www.gov.mb.ca/natres/parks/contents.html

**Provincial Parks of Ontario**
http://www.ontarioparks.com/

**Parcs provincial du Québec**
http://www.sepaq.com/Fr/carteParcs.cfm

**Provincial Parks of New Brunswick**
http://www.tourismnbcanada.com/web/english/outdoor_network/default.htm

**Provincial Parks of Nova Scotia**
http://parks.gov.ns.ca/index.htm

**Provincial Parks of Newfoundland & Labrador**
http://www.wordplay.com/parks/welcome.html

**Provincial Parks of Prince Edward Island**
http://www.gov.pe.ca/visitorsguide/explore/parks/index.php3

**Yukon Territorial Parks**
http://yukonweb.com/notebook/tparks.html

**Nunavut Parks**
http://www.nunavutparks.com/

**Canadian Parks & Wilderness Society**
http://www.cpaws.org/

**Canadian Parks Partnership**
http://www.canadianparkspartnership.ca/english/

**Committee on the Status of Endangered Wildlife in Canada**
http://www.cosewic.gc.ca/COSEWIC/

**Birding the Americas Trip Report and Planning Repository**
http://www3.ns.sympatico.ca/ns/maybank/Trips.htm

**Canadian Amphibian and Reptile Conservation Network**
http://eqb-dqe.cciw.ca/partners/carcnet/

FLORA

Newcomb, Lawrence (1989) *Newcomb's Wildflower Guide*. Little, Brown and Co., Toronto

Lloyd, Dennis, Parish, Roberta, and Coupé, Ray (1996) *Plants of Southern Interior British Columbia*. Lone Pine Publishing, Vancouver.

Johnson, Karen L. (1987) *Wildflowers of Churchill and the Hudson Bay Region*. Manitoba Museum of Man and Nature, Winnipeg.

Vance, F. R., Jowsey, J. R., Switzer, F. A., and McLean, J. S. (1999) *Wildflowers Across the Prairies*. Greystone Books, Douglas & McIntyre, Vancouver, Saskatoon.

Burt, Page (1991) *Barrenland Beauties - Showy Plants of the Arctic Coast*. Outcrop Limited, Yellowknife.

Hosie, R.C. (1979) *Native Trees of Canada*. Fitzhenry & Whiteside.

Cobb, Boughton (1999) *Field Guide to Ferns*. Peterson.

Lloyd, D., Parish, R., and Coupé, R. (1996) *Plants of Southern Interior British Columbia*. Lone Pine Publishing, Vancouver.

MacKinnon, A., Pojar, J., and Coupé, R. (1992) *Plants of Northern British Columbia*. Lone Pine Publishing, Vancouver.

MacKinnon, A., and Pojar, J., (1994) *Plants of Coastal British Columbia*. Lone Pine Publishing, Vancouver.

Guide d'identification Fleurbec (1985) *Plantes Sauvages du bord de la mer*. Diffusion Dimedia Inc.

FAUNA

Finlay, J. Cam (editor) (2000) *A Bird-finding Guide to Canada*. McLelland & Stewart, Toronto.

Godfrey, W. Earl (1986) *The Birds of Canada*. Canadian Museum of Nature, Ottawa.

(1999) *Field Guide to the Birds of North America*. National Geographic Society, Washington.

Layberry, Ross A., Hall, Peter. W., and Lafontaine, J. Donald (1998). *The Butterflies of Canada*. University of Toronto Press, Toronto.

Glassberg, Jeffrey (1999) *Butterflies through Binoculars*. The East Oxford University Press, New York.

Dunkle, Sydney W. (2000) *Dragonflies Through Binoculars: A Field and Finding Guide to Dragonflies of North America*. Oxford University Press U.S.A.

Banfield, A.F. (1974) *The Mammals of Canada*. University of Toronto Press, Toronto.

Breton, Mimi *Guide To Watching Whales In Canada*. Department of Fisheries and Oceans, Ottawa.

Hoyt, Erich (1988) *Whales of Canada*. Camden House Publishing.

Scott, W.B. (1967) *Freshwater Fishes of Eastern Canada*. University of Toronto Press, Toronto.

GENERAL

Cannings, Richard and Cannings, Sydney (1996) *British Columbia - A Natural History*. Greystone Books, Douglas & McIntyre, Vancouver.

# INDEX

Page numbers in **bold** refer to illustrations


Acadian forest 128, 129, 133 142
accessibility 14-15
Arctic travel 168-9
*see also* individual park information panels
Adams Lake 66, **66**
Ajawaan Lake 48
Aksayook Pass 155-6
Alberta 12, 43, 51-9, 71-2, 77-81
Alberta Plateau 57
Albertosaurus 77
Algonquin Provincial Park 11, **82-3**, 83, 93-5, **93-5**, 171
autumn colours 93, **94**
Gallery 93
interpretative programs 93, 94
Logging Museum 93
trails 94, 95
Wolf howls 93, 95
Algonquin people 105
alpine meadows 19, 27, 29, 39, 52, 61, 71, 110, **148**, 151, **152-3**
alpine tundra *see* tundra
Mt Alsek **150**
Alsek River 151
altitudinal variation 29, 62
Anemone
Canada 73
Cut-leaved **56**
Rue 99
Small Flowered 110
Anishnabe people 88
L'anse aux Meadows Viking settlement 119
Antelope, Pronghorn 67, **69**, 77
Appalachian Mountains 12, 103, 109, 119, 121, 138
Arctic National Wildlife Refuge 166
Arctic Ocean 147, 155
Arctic Region 13, **13**, 15, 61, 103, 119, 147-69
High Arctic 147
SubArctic 43, 83, 103
Arnica, Mountain 71
Arum, Water 47, **75**
Mt Asgard 155
Ash, Red 74
Aspen, Trembling **44**, 46, 62, **64**, 80, 137, 151, **151**
aspens **15**, 43, 48, 73, 81
Assiniboine people 65-6
Astotin, Lake **81**
Athabasca, Lake 57
Athabasca River 57, 59, 61, 63
Athapaskan people 160
Atlantic coast **14**, 103, 106, 119-45
coastal plain 121, 122, 123
Attikamek people 105
Attikamek-Montagnais people 115, 117
Audy, Lake 73
Auklet, Rhinocerous 35
Aulavik National Park 167-8, **167**, **168**, 171
auto-tours 65, 66, 67, 79
autumn colours 93, **94**, 127, 161, **162**
Auyuittuq National Park Reserve **13**, **148**, **154-7**, 155-7, 171
Avalanche Mountain **31**
Avalon Peninsula 119
Aven
Mountain 59, 62, 162
Yellow Mountain 110

backcountry travel *see* wilderness areas
backpacking *see* hiking
badgers 67, 72
badlands 43, 67, **76-8**, 77-8, 167
Baffin Island 144, 147, 156
Bald Butte 66
Banff National Park **6-7**,11, 12, 27, 33, 43, **50-55**, 51-3, 61, 170
Castleguard Caves 52-3
Fenland Trail 52
Hoodoo Lookout **50**
hoodoos 53
hot springs 51, 53
Johnstone Canyon Trail **51**, 52
Parker Ridge Trail 52
Sunshine Meadows 52
waterfalls **51**, 52
Banks Island 168
Mt Barbeau 168
Barley, Foxtail **69**
Barnacle, Acorn 22
barrachois areas 141
Bat, Silver-haired 73
bats 53
Bear
Barren-ground Grizzly 167
Black 15, 22, 33, 35, 45, 47, **49**, 62, 71, 73, 83, 93, 94, 110, **133**, 149, 151, 162
Brown 15
Grizzly 19, 29, 30, **60**, 62, 63, 71, **148**, 149, 151, 162, 165
Polar 15, 43, 155, 161-2, **163**, 165, 167,168
Bearberry **162**
bears
poaching of 75
risks posed by 15, 62, 162
Beausoleil Island **90**, 91, 92
Beaver Hills 79
Beaver people 59
Beaver River 57
beavers 29, 37, 45, 46, 47-8, 52, 59, 62, 73, 74, 79, **79**, 80, 93, 94, 105, **106**, 111, 129, **129**, 141
Bedstraw
Northern 81
Sweet-scented 46
beech 91
Belaney, Archibald Stanfeld *see* Grey Owl
Berry, Saskatoon 74
Beulach Ban Falls 128
biogeographical development 12-13
Birch, Yellow 129, 137
Birch Uplands Plateau 57
birches 92, **151**
bird species 13, 19, 21-2, 23-4, 35, 47, 59, 65, 67, 73, 79, 85, 87, 88, 93, 99-100, 119, 161, 165, 167, 168
migratory 13, **23**, 24, 52, 59, **84**, 85, 131, 132, 137, 165, 168
birdwatching 21-2, 33, 45, 52, 61, 65, 77, 85, 91, 99, 105, 109, 113, 115, 127, 129, 131, 135, 137, 141, 149, 161, 162
Bison
Plains 45-6, 58, 79
Wood 58, **58**, 79
bison 57, 59, 68, 73
Bittern, Least 99, **99**
Bittersweet 74
Black Brook Bay **128**
Black-eyed Susan **138**
Blackfoot people 33, 65, 71
Black Tusk Mountain **10**, 39, **40**
Blackbird
Red-winged **142**
Yellow-headed 79
Bladderwort, Common **47**
bladderwort 46, 129
Mt Blakiston 71
Blomidon Provincial Park 119
Blueberry, Alpine 88
Bluebird, Mountain 77
boating/sailing **28**, 35, 45, 51, 65, 71, 73, 79, 87, 91, 99, 115, 121, 122, 149, 151
glass-bottom boats 97, 98
salt-water 109, 111, 143-4, **144**, 145
bobcats 47, 67
Bobwhite, Northern 83
bog areas **15**, 45-6, **46**, 73, 74, **75**, 80, 91, 94, 110, 123, 128-9, **129**, 131, 136, 137, **139**, 141, 143, 161
Bonaventure Island Provincial Park **108**, 109, 111, **111**, 171
Bonne Bay **118**, 121, 123
Boom Lake **32**
Boreal Ecological Region 43, 45, 49, 59, 83, 88, 103, 119
boreal forest **13**, 15, 43, **44**, 48, 73, 74, 119, 161
fire regime 74
Bow River **50**, 51, **51**, 52, 53
Brackendale Eagle Reserve 40
Brazeau River 61
Breadroot, Indian 68
Breton, Cape 119
Brier Island 119
British Columbia 12, 18-41
British Mountains 165, **166**
Brock River 167
Broken Group Islands Marine Park 23, 24
Broome, Smooth 68
Bruce Peninsula National Park **96-8**, 97-8, 170
Bruce Trail 97-8
buffalo 57-8
Buffalo River **56**
Buffaloberry, Silver 81
Bunchberry **45**, 46, 74
Bunting
Indigo 74
Snow **168**
burbots 73
Burgess Shales fossil site 28
Burning Bush 83, 86
Burnet, Canadian **15**
Buttercup, Prairie 68
butterflies 68, 81, 85, 161
Butterfly
Callipe Fritillary 81
Cranberry Blue 162
Gorgone Checkerspot 81
Monarch 85-6, **85**
Spring Azure 81
Theano Alpine 162
White-veined Arctic 162
Butterfly Weed 83, 86-

Cactus
Ball 78
Prickly Pear 47, 68, **77**, 78, 83
camping/camp sites 14, 21, 27, 29, 33, 37, 39, **41**, 77, 85, 87, 88, 93, 94, 97, 98, 99, 115, 121, 123, 127, 131, 135, 141, 149, 165
Campion, Moss 27, **157**
Canadian Heritage Rivers 61
Canadian Precambrian Shield 13, 45, 83, 87, 88, **90**, 91, 99, 101, 103, 105, 107
Canadian Rocky Mountain Parks *see* Banff; Jasper; Kootenay; Yoho
canoeing 14, 21, 27, 33, 35, 45, 51, 57, 71, 73, 77, 79, 85, 87, 93, 94, 97, **104**, 105, 107, 131, **134**, 135, 137, **138**, 143, 149, **158**, 159, 161, 165, 167
Cape Breton Highlands National Park **126-9**, 127-9, 171
autumn colours 127
Bog Trail **127**
Cabot Trail 119, 127-8, **127**, **128**
trails 128-9
Cape Sable Island 119
Cardinal Flower **91**
Caribou
Bluenose 167
Mountain 30
Peary 168
Porcupine **164**, 165, 166
Woodland 47, 62, 88
caribou 48, 61, 62, 121, **124**, 149, 155, **157**, 162, 167
Caribou Uplands Plateau 57
Mt Carleton 119
carnivorous plants 46, 47, 129, **129**, 135, 136, **138**
Carolinean Forest 83, 85, 86
Les Cascades River **102**
Castle Mountain **6-7**
Castleguard Cave system 52-3
Catechu Provincial Park 83
Cathedral Grove 19
Cave and Basin Hot Springs 51, 53
caves/caving 29, 30, 52-3
Cedar
Eastern White 98, 137
Red 21
cedars 29
Celestine, Lake **60**
Chat, Yellow-breasted 78
Cherry, Choke 74
Chéticamp River 128
Chickadee
Black-capped 29, **30**
Boreal 29, 93, 121
Chestnut-backed 29
Mountain 29
Chignecto Provincial Park 119
Chinook (wind) 72
Chipewyan people 59
Chipmunk
Eastern 111
Least **119**, 143
Churchill, Cape 162
Churchill National Park 43, 161, 162
Churchill River 46, 162
La Chute waterfall **110**
Cinquefoil
Shrubby 72
Snowy 110
climatic conditions *see* individual park information panels
Columbia Icefields 51, 61
Columbia Mountains 29, 30
Conglomerate Cliffs 66
coniferous forests **13**, 19, 65, 81, **89**, 91, 99, 123, 137
conservation *see* environmental issues
Continental Divide 27, 51, 53
Coralroot, Striped 47
Cormorant
Brandt's 24
Double-crested 79, **110**, 111, 136
Great 111
Pelagic 24
Corydalis, Pink 91
Corythosaurus 77
Cottonwood 41, 78
cougars 22
coyotes 33, 47, 62, 67, 77, 79, **80** 110, 143
Crab, Purple Shore 22
crabs 132
Crane
Sandhill 57, **58**
Whooping 43, 57, 58, **58**, 59
Cree people 27, 59, 65, 88, 161, 162
Creeper, Brown 22
Crocus, Prairie 68
Cuckoo, Yellow-billed **84**
Cumberland Sound 156, **157**
Curlew, Long-billed 68, 78
Cypress Hills Interprovincial Park 11, 43, **64-6**, 65-6, 170
fire suppression 66
Lookout Point 66, **66**

Daisy, Subalpine 71
Dalvay-by-the-Sea 142
Dan people *see* Southern Tutchone people
deciduous forest 73, 74, 103, **136**, 137, **151**
Deer
Mule 22, 27, **32**, 33, 45, 46, **50**, 62, 67, 71, 77
White-tailed 29, 33, 45, 46, 62, 77, 79, 83, **83**, 86, 93, 94, 103, 131
deer 37
Deerberry 99
Dene people 162
Devil's Club **30**
Dickson Falls **130**
Dinosaur Provincial Park 11, 43, **76-8**, 77-8, 170
Badlands Trail 77
hoodoos **76**
Coulee Viewpoint Trail 77, **78**
Natural Preserve 77
trails 77, **78**
Dipper, American 52
disabled access 14-15
Dog, Black-tailed Prairie 43, 67, **68**
dog sledding 93, 149, 155
Dogwood, Red-Osier 81
Duck
American Black 132
Canvasback 79, 80, 99, 100
Common Goldeneye 99, 100
Harlequin 52
Oldsquaw 99
Ruddy 79, 80
ducks, sea 24

Eagle
Bald 39, 40, **41**, 46, 99, 119, 121, **143**, **144**, 159
Golden 19, 30, 67, 151, 159, 167
earthquakes 12, 21
Eastern Deciduous Hardwood Forest 74
Eastern High Arctic Glacier region 169
Eastern Newfoundland Atlantic region 145
Eastport bay **145**
Eider, Common 113, 136
elk 15, 27, 29, 33, 45, 46, 48, **60**, 61, 62, 65, 67, 73, 79
Elk Island National Park 43, 79-81, **79-81**, 170
Amisk Wuche Trail **80**
trails 79, **80**
Ellesmere Island *see* Quttinirpaaq National Park
Elm, White 74
Emerald Lake 28, **28**
endangered species 63, 67, 85, 91, 99, 107, 119, 132, 135, 137, **142**
endemic species 13, 143
environmental issues 11, 13, 19, 14, 18, 34, 37, 40-41, 48, 53, 59, 63, 75, 81, 83, 86, 88, 92, 101, 103, 111, 117, 123, 129, 132, 136, 137, 138, 142, 145, 151, 160, 166, 169
Erie, Lake **84**, 85, 86
ermine 111

Falcon
Peregrine 132, 159, 165, 167
Prairie 67, 77, 78
Farwell, Abe 65
Fathom Five National Marine Park **96**, 97, 98, 170
Cove Island lighthouse **97**, 98
fees and charges 14
Fern
Bog 136
Curly-grass 136
Dwarf Chain 136
Licorice 21
Northern Holly 98
Oak 136
Rock Polypody 91
ferns 21
Fir
Balsam 45, 137
Douglas 62
Subalpine 62
Fireweed 74, **152-3**
First Nations people 11-12, 13-14, 160
*see also* individual groups
Firth River 165
fish species 73
fishing 37, 41, 123, 145, 162
ice-fishing 65
salt-water 109
sport fishing 14, 39, 48, 57, 65, 73, 77, 85, 87, 91, 94, 97, 105, 106, 121, 127, 131, 135, 143, 149, 155, 167
Flat River 160
Fleabane, Divided-leaf 110
Flicker, Northern 142
Flies
Black 15, 121, 143
Damselfly 91
Deer 15
Dragonfly 46, 85
Horse 15
Sand 15
flora 13, **15**, **42**, 46, 52, 65, 71, 73, 77, 93, 110, 121, 143, 161, 162, 168
*see also* individual species
Flowerpot Island **96**, 97, 98
Flycatcher
Arcadian 83, 86
Cordilleran 52
Greater Crested 136
Least 142
Olive-sided 30
flycatchers 99
Flying-Squirrel
Northern 73
Southern 83, 86, 136
Forillon National Park **108-11**, 109-11, 171
International Appalachian Trail 109
Fort Benton 65
Fort Conger 168
Fort Walsh 43, **65**, 66
fossils/fossil species 27, 28, 43, 67, 77-8
Fox
Arctic 155, **156**, 162, 168
Red 45, **98**, **107**, 110, 141, 162
foxes 15
Frenchman River 67
Freshwater Lake 129, **129**
Frog
Bullfrog 136
Green 136
Leopard 73, **75**, **80**
Northern Spring Peeper 136
Pacific Tree 22
frogs 135, 136, 143
Fulmar, Northern 168
Fundy, Bay of 119, 131, 132
intertidal zone 131-2
Fundy National Park **130-33**, 131-3, 171
Alma Beach 131
Greater Fundy Ecosystem Project 133
fungi **22**

games 21, 45, 71, 73, 109, 127, 131, 141, 143
*see also* individual sports
Gannet, Northern **108**, **110**, 111, 113, 141
Garibaldi Lake 39, **41**
Garibaldi Provincial Park **10**, 11, 19, **38-41**, 39-41, 170
Singing Pass 39
Gaspé, Cap **108**, 109, 111
Gaspé Peninsula 109, 111
Gaspé Provincial Park 103
Gatineau Provincial Park 103
Gayfeather, Dotted **74**
geological features 53, 57, 65, 71, 73, **76**, 78, 97, **108**, **111**, 115, **117**, 121, 122, **123**, 132, **132**, **140**, 155, 161
Georgia, Strait of 40
Georgian Bay Islands National Park 83, **90-92**, 91-2, 97, 171
Fairy Lake Trail **90**
Glacier Lake 155
Glacier National Park 29, 30
Nakimu Caves 29, 30
glaciers/glaciation 13, **13**, 29, 40-41, 53, 59, 61, 72, 79, 131, 143, 144, **148**, 150-51, **150**, 155, **156**, 161, 168
Glascow Lakes 128
Goat, Mountain 19, 27, **32**, 33, 61, 62, 71, 149, 151
Godwit, marbled 78
Goldeneye, Barrow's 79
Goose
Brant 168
Canada **44**, **81**
Lesser Snow 168
Snow 103, 161, **167**
gophers *see* Ground-Squirrel: Richardson's
Grande Anse Valley **128**
Grands Jardins Provincial Park 103
grasslands **42** 43, 67, 68, 73
fescue 46-7, 48, 71, 72
fire regime 68
grazing of 68
Grasslands National Park **12**, 43, 67-8, **67-9**, 170
Great Lakes 13, 92, 101, 103
*see also* Erie; Huron; Superior
Great Sand Hills 66
Grebe, Red-necked 79
grebes 24
Green Gables House 142
Green Point **120**
Greenland 144
Grenadier Island 95
Grey Owl (Wa-Sha-Quon-Asin) 11, 45, 47-8, 128
Gros Morne National Park **120-5**, 121-3, 171
fjiord/ponds 122, 123, **124-5**
Green Gardens Trail 123
James Callaghan Trail 123
Lobster Cove Head lighthouse 123
trails 121, 123
Grosbeak, Rose-breasted 142
Grosbeak, Lake 57
groundhogs 111
Ground-Squirrel
Arctic 151
Colombian 62
Golden-mantled **71**
Richardson's 67, 80
Grouse
Blue 22, 29
Ruffled 62, 83, **139**, 143
Sage 67
Sharp-tailed 67
Spruce 62, 93, 143
guides 36
Guillemot, Black **109**, 111, 141
Gull
Glaucous 168
Great Black-backed 111, 115, **116**
Herring **84**, 92, 111
Ivory 167, 168
Ross's 162
gulls 137
Gypsum Karst topography 57
Gwaii Haanas National Park Reserve 19, 35-7, **35-7**, 170
Principe Channel **36-7**
gyrfalcons 151, 155, 165, 167

Hackberry Tree 83, 86
Haida Gwaii Watchmen 36
Haida Heritage Site 36, 37
totem poles **35**, 36
Haida people 35, **35**, 36, 37
hardwood forests 91-2, 99
Hare
Arctic 121
Snowshoe 111, **111**, 141, 143
hares 168
Harkin, James B. 12
Harrier, Northern 141
Hawk
Ferruginous 67, 68
Red-tailed **61** 80
Rough-legged 167
Swainson's 78, 80
Hawk-Owl, Northern 30, **126**
Hazen, Lake 168
Hazlenut, Beaked 74
Head-Smashed-In Buffalo Jump, Alberta 43
health and safety issues 36, 57, 61, 62, 85, 121, 131, 143, 155, 156, 159, 165, 167
Arctic travel 168-9
hypothermia 15, 162
Hecate Strait 37
Hemlock, Western 19, 21, **22**
Heron, Great Blue 79, **131**, **140**, 141
herons 99, 132
herptile species 67, 73, 86, 91, 135, 136
Hickory, Shag Bark 99
High Arctic Region 147
Highway Glacier 155
hiking 14, 21, 27, 29, 33, 39, **41**, 45, 51, 57, 61, 65, 67, **70**, 71, 73, 77, 79, 85, 91, 93, 94, 97, 105, 109, 115, 121, 123, 127, 128-9, 131, 135, 136, 137, 141, 143, 149, 155-6, 159, 161, 165
*see also* wilderness areas
Hind, Henry 73
historical survey 11-12
Honey Locust Tree 86
hoodoos 53, **76**
Hopewell Rocks **132**
Hornaday River 167
horse riding 14, 27, 33, 51, 61, 65, 67, 71, 73, 93, 109, 149
hot springs *see* thermal springs
Hudson Bay 27, 61, 147, 161, 162
Hudson Bay Company 117
Huron, Lake 91, 97
Huron people 105
hypothermia 15, 162

icebergs 144-5
icefields *see* glaciers/glaciation
Icefields Parkway 51, 61
Ingonish Bay 129
insect species 13, 15, 68
Interior Plains 13
intertidal areas 131-2
*see also* mudflats
introduced species 37, 75, 81, 86, 106, 133, 143
Inuit people 155, 156, 162, 167
Inuvialuit people **164**, 165, 167
invertebrate species 132
Iris
Blue Flag **145**
Dwarf Lake 98
Iroquois people 105
Ivvavik National Park **164**, 165, 166, 171
climatic conditions 166
coastal plain 166

Jackrabbit, White-tailed 67
Jacques Cartier River Valley **8-9**
Jaeger, Long-tailed 165, 167
Jasper National Park 11, **13**, 27, 33, 51, **60-63**, 61-3, 170
thermal springs 61
waterfalls 61
Jay
Gray 73, **74**, 83, 88, **88**, 93
Steller's **24**, 35
jellyfish **145**
Joe Lake **95**
Juniper, Creeping 91

Kaskawulsh Glacier **150**
kayaking 21, 27, 33, 35, 45, 51, 87, 97, 99, 121, **158**, 159, 167
sea-kayaking 109, 115
Kejimkujik National Park **134-6**, 135-6, 171
Seaside Adjunct 135, 136
trails 136

Kekerten Island Territorial Park 156
killdeer 139
Killdeer badlands 67
Kingbird
 Eastern 78, **78**
 Western 72
Kingfisher, Belted 46
Kittiwake, Black-legged **108**, 111, 113, **126**
Kluane National Park Reserve 11, 14, **148-53**, 149-51, 171
 trails 149
Knot, Red 168
Kootenai (K'tunaxa) people 33, 34
Kootenay National Park 11, 19, 27, **32-4**, 33-4, 51, 61, 170
 Clear Lake Trail 33
 Fireweed Trail 33
 Marble Canyon 33, **34**
 thermal springs 33, **33**, 34, **34**
Kouchibouguac National Park 137-8, **137-9**, 171
 beaches 137
 boardwalk **139**
 Kelly's Beach 137
 trails **137**

Labrador *see* Newfoundland and Labrador
Laughing Falls 27
Laurentian Boreal Highlands 107
Lavallee Lake 45, 47
lichens 45
Lily
 Avalanche 71
 Corn 92
 Western Wood **19**, 92
 Wood 73
 Yellow Dog **130**
 Yellow Glacier **31**
limestone cliffs 97
Limpet, Finger 22
Lion, Mountain 62
Little Buffalo River Falls **56**
Lizard, Eastern Short-horned 67
Locoweed, Yellow 47
Mt Logan 149
logging industry 19, 24, 28, 30, 34, 48, 59, 63, 83, 88, 93, 95, 103, 111, 123, 129, 133, 145
Long Point Provincial Park 83
Long Range Mountains 119, 121, 122
Longspur
 Chestnut-collared 68
 McCown's 68
 Smith's 162
Loon
 Common 46, 79, 83, **104**, 105, 129
 Great Northern *see* Common
loons 24, **95**, 105, 106, 107
Louise, Lake 27, 28, 51, **52**, 53, 61
Lowell Glacier 151
Lower Fort Garry 43
Lupin, Alpine 71
lynx 47, **48**

MacKenzie Delta Natural Region 166
MacKenzie Mountains 147, 160
McLeod brothers 160
McNab's Island Provincial Park 119
Magpie, Black-billed 62
Maligne Canyon/Lake 61, **62-3**
mammal species 13, 24, 35, 45, 62, 67, 73, 79, 149, 151, 155
Manitoba 43, 161, 73-5
Maple
 Manitoba 74
 Red **107**, 137
 Sugar 91, **107**, 129
maples 92
Marigold, Alpine Marsh 62
Maritime Plain Natural Region 142
Marmot
 Golden-mantled 71
 Hoary 19, 29, 52, **53**, 62, 151
Marram Grass 141
Marrella fossil species 28
Marten
 American 132
 Pine 35
Mary's Point 132
La Mauricie National Park **4-5**, **102**, **104-7**, 105-7, 171
 Andrew Lodge 106
 fire regime 107
 Ile Les Pins viewpoint **106**
 Shewenegan recreational area **104**
 trails 105
 Wabenake Lodge **104**, 106
Meadowlark, Western 67, 79, 81
Mermaid Island 99
Mersey River **134**
Métis people 59, 65, 160, 162
Mew Lake 93
Miette Hot Springs 61
migratory birds 13, **23**, 24, 52, 59, **84**, 85, 131, 132, 137, 165, 168
Mi'kmaq people 135, 137-8, 142
 petroglyphs by 135
Milkweed 86
Minas Basin 131
mineral springs *see* thermal springs
Mingan Archipelago National Park Reserve 115-17, **115-17**, 171
mining industry 63, 150, 160, 165
minks 67, 111
Minnewanka, Lake (man-made) 51
Mississaugas people 99
Mistaya River 62
Mitchell Mountain Range 33
Mizzy, Lake **95**
Mont Jacques-Cartier Provincial Park 103
Mont Tremblant Provincial Park 103
montane forest 62
Montgomery, Lucy Maude 142
Moon Lake **74**
moose 15, 33, 45, 57, 59, 62, 65, **66**, 73, 79, **80**, 83, 93, 94, 105, 110, 121, **122**, 128, 131, 143, 149, 151, 159
Moraine Lake 53, **54-5**
mosquitoes 15, 121, 143
Moss
 Feather 21
 Ground Cedar 45
 Running Pine 45
 Sphagnum 45-6, 47, **48**, 137
mosses 21
 club 45
Mount Revelstoke National Park 29-30, **29**
 Giant Cedars Nature Trail 29, **30**
 Rogers Pass 27, 30, **31**
 Skunk Cabbage Nature Trail **29**
mountain biking/cycling 14, 27, 33, 39, 45, 71, 73, 85, 91, 93, 105, 109, 127, 131, 135, 137, 149
mountain climbing 14, 15, 27, 29, 30, 51, 61, 149, 155
mudflats 132, 137, 141, 162
mudpuppies 91
Murre
 Common **108**, 111, **144**
 Thick-billed 168
Murrelet
 Ancient 35
 Marbled 19
muskrats 29, 59, 80, 141, 162

Naha Dene people 160
Nahanni National Park 11, **158-60**, 159-60, 171
 trails 159
Nakimu Caves 29, 30
Nanook *see* Bear: Polar
narwhals 168
National Historic Sites 43, 53, **65**, 66, 98, 119, 141, 142
national/provincial parks 11, 12, 13, 43
 *see also* individual parks
Navaho Indians 160
New Brunswick 12, 119, 131-3, 137-8
Newfoundland and Labrador 12, 119, 121-3, 143-5
Newman Sound **144**, **145**
Niagara Escarpment **96**, 97-8
Niagara Falls 97
Night-Heron, Black-crowned 79
North American tectonic plate 12
North Swallow River 87, **88**
Northern Yukon Natural Region 166
Northern Lights 57, 161
Northwest Mounted Police **65**, 66
Northwest Territories 57-9, 147
Nova Scotia 12, 119, 127-9, 135-6
nunataks 168
Nunavut 147
Nutcracker, Clark's 27, 62, **62**, 71
Nuthatch, White-breasted 128
Nuu-chah-nulth people 21

Oak, Bur 74
oaks 92
O'Hara, Lake 27
Ojibway people 88
Okanagen Valley 19
Ontario 83-101
Opabinia fossil species 28
Opeongo Lake **94**
Orchid
 Alaskan Rein **98**
 Calypso 47, **56**, 97
 Franklin's Lady's Slipper 88
 Mountain Lady's Slipper **70**
 Purple-fringed 135, **135**, 136
 Round-leaved 73
 Showy Lady's Slipper 98
 White-fringed **98**
 Yellow Lady's Slipper 81, 92, 98
orchid species 92, 98
Oriole, Baltimore **84**
ospreys 99, 137, 159, **160**
Otter
 River 22, **34**, 46, 151
 Sea **20**
otters 47
Ovenbird 79, 99
Mt Overlord 155
Owl
 Burrowing 68
 Great Gray 45, **47**, 73
 Great Horned 78
 Saw-whet 35
 Short-eared 141
 Snowy 141, 155, 165, 167
owls 47
Oxen, Musk 165, **166**, 167, 168
Oystercatcher, Black 24

Pacific Coast mountain region 24, 37
Pacific Flyway **23**, 24
 *see also* migratory birds
Pacific Ocean 12, **14**, 19, **20**, 21, 23, 24, 27, 61, 106, 150, 151
Pacific Rim National Park Reserve **18-25**, 19, 21-4, 170
 Botanical Beach **20**
 Broken Group Islands 21, 23, 24
 Long Beach 21-3, **23**, 24
 Rainforest Trail 21
 West Coast Trail **20**, 21, 23, 24
Paint Pot springs 33, **33**, **34**
Paintbrush
 Common Yellow **70**
 Indian 72
Pangnirtung Fjords 155
Parks Canada 12, 14, 15, 37, 169
Peace-Athabasca Delta 57, 59
Peary, Robert 168
Pelican, American White **43**, 45, 58, **59**
Penny Highlands 155-6
Penny Ice Cap 155
Pennywort, Water 135
Percé Rock **108**, 109, 111, **111**
periwinkles 132
permafrost 13, **13**, 161
 La Perouse Bay 161
Phalarope, Red-necked 165, **165**
Phoebe, Say's 7, 78
photography 33, 35, 39, 57, 65, 67, 77, 78, 85, 87, 91, 94, 99, 113, 115, 127, 131, 135, 137, 141, 159, 165, 167
Pikaia fossil species 28
pikas 19, 52, 62
Pine
 Eastern White 91, 107, 138
 Jack 79, 129
 Lodgepole 65, 66
Pitch 99
pines 29, **62**, 65
 fire-dependent 66
Pipit
 American 30, 52
 Sprague's 67
Pitcher Plant 46, 47, 129, 135, 136, **138**
Plantain, Indian 98
Pleasant Bay 127-8
Plover
 Common Ringed 168
 Mountain 68
Piping 119, 135, 137, 141, 142
Plum, Wild 74
Point Pelee National Park 83, **84-6**, 85-6, 151, 171
 East Point Beach **84**
 Marsh Boardwalk **86**
 reclamation work 85, 86
 trails 85
Polar Bear Provincial Park 83
polar deserts 168
Poplar, Balsam 151, **151**
poplars 92
Poppy, Arctic **147**, 155
population figures 11, 12
porcupines 67, 111
Prairie Provinces **12**, **42**, 43-81
Prince Albert National Park 43, **44-9**, 45-8, 170
 Boundary Bog Trail **44**, 45-6, **46**
 Height-of-Land Tower **46**
 Mud Creek Trail **45**, 46
 Treebeard Trail 45
Prince Edward Island 12, 119
Prince Edward Island National Park **140-42**, 141-2, 171
 beaches 141, **141**, 142
 coastal erosion 141, 142
 dunes 141
 Greenich adjunct 141
Ptarmigan
 Rock 121, 155
 White-tailed 19, 30, 52, 62, 151
 Willow **103**
Puffin
 Atlantic 111, 115-16, **115**, **116**, 143-4
 Horned 35
 Monk *see* Atlantic
 Tufted 24, 35
Pukaskwa National Park 87-8, **87-9**, 170
 Coastal Hiking Trail 87-8, **88**
 fire regime 88
 Headland Trail **89**
 stone circles 88
Purcell Sill 71

Québec 12, 13, 103-17
Queen Charlotte Islands 37
 *see also* Gwaii Haanas National Park Reserve
Queen Elizabeth mountain range 62-3
Quttinirpaaq National Park 167, **167**, 168, **168-9**, 171

Rabbit, Prairie Cottontail **78**
Rabbitkettle Hotsprings 159
racoons 15, 22, 37, **142**
Radium Hot Springs 33, 34
rafting 33, **62**, 87, 149, 159, 165, 167
Rail, King 83
Rainbow Falls Provincial Park 83
rainforest **18**,19, 21, 24, 35
Raspberry, Stemless **161**
Rattlesnake
 Massassauga 91, 92, **92**
 Prairie 67, 68, 77, 78
rattlesnakes 15
Raven, Common 27, 62
ravens 159
razorbills 111
Red Deer River 77, 78
Red River 128
Red Rock Canyon **70**
redheads 79
Redstart, American 128
Mt Revelstoke *see* Mount Revelstoke National Park
Rhododendron, White Mountain 27, 62
Riding Mountain National Park 43, 73-5, **73-5**, 170
 Arrowhead Trail 73, **74**, **75**
 Brulé Trail 74
 Burls and Bittersweet Trail 74
Rocky Mountain Park *see* Banff National Park
Rocky Mountains 12, 34, 43, 53, 63, 65, 71
Rocky Mountains National Parks *see* Banff; Jasper; Kootenay; Yoho
Rogers, Major A. B. 30
La Roncière Falls 167
Rondeau Provincial Park 83
Rose, Wild 62, 72
Rosebay, Lapland 155, 162
Roseroot 132
Rosy-Finch, Gray-crowned 30, 52
Mt Royal 103
Russel Island **98**
Rye, Russian Wild 68

Sage, Prairie 78
sagebrush 68
Saguenay-St Lawrence Marine Park **12**, 103, **112-14**, 113-14, 171
St Catherine's River 135
St Elias Mountains **148**, 149, 150-51
St Lawrence Bay 128
St Lawrence Gulf **12**, 103, 113, **113**, 115, 128, 137
St Lawrence Islands National Park 83, 99-101, **99-101**, 171
 Lookout Tower **100**
St Lawrence Lowland Region 98, **98**, 101, 111, 117
St Lawrence River 13, 83, 99, 100, 103, **112-14**, 113-14
St Paul's Bay 121
Salamander, Blotched Tiger 78
salamanders 135, 136
Salmon
 Atlantic 132
 Chum 40, 41, **41**
salt marshes 132, 137, 141
 *see also* bog areas
salt plains 57
San Christoval mountain 35
sanderlings **87**
Sandpiper
 Rock 22
 Semipalmated 132
 Western **23**
sarsaparillas 73
Saskatchewan **12**, 43, 45-8, 65-8
Saskatchewan River **46**, 61
Sassafras 83
Saxifrage
 Encrusted 88
 Purple 162
 Tufted 110
scuba diving/snorkelling 91, 97, 98, 99, 105, 109, 113, 115, 143
Sculpin
 Deepwater 72
 Tidepool 22
Sea Lion, Steller's 35, **37**
sea lions 21
Sea Parrott *see* Puffin: Atlantic
Sea Slug 132
sea wolves *see* Seal
sea-ice 144, 155, **157**, 168, **168**
Seal
 Bearded 168
 Grey 116, 137
 Harbour 116, **117**, 121, 136
 Harp 116
 Ringed 168
seals 21, 155, 161
Selkirk Mountains 30
Shannon Falls **38**
Sheep
 Bighorn 33, **50**, **60**, 61, 62, 71
 Dall **148**, 149, 151, 159, 165, **166**
Shooting-Star, Saline **56**
Shrew, Masked 143
Shrike, Loggerhead 68
Shrimp
 Mud 132
 Opossum 72
Sioux people 65
skiing/snowshoeing:
 alpine 39
 cross-country 14, 29, 33, 39, 45, 51, **52**, 57, 61, 65, 71, 73, 77, 79, 93, 94, 97, 99, **104**, 105, 109, 123, 127, 131, 135, 137, 143, 149
 downhill 51, **52**, 61, 127
 Nordic 155
Skink, Five-lined 83, 86
Skunk, Striped 67, 72
skunks 15
Slave River 57, 59, **59**
Slavey people 59, 160
Snake
 Black Rat 99
 Bull 78
 Eastern Fox 83, 86, 91, 92
 Eastern Yellow-bellied Racer 68
 Maritime Garter 136
 Northern Red-bellied 136
 Northern Ribbon 136
 Red-sided Garter 58, 73, **98**
 Water 91
snakes 15, 131, 136
snowmobiling 155
Solitaire, Townsend's 65
Soloman, Moses 65
Southern Boreal Plains 75
Southern Tutchone people 149, 151
Southesk River 61
Sparrow
 Baird's 68
 Brewer's 151
 Clay-colored 79, 80-81
 Fox 111
 Golden-crowned 151
 Harris's 162
 Lincoln's 128
 Nelson's Sharp-tailed 132
 Savannah 72, 142
 Swamp 141
 Timberline *see* Brewer's
 White-throated 83, 88
Springbeauty 92
Spruce
 Black 74, 161
 Engleman 62
 Red 137
 Sitka 21, **22**
 White **44**, 45, 46, 151
Squamish River 39-40, 41, **41**
Squirrel, Red 62, **105**, 111, 143
Starfish, Ochre 22
Stegosauras 77
Stoney people 53
Storm-Petrel, Leach's 35
subalpine forest 62
SubArctic Region 43, 83, 103
Sulphur Mountain 51, 53
Summit Lake **146**, 155
Sundew **15**, 46, 129
Sunflower, Woodland **75**
Sunwapta Falls 61
Sunwapta Pass 61
Sunset Pass 51
Superior, Lake 87, 88, **89**
surfbirds 22
Swallowtail, Tiger **57**
Swamp Candle **130**
Swan, Trumpeter 65, 79, 80, **158**, 159
Swift
 Black 30, 52
 Vaux's 30
swimming/surfing 14, 21, 33, 45, 65, 73, 79, 85, 87, 91, 97, 99, 105, 109, 121, 127, 131, 135, 137, 141

The Tablelands 121, 122, **123**
Taiga region 45-6, 83, 91
Takakkaw Falls 27, **28**
tamaracks 161
Tanager, Scarlet 74, 136, **136**
Teal, Blue-winged 80
Ten Peaks Valley **54-5**
Tern
 Arctic 122, 165, 168
 Common 92, 137, **139**
terns 99
Terra Nova National Park 143-5, **143-5**, 171
 boat tours 143-4, **144**, 145
 icebergs 144-5
 trails 143
 viewing towers 145
thermal springs 12, 33, **33**, 34, 51, 53, 57, 61, 159
Thompson, Tom 93
Thomsen River 167, **167**, 168
Mt Thor **154**, 155-6
Thousand Islands region 99, 100, **100**, **101**
Thrush
 Bicknell's 103, 111, 129
 Grey-cheeked 162
 Hermit 142
 Varied 22
 Wood 136
Thule people 156
Tick, Black-legged 85
Tlingit people 149
Toad
 American 136
 Plains Spadefoot 77, 78
toads 135, 136
Tobeatic Management Area 135
Tobermory Islands 97
totem poles **35**, 36
Towhee
 Eastern 74
 Spotted 78
trapping 59, 149-50, 160, 162
Tree-Frog, Gray 91
treeline 62, **62**, 151
trees **13**, **15**, **15**
 *see also* individual species
trekking *see* hiking
Trillium
 Purple **107**
 Red 92
 White 92
Tuktut Nogait National Park 167, **167**, 171
Tulip Tree 83, 86
tundra 29, 43, 62, 103, 147, 161, 162, **162**, 165, **165**, 167, 168, **168**, 169
Tundra Hills 147
Turkey, Wild 99
Turner Glacier 155
Turnstone
 Black 22
 Ruddy 22, 168
Turtle
 Blanding's 136
 Musk 91
 Painted **86**
 Spotted 91
 Western Painted 73
turtles 135, 136
Twayblade, Northern 88
Twin Falls 27
Twinflower 46, 74
Tyrrell Museum, Drumheller 77, **78**

UNESCO World Heritage Sites 11, 27, 28, 33, **35**, 36, 51, 57, 61, 77, 121, 159
Upper Salmon River **131**, 132
Vancouver Island 21-4, **21-5**
vascular plants 73
Vermilion Lakes 51, 52, **53**
Vermilion Pass/River Valley 33
Victoria Glacier 53
Virginia Falls 159, **159**, **160**
visitors, advice for 14-15, 21
 *see also* health and safety issues; individual park information panels
Vuntut National Park **164**, 165-6, **165**, 171
 climatic conditions 166
 Old Crow Flats 165
Vuntut Gwitchin people 165

Walcott, Charles D. 28
walleyes 73
walrus 103, 155, 168
Wapiti *see* elk
Wapta ice-sheet/waterfall 27
Wapusk National Park 43, 161-2, **161-3**, 170
 autumn colours 161, **162**
Waputik ice-sheet 27
Warbler
 American Redstart **84**
 Bay-breasted 88
 Blackburnian 73, **89**, 128
 Black-throated Green 79, 142
 Connecticut 46, 103
 Golden-Winged 73, 74
 MacGillivray 29, 65
 Mourning 93, 128
 Pine 100
 Prairie 91
 Prothonotary 83
 Yellow 72, 79
warblers 99, 121
Warren lake 129
Waskesiu Lake **44**, 46
waterfalls 27, 29, 33, **38**, **51**, 52, **56**, 61, **110**, 128, **130**, 159, **159**, **160**, 167
Waterton Lakes National Park 11, 43, **70-72**, 71-2, 170
 Bison Paddock 71, 72
 Upper Waterton Lake 72
Weasel
 Long-tailed 67
 Short-tailed 35
Weasel River **146**, 155, 156, **156**
weasels 72
Wedgemount Lake 39
West Coast Trail **20**, 21, 23, 24
Western Arctic Lowlands 168
wetlands 91, 92, 97, **145**
Whale
 Beluga 43, 114, **114**, **157**, 161, 162, 168
 Blue 110, 113, 116
 Fin 35, 110, 113-14, **114**, 116
 Gray 19, 21, 35, **36**
 Humpback **14**, 35, 110, 116, 144
 Killer *see* Orca
 Minke 35, 110, **114**, 116
 Orca **11**, 19, **20**, 35
 Sei 35
whales 103, 109, 110, 114, 116, 119, 155, 156
 baleen 113
whale-watching 19, **21**, 109, 110, 113-14, 121, 127, 143
Wheatgrass, Crested 68
Whelk, Dog 132
White River 87
Whitefish, Pygmy 72
wilderness areas 14, 15, **20**, 21, 23, **24-5**, 27, 35, 36, 39, 45, 73, 83, 87-8, 94, 105, 131, 132, 135, 147-69, **147-69**
willets 46, 132
Willow, Arctic **162**
Windy Lake 155
Wolf
 Arctic 165, 167, 168
 Gray 74
 Newfoundland 143
 Timber 47, 83, 93, **93**
Wolfe Point **132**, **133**
Wolfe River 132
wolverines **14**, **149**, 151
wolves 22, 43, 62, 73, 95, 132, **151**, 155, 168
Wood Buffalo National Park 11, 43, **56-9**, 170
 salt plains 57
 thermal springs 57
Woodpecker
 Black-backed 45, 74, 79, 93
 Hairy 35
 Pileated 22, 45, 74
 Red-bellied 86
 Three-toed 30, 74
Wood-Pewee, Eastern 100
Worm
 Bamboo 132
 Blood 132
 Clam 132
wreck diving **96**, 97, 98
Wren
 Carolina 83, 86
 Marsh 141
 Rock 77, 78
 Winter 22

Yellowthroat, Common 79
Yoho National Park 11, 19, **26-8**, 27-8, 33, 51, 61, 170
 Kicking Horse Pass 27
 waterfalls 27
Yotin Lake 46
Yukon Territory 12, 147, **148-53**, 149-51, 160, **164-6**, 165-6

# ACKNOWLEDGEMENTS

The author would like to give sincere thanks to the following people and organizations, without whose help this book would have been impossible.

The following former or current Parks Canada staff: Merv Syroteuk, Martine Dufresne, Ron Seale, Mike Jones, Suzanne Henry, David Henry, Donna Bruce, Shelley Ross, Dave Huddlestone, Ben Johns, Achim Jankowski, and Grey Owl.

Also: Dick Cannings, Margo & Meaghan Jankowski, Joan Waldron, and Joel Ellis.

### PHOTOGRAPHIC ACKNOWLEDGEMENTS

All the photographs in this book were taken by Peter Mertz with the exception of the following:

*Frank Hecker:* p1: p14 (bottom left); p34 (centre left); p100 (bottom); p103; p116 (below left); p117(bottom); p126 (bottom left); p149 (top); p165 (top); p168 (bottom)

*J. D. Henry:* p164 (top and bottom); p168 (top left); p169

*Johnny Johnson (Bruce Coleman Collection):* p66 (bottom)

*Gordon Langsbury (Bruce Coleman Collection):* p160 (bottom)

*Joe McDonald (Bruce Coleman Collection):* p92 (bottom)

*Blake Maybank:* p27 (top); p84 (top left, bottom left); p89 (top left); p99 (top); p144 (bottom); p157 (bottom right); p161 (top); p162 (top and bottom); p163; p167 (top)

*A & E Morris (Windrush Photos):* p89 (top left)

*Hans Reinard (Bruce Coleman Collection):* p93 (top)

*José Schell/Louis Gagnon:* p109 (top); p121 (top); p156 (top)

Left: *Colourful Maple leaves in the fall*